Asia in Transition

Volume 26

This book series, indexed in Scopus, is an initiative in conjunction with Springer under the auspices of the Universiti Brunei Darussalam – Institute of Asian Studies (http://ias.ubd.edu.bn/). It addresses the interplay of local, national, regional and global influences in Southeast, South and East Asia and the processes of translation and exchange across boundaries and borders. The series explores a variety of disciplinary and interdisciplinary perspectives.

Submission and Peer Review:

Proposal submissions are to be sent to the Series Editor, Dr Bruno Jetin: bruno.jetin@ubd.edu.bn and Springer Publishing Editor Alex Westcott Campbell: alexandra.campbell@springernature.com using the Book Proposal Form available in the sidebar. All proposals will undergo peer review by the editorial board members. If accepted, the final manuscript will be peer reviewed internally by the editorial board as well as externally (single blind) by Springer ahead of acceptance and publication.

Hong Yu

Understanding China's Belt and Road Initiative

INSTITUTE OF ASIAN STUDIES

Springer

Hong Yu
East Asian Institute
National University of Singapore
Singapore, Singapore

ISSN 2364-8252 ISSN 2364-8260 (electronic)
Asia in Transition
ISBN 978-981-99-9632-2 ISBN 978-981-99-9633-9 (eBook)
https://doi.org/10.1007/978-981-99-9633-9

This Springer imprint is published by the registered company Springer Nature Singapore Pte Ltd.
The registered company address is: 152 Beach Road, #21-01/04 Gateway East, Singapore 189721, Singapore

Prologue

My Research Journey with the Belt and Road Initiative

This book is a result of my decade-long research endeavour. My research journey began with economic geography and the role of infrastructure facilities in unlocking the development potential of the mountainous landlocked regions in China. This triggered my enduring interest in the Belt and Road Initiative (BRI), which was first proposed by China in 2013 and is centred on promoting infrastructure connectivity, and its impacts on China's regional outreach endeavour, cross-border economic-social development and diplomacy with the regional countries.

The BRI name was coined by China's President Xi Jinping in 2013, drawing inspiration from the concept of the ancient Silk Road, which was established 2,000 years ago during the Han Dynasty. The ancient Silk Road was essentially an ancient network of trade routes connecting China to the Eurasian continents, Southeast Asia, South Asia, Arab-Persian Gulf and the Mediterranean.

My research in and about China and the BRI explores the ambitious new Silk Road initiatives. The BRI remains a popular topic for both academia and the policy research community with an interest in China, regionwide as well as worldwide.

The BRI cooperation framework, which contains the multidimension of political, infrastructure financing and construction, economic, social and security has brought China into the limelight of geopolitics and geoeconomics of the world. Perceived as the world's largest infrastructure financing and connectivity initiative, arguably, no previous development initiative has stirred such intense debate among governments, academics, media and business communities around the world as the BRI.

Nevertheless, although the BRI has received much international media attention, the relevant topics have rarely been exposed to academic scrutiny. This book is about unpacking the origins, motivation and evolution of the contemporary version of the Silk Road project, mapping out the decision-making processes and areas of BRI implementation by Chinese central and local authorities, as well as the Chinese companies. It also aims to explain the geopolitical and geoeconomic consequences of the globally oriented Silk Road initiative for the participating countries and beyond.

The colossal infrastructure investments under the BRI framework could usher in a new era of investment, and trade and economic growth for the participating countries and beyond, while the initiative has faced significant criticism. The development of the Belt and Road Initiative has had significant influence on China's relations with the world and on the participating countries' own growth. The BRI will continue to have profound consequences for China and the world.

As the BRI reaches the 10th anniversary of implementation in 2023, it is the right time to evaluate the achievement, evolution, issues and challenges faced by China's grand initiative, and assess its future prospects. This book intends to make sense of the origins, scope and scale of the Belt and Road Initiative, as well as the debates surrounding the BRI through the case studies of the participating countries in Southeast Asia, Central Asia and the Middle East.

Southeast Asia and Central Asia are two priority regions under China's push for the Belt and Road Initiative. Against the backdrop of the rise of China and his ambitious vision to pursue the great rejuvenation of the Chinese nation, in 2013, China's President Xi Jinping unveiled the Silk Road Economic Belt, the overland component of the BRI in Kazakhstan, and the Maritime Silk Road of the 21st Century, the maritime component of the initiative in Indonesia, individually during his state visit to both countries in 2013. Shortly after that, the Silk Road Economic Belt and the Maritime Silk Road of the 21st Century were combined as the Belt and Road Initiative (or the BRI in short).

Literally, the seeds of the contemporary version of the Silk Road were sown in Southeast and Central Asia. Historically, Central Asia and Southeast Asia were the key participants in the ancient Silk Road trade until its decline by the mid-fifteenth century. For example, Uzbekistan's Samarkand and Malaysia's Malacca are two ancient Silk Road cities. Many local people in Southeast Asia and Central Asia are familiar with the Silk Road concept and thus tend to be more amenable to the concept of the BRI.

The BRI has a historical resonance with the centuries-old Silk Road linking the vast Eurasian continent to East Asia. China intends to connect the ancient Silk Road to the BRI in the 21st century. From the ancient Silk Road to the BRI, China's past adventure along the Silk Road routes is guiding China's present global outreach under the BRI, and towards the future.

For China, as the rising superpower, connectivity has trumped resources and territory to become a key element of building national power and exerting influence. Developing interconnectivity of infrastructure development forms a central part of China's national BRI strategy for accelerating infrastructure development in Asia and beyond, gaining control over markets and industrial supply chains and boosting bilateral trade and investment in the BRI countries. China holds a strong belief that whoever controls the interregional connectivity routes will dominate the world in the 21st century.

Xi Jinping has emerged as the most powerful leader in China since the Mao era. The Chinese government under Xi Jinping has been promoting proactive foreign policy, a clear departure from the low-profile foreign policy advocated since the 1980s by the former paramount Chinese leader Deng Xiaoping. The BRI, which is

President Xi's pet project, demonstrates China's more assertive and proactive stance on regional and global affairs. China's foreign policy is undergoing a shift from passively following the international system in the past to actively participating in the reform of global governance and the international institutional system.

President Xi views the change to China's foreign policy as necessary to match its ascendancy as the rising global power. Xi intends that China will one day become a rule-shaper in the global arena and regain a position of pre-eminence in the world via the BRI platform. China has now determined to reshape the world order in China's favour, rather than be shaped by the changing world. The BRI could transform China's formidable economic might into geostrategic leverage and influence.

The BRI is important for the sustainable development of the Chinese economy, to secure global market access for the Chinese firms, to promote close trade and economic cooperation between China and the BRI countries via improving infrastructure connectivity, and Beijing's pursuit of its regional and global geostrategic ambitions.

Against the backdrop of change to the global geostrategic landscape, driven by the deepening strategic competition between the United States and China and the global COVID-19 pandemic, the BRI is apparently becoming even more important for China.

China's economy had previously undergone remarkable growth since the early 1980s. Nevertheless, the Chinese domestic economy has been slowing down quite dramatically since 2010. In addition to downward pressure due to the weakening of economic comparative advantages such as supplies of cheap skilled labour and land costs, China's economy is now facing significant headwinds from the challenging global geostrategic environment, the long-standing structural issues riddling the domestic economy (e.g. regional economic inequality, property market downturn and the sluggish productivity growth) and fast population ageing.

Many developing BRI countries, from Asia to Africa, from the Pacific Islands to Latin America, are still facing bottlenecks for boosting trade within or across their borders due to chronic infrastructure shortage and poor interregional connectivity. China is promoting the BRI to the developing countries in Asia and beyond through multilateral forums and platforms including the Shanghai Cooperation Organization (SCO), ASEAN (Association of Southeast Asian Nations), the African Union and Asia-Pacific Economic Cooperation (APEC).

China also encourages the BRI countries to align their own development strategies with the initiative. These countries have huge investment demands for infrastructure development, and they are still welcoming the Chinese investment in their infrastructure sector. China's investment in the BRI countries has remained robust even amidst the pandemic.

BRI implementation has been demonstrated to be adaptable and flexible in practice. Due to the criticism and pressure from the international community, the Chinese authorities and Chinese companies have been implementing readjustment measures in the push for the Belt and Road Initiative. I refer to it as China seeking to rebrand the initiative as the BRI 2.0. This book assesses the modified BRI 2.0 through the case study of Central Asian countries.

The modified BRI 2.0 focuses on promoting both more financially and more environmentally sustainable projects in the BRI countries. It is also intended to expand the Belt and Road cooperation to new areas such as the digital and health fronts in the BRI countries in the post-COVID-19 era, departing from the initial infrastructure-centred outreach approach.

This book is based on assessment of the relevant central and local government plans and policy initiatives of China, statistical data collected from China, regional countries and multilateral development institutions, such as the World Bank and International Monetary Fund. In addition, over the past decade I have travelled to many Southeast Asian countries, and several Chinese provinces and cities to conduct interviews that would enhance my understanding of the BRI and its execution from the Chinese central and local perspectives.

Through the BRI framework, local governments pursue their local interests, formally or informally, by participating in foreign affairs and strengthening interregional connectivity and external ties. These local endeavours also help China achieve the national policy goals of the initiative. Economic globalisation and China's deep integration into the world economy have pushed Chinese provinces into the trend of internationalisation and strengthening international ties.

For Chinese government officials, scholars, corporate personnel and other individuals who are based in China, the book follows the Chinese convention, that is, with the surname followed by the given name, in reversal of standard Western practice. For other individuals who are based outside China, their names are spelled following the Western practice; that is, the first name is followed by the surname. This convention is used in the footnotes and bibliography as well.

The structure of book is organised as follows: Chapter 1 assesses the driving forces and rationale behind Beijing's push for the Belt and Road Initiative. Chapter 2 discusses the BRI as a platform for China to advance economic globalisation. Chapter 3 analyses China's economic relations with the ASEAN countries, as well as the BRI implementation in the Southeast Asian countries. Chapters 4–6 zoom in on case studies of Vietnam, Singapore and Cambodia, three Southeast Asian countries respectively. Chapter 7 discusses China's ties with the Arab and Persian Gulf countries under the BRI, with reference to country cases, namely Saudi Arabia and Iran. Chapter 8 assesses the launch of the Partnership for Global Infrastructure and Investment (PGII) initiative by the G7 countries to counter China's Belt and Road Initiative. Chapter 9 focuses on the China-led Asian Infrastructure Investment Bank and its role in regional infrastructure financing. Chapter 10 analyses Beijing's readjustments to the Belt and Road Initiative amid its criticism, and the progress of BRI 2.0. Finally, Chap. 11 presents reflections on the BRI over the past decade, and its implications for the region and beyond.

Singapore
September 2023

Hong Yu

Acknowledgments

This book has taken a decade-long time to write. I started to research the Silk Road Economic Belt and the Maritime Silk Road of the 21st Century in 2012, before they were later combined to become China's ambitious and carefully crafted Belt and Road Initiative (BRI).

Numerous debts have been incurred during this long writing journey. It would not have been possible to understand the origins of the BRI, and its evolutions, without the many discussions and conversations over the years with academic scholars, policy analysts, career diplomats and entrepreneurs from China, Southeast Asian and Central Asian countries, Australia, Japan, Republic of Korea, India, United States, United Kingdom, Canada, among other countries. Many of them were generous in giving their time, and this book would have been poorer without their deep knowledge and frank insights. I would also like to express my gratitude to the following individuals: Gungwu Wang, Suisheng Zhao, Bert Hofman, Katherine Morton, Paul Haenle, Mingjiang Li, Chulanee Attanayake, Lin Minwang, Baogang He, Hoo Tiang Boon, Zheng Yongnian, Justin Lin Yifu, Ernesto Braam, Wu Shicun, Lam Peng Er, Chen Gang, Lye Liang Fook, Lim Tai Wei, Ngeow Chow Bing, P.S. Srinivas, Erik Baark, Mao Yanhua, Selina Ho, Nur Shahadah Binti Jamil, Lu Guangsheng, Kong Tuan Yuen, Charmaine Willoughby, Danny Alexander, Paul Evans, Agatha Kratz, You Ji, Guo Yanjun, Gao Fei, P. S. Suryanarayana, Kevin Hewison, Ninad Deshpande, Michael Clarke, Jingdong Yuan, Francesca Ghiretti, Jean-Pierre Cabestan, Yuqing Xing, Xue Gong, Wendy Leutert, Sivarin Lertpusit, Merethe MacLeod, Qingyang Gu and Pou Sothirak, for their valuable advice.

I wish to give special mention to the senior Chinese central and local government officials and senior career diplomats who provided their candid and insightful views on Chinese domestic development, China's foreign policy and the BRI implementation. Out of respect for their privacy, they are not named here.

Throughout the years, I have benefited enormously from the collegiality and thoughtful interactions with the China watchers at the East Asian Institute of the National University of Singapore, where I have been doing research on China and East Asia as a Senior Research Fellow.

I would like to acknowledge the generous support of the University of Brunei Darussalam through the Open Access grant for the publication of the "Asia in Transition" book series. This will ensure my book is freely accessible and discoverable by communities across economics, politics, international relations, technology, the humanities and social sciences. It will also enable my work to be available to readers around the world via SpringerLink, Springer Nature's content platform.

The anonymous reviewers of this book made me think harder about what I was trying to argue; their criticism and comments helped considerably. I wish to thank Alex Campbell, Senior Editor for Humanities and Social Science (Southeast and East Asia) at Springer Nature for her professional advice. She saw merit in the book proposal and shepherded it expeditiously. In addition, I wish to thank Springer's editorial and production team, who oversaw the book's timely production. I also wish to express my gratitude to Rachel Grantham for proofreading the draft book manuscript. Rachel has served me well over the years.

I would like to thank my family for supporting my scholarly pursuit. This volume would not have been written without the love and support of my family and especially my very understanding wife Danlu and my son Alvin, who often critiqued my book manuscript. Indeed, my family is part of this book's creation.

Readers might find a small number of chapters and paragraphs familiar. This book project has been under way for quite some time and the initial versions of a few chapters first found their way into publication via academic journals or newspaper magazines. The work has of course been extensively reworked, updated and expanded since then.

Contents

About the Author

Hong Yu is a Senior Research Fellow at the East Asian Institute, National University of Singapore. His research interests cover regional economic development in China, the Belt and Road Initiatives, the Asian Infrastructure Investment Bank, China's state-owned enterprises and railway sector reform. His research and review articles have appeared in many internationally peer-reviewed journals such as *Cambridge Review of International Affairs*; *Journal of Contemporary Asia*; *Journal of Contemporary China*; *Pacific Affairs*; *Asian Survey*; *China: An International Journal*; *Asian Studies Review*; *Asia Policy*; *East Asia: An International Quarterly*; *The Copenhagen Journal of Asian Studies* and *Asian Politics and Policy*. He is the author of the three monographs *Economic Development and Inequality in China: The Case of Guangdong* (Routledge, London and New York: 2011); *Chinese Regions in Change: Industrial Upgrading and Regional Development Strategies* (Routledge, London and New York: 2015) and *Belt and Road Initiative, The Rise of China and International Cooperation: What Does it Mean to China and the Region?* (in Chinese) (World Affairs Press, Beijing: 2017).

His academic article entitled "Motivation behind China's 'One Belt, One Road' Initiatives and Establishment of the Asian Infrastructure Investment Bank", which was published by the *Journal of Contemporary China* in 2017, has been one of the most read and cited articles on the topic in the academic journals. He is the recipient of the fifth annual John and Vivian Sabel

Award for the best article by the Journal of Contemporary China. He has been interviewed as an expert on China by various international and local media. He obtained his doctorate degree from the University of Sheffield, UK.

Abbreviations

ADB	Asian Development Bank
AIIB	Asian Infrastructure Investment Bank
APEC	Asia-Pacific Economic Cooperation
ASEAN	Association of Southeast Asian Nations
AUKUS	Trilateral Military Partnership between US, UK and Australia
BRF	Belt and Road Forum
BRI	Belt and Road Initiative
BRICS	Brazil, Russia, India, China and South Africa
CAFTA	China-ASEAN Free Trade Area
CCFTA	China-Cambodia Free Trade Agreement
CCP	Chinese Communist Party
CNPC	China National Petroleum Corporation
CPP	Cambodian People's Party
CPTPP	Comprehensive and Progressive Agreement for Trans-Pacific Partnership
CSTO	Collective Security Treaty Organization
DSR	Digital Silk Road
EAEU	Eurasian Economic Union
ECRL	Malaysia's East Coast Rail Link
FDI	Foreign Direct Investment
GCC	Gulf Cooperation Council
GDP	Gross Domestic Product
GSI	Global Security Initiative
HSR	Health Silk Road
ICT	Information and Communications Technology
IMF	International Monetary Fund
IPEF	Indo-Pacific Economic Framework
MDB	Multilateral Development Bank
NDB	New Development Bank
ODA	Official Development Assistance
PGII	Partnership for Global Infrastructure and Investment

PPP	Public-Private Partnerships
QUAD	Quadrilateral Mechanism
RCEP	Regional Comprehensive Economic Partnership
RMB	Renminbi (Chinese Currency)
SASAC	State-owned Assets Supervision and Administration Commission of China
SCO	Shanghai Cooperation Organization
SCS	South China Sea
SINOPEC	China Petroleum and Chemical Corporation
SOE	State-Owned Enterprise
SSEZ	Sihanoukville Special Economic Zone
SWIFT	Society for Worldwide Interbank Financial Telecommunication
US	United States
WB	World Bank
WHO	World Health Organization
WTO	World Trade Organization

List of Figures

List of Tables

List of Maps

Chapter 1
China's Push for the BRI in a Changing World: Origins and Motivations

1.1 Unveiling of the Belt and Road Initiative: How Significant Is It?

The Belt and Road Initiative (BRI) is at the heart of the paradigm shift of Chinese foreign policy. Since its announcement by China's President Xi Jinping in 2013, the BRI has emerged as the centrepiece of China's aspiration to become a global power. China's BRI is rooted in history and inspired by the historic Silk Road, an extensive network of maritime and land routes for trade, communication and cultural exchanges that once linked China with the Eurasian countries. It felt into disuse around the 1600s after a few glorious centuries. China is now keen for this historical Silk Road to be revived.

Since the implementation of the Belt and Road Initiative in 2013, China has made every effort to expand cooperation with the BRI countries in the fields of infrastructure, investment, trade and people-to-people exchanges. The BRI is a globally oriented strategy, and therefore, it has no clear physical boundaries. It is a carefully crafted long-term strategy with an ambitious agenda.

The Chinese central leadership team for implementation of the BRI, headed by the Executive Vice Premier of the State Council, has been established since 2013. In October 2017, the BRI was incorporated into the Chinese Communist Party's Constitution, demonstrating the Party-state's determination to push through implementation of this grand initiative. No other countries have ever incorporated their economic initiatives or development plans into their constitutions.

China is keen to project a "Global China" image under the BRI. The Initiative has been opened up to all countries which are interested, and there has subsequently been a gradual shift away from the ancient Chinese Silk Road narrative based on the historical and cultural significance. Essentially, the BRI is China's outreach, connecting the world with China as the core hub. Nevertheless, several regionally

---

An initial form of this Chapter was published as an academic article, please see Yu (2017a).

H. Yu, *Understanding China's Belt and Road Initiative*, Asia in Transition 26,
https://doi.org/10.1007/978-981-99-9633-9_1

or globally influential countries have not signed up for the BRI to date, including the United States, the United Kingdom, Canada, Mexico, Australia, India and Japan. Surprisingly, North Korea, China's close ally, is not in the BRI mapping.

Moreover, some countries which have signed up for the initiative have yet to host large-scale infrastructure projects under the BRI framework, for example, Vietnam. Some countries have merely endorsed the BRI formally as a concept and pledged to cooperate with China to promote the initiative. Even if some BRI countries are not hosting BRI projects, their endorsement of the initiative lends credibility to it.

Among the major global cooperation initiatives to promote infrastructure connectivity, the Belt and Road Initiative has achieved the largest financial scale and the greatest impact (see Table 1.1). This is a reflection of China's ascendance in the global arena, economically, politically and strategically. The BRI accurately reflects China's rising global influence.

The world cannot ignore the impact of China's rise and BRI implementation. According to a report published by the World Economic Forum (2022), Chinese enterprises and banking institutions have announced their participation in about 3800 overseas projects under the BRI since 2013, involving a total investment of US$4.3 trillion. A poll released in 2022 by the Centre for Future Democracy at the University of Cambridge found that 62% of respondents in the developing countries around the world have a favourable opinion of China, compared with 61% of respondents who have a favourable opinion of the United States. Almost two-thirds of respondents from the BRI countries have a favourable opinion of China. According to the Cambridge survey report, for the first time, China leads the United States in public favourability in developing countries, especially in Asia and Africa. To the Chinese intelligentsia, this survey data documents well the rise of China's geostrategic influence in contrast to the United States' diminishing influence in the world, commonly described as the "rise of the East and decline of the West" by China.

Under the implementation of the Belt and Road Initiative, China has continuously expanded economic and trade ties with other countries, improved the cross-border connectivity of international trade routes, and promoted the sustainability of China's economic development (Office of the Leading Group for Promoting the Belt and Road Initiative 2019). Over the past four decades, China has pursued a national policy of domestic reform and opening up to the outside world, and its development achievements have attracted worldwide attention.

China's "reform and opening up" strategy since the early 1980s has two strands: the first is to promote reform, and the other is to expand the open market throughout the world. The 40 years of reform and opening up, especially since China's accession to the World Trade Organization (WTO), have been a period of rapid development and integration into the world economy. China's great development achievements have been made possible by opening its doors and embracing the world economy.

Since the announcement of the BRI in 2013, the Chinese government has been deploying its full political, economic and diplomatic resources in order to forge a positive image of the BRI among the international community. The success of the

Table 1.1 List of competing regional/global connectivity initiatives

Year	Dominant country/ Organisation	Name of connectivity initiative	Investment committed/Spent	Investment sector
2009	Australia	Australia-ASEAN Development Cooperation Programme Phase II	US$39 million	Technical service for infrastructure development and regional integration
2010	ASEAN	ASEAN Master Plan for Connectivity	N/A	Infrastructure development; technical service
2013	China	Belt and Road Initiative	US$156.2 billion–US$332.6 billion*	Infrastructure development; technical service
2015	Japan	Partnership for Quality Infrastructure	US$110 billion	Infrastructure development; technical service
2015	Russia and Kazakhstan	Eurasian Economic Union	N/A	Regional economic integration and infrastructure development
2016	India and Japan	Asia- Africa Growth Corridor (AAGC)	N/A	Infrastructure development
2017	Republic of Korea	ASEAN-Korea Infrastructure Fund	US$200 billion	Infrastructure development; technical service
2019	United States, Japan and Australia	Blue Dot Network	US$60 billion	Infrastructure investment and technical service
2021	European Union	Global Gateway	€300 billion	Infrastructure development; technical service

(continued)

Table 1.1 (continued)

Year	Dominant country/ Organisation	Name of connectivity initiative	Investment committed/Spent	Investment sector
2021	United States with other G7 countries	Build Back Better Initiative	US$6 million	Climate change; digital infrastructure; gender equality; health systems
2022	United States with other G7 countries	Partnership for Global Infrastructure and Investment (PGII)	US$600 billion	Climate change and energy security; digital infrastructure; gender equality; health systems

Note *According to China's Ministry of Commerce, US$156.2 billion were invested in the BRI countries between 2013 and 2021, while, as estimated by American Enterprise Institute's China Global Investment Tracker, Chinese firms had invested US$332.6 billion in the Belt and Road countries from 2013 to 2021

Source Compiled by the author

BRI will testify to China's rise as a full-fledged global power and boost the legitimacy of the Chinese Communist Party and the Chinese leader's rule at home.

The BRI puts China at the centre of geoeconomics and geopolitics in the region and beyond, a position from which it hopes to strengthen its political and economic ties with the participating countries. Most of the fast-growing emerging countries, such as Indonesia, Turkey, Saudi Arabia, Egypt, South Africa, Argentina and Chile, are concentrated along the Belt and Road routes. By deeply cultivating the markets of countries along the BRI, Chinese enterprises have seized new opportunities, expanded foreign investment and developed new economic and trade ties.

After a decade of development since 2013, the BRI has gradually transformed into a loose institutionalised framework for international cooperation. The projects presently covered by the Belt and Road, extending from infrastructure to manufacturing, finance, energy, services, logistics, digital economy and health, will help developing countries along the route accelerate the industrialisation process. The BRI provides a platform for Chinese companies and capital to invest in other countries by leveraging on China's strengths in manufacturing and infrastructure development and financial power.

The BRI is building a new model of interaction between China and the world: China is going to the world, and the world is going to China. Building on the ancient maritime and terrestrial Silk Road, China seeks to build a new circle of cooperation that extends across Asia and Europe to the African continent and Latin America. To borrow from President Xi's own words: "to expand China's circle of friendly countries".

China has successfully transformed the economic power it has built up since its reform and opening up into expanding influence in the world (Yu 2017b). China's ability to grant or deny access for foreign companies to its huge domestic markets gives it geoeconomic and geopolitical leverage.

While geopolitics and geoeconomics are different concepts with different meanings, the two are closely interrelated. The concept of geopolitics is defined as "an old expression shaped by both academic and popular usages going back to imperial concerns with the links between geography, state territoriality, and world power politics". In contrast, geoeconomics is a relatively new concept: "geoeconomic visionaries tend as a result to anticipate capitalist inclusion rather than the expulsion or containment of evil others. Their focus is on networks not blocs, connections not wall, and transborder ties instead of national territories" (Sparke 2007). In essence, geopolitics studies the influence of such as the military, political, human resources and other hard power elements on the policy of a state, particularly its foreign policy. Meanwhile, geoeconomics focuses more on economic space, covering transportation connectivity, networks, commerce, trade, investment, and financial and economic strengths. Geoeconomics concerns a nation's pursuit of strong economic performance and sustainable economic competitiveness. However, geopolitics and geoeconomics are two sides of the same coin, the political dimension of geoeconomics being strongly intertwined with the competitive economic dimension of geopolitics.

China has leveraged on its formidable economic power to pursue its long-term strategic goals and aims to further deploy the BRI to expand its geopolitical and geoeconomic influence in the world. The countries along the Silk Road routes will thus be brought into China's economic orbit. As Graham (2015) comments:

> The preeminent geostrategic challenge of this era is not violent Islamic extremists or a resurgent Russia. It is the impact that China's ascendance will have on the U.S.-led international order, which has provided unprecedented great-power peace and prosperity for the past 70 years.

1.2 Motivations and Rationale Behind China's BRI Implementation

On 28 March 2015, China's National Development and Reform Commission, Ministry of Commerce and Ministry of Foreign Affairs jointly released the lengthy "*Vision and Actions on Jointly Building the Silk Road Economic Belt and 21st Century Maritime Silk Road*" (the Blueprint) outlining relevant frameworks, principles and action plans. This Blueprint provides the clearest overall picture yet of the ambitious BRI and demonstrates China's serious attempt to materialise its grand vision. In China's view, the BRI is an initiative calling for infrastructure development and economic cooperation that will foster economic growth and industrial development for the participating countries, to create trade and investment opportunities and promote stability and peace in the world.

China stresses that BRI implementation is based on extensive consultation with the countries involved. The Chinese authorities insist that the BRI has no geostrategic motivations or geopolitical ambitions. However, promoting the notion that China is a great growing power but without geostrategic motivations is a hard sell for Beijing, and few outside China believe it.

The author's view remains firmly that pursuit of interregional connectivity through the BRI is being driven by domestic economic, geopolitical and historical motivations. First, against the backdrop of domestic economic slowdown, sustaining Chinese economic growth has been one of the main drivers of BRI implementation. However, in the shifting international geopolitical environment, China is facing daunting external challenges to its economic development.

At the same time, internal contradictions and problems accumulated over many years of economic growth, from environmental degradation, uneven regional development, to widening of the wealth gap between the rich and the poor, are also increasingly affecting the sustainable development of China's economy. BRI implementation could enable China gradually to resolve these various domestic issues and build a high-quality, high-income economy.

The shifting global geostrategic environment and COVID-19 pandemic have pushed China to rely more on the domestic market and resources for generating economic growth. The new development paradigm of "dual (domestic and international) circulation" strategy emphasises the domestic market, while the other side of this dual-circulation strategy is to open up more to the outside world. The BRI will be at the heart of international circulation under China's new development paradigm.

Although China is pursuing more balanced economic growth in which domestic consumption will play a major role, this will take time. Foreign trade is thus still vital to boost the Chinese economy and domestic industrial development. The export of "Made in China" goods to the Asian countries will help to absorb many of China's manufactured goods, such as iron and steel, which will help to address domestic production overcapacity and stimulate domestic economic growth through upgrading of its industries. With its push for BRI implementation, China will continue to expand its global trading and investment ties to enhance its economic resilience and to gain wider market access to the BRI countries.

The Belt and Road Initiative is in line with the Chinese government's "going global" strategy for Chinese enterprises, encouraging and supporting Chinese enterprises to go overseas to find new markets and investment opportunities. More and more Chinese enterprises are confidently expanding into overseas markets and expanding their presence in the global market.

China's economic growth is powered by its massive export-oriented manufacturing industries, while it has to import large amounts of intermediate components and raw resources to power these industries. As the transport of these raw materials and semifinished goods to China largely depends on maritime shipping, a secure and reliable maritime trade shipping line is crucial to China. It is anticipated that a comprehensive and efficient transport network based on land, air and sea transport will facilitate the flow of goods and trade, as well as contributing to people exchanges and stimulation of economic prosperity in China and the BRI countries.

China's accelerated economic transformation and industrial upgrading, and the transfer of some low value-added manufacturing industries to developing countries along the Belt and Road with relatively low production costs will drive China's investment in the regional countries and will also provide opportunities for relevant countries to develop manufacturing industries. Access to the BRI countries' markets has helped China to promote its market diversification strategy for foreign trade and investment, by reducing its dependency on the Western markets, and helped to consolidate and enhance China's position at the centre of global supply chains.

In seeking to gain more profits and expand their global business operations, Chinese companies have strong incentives under the BRI to invest their capital in other nations and implement a "going global" strategy. China is eager to participate in infrastructure construction abroad as such outward infrastructure investment will boost its manufacturing investment and hence its economic growth. For example, Chinese state-owned firms, such as COSCO Pacific, have made huge investment in the container terminals across many BRI countries in order to gain a market foothold through building a better and efficient port infrastructure network for maritime shipping (see Table 1.2). These projects, while currently representing a tiny portion of the completed BRI infrastructure projects, could have major geopolitical and geoeconomic impact across the world moving forward into the future.

Second, from the geopolitical perspective, China's foreign policy direction has changed substantially over the past decade, in particular after the Global Financial Crisis in 2008, and it is now far more proactive, assertive and globally driven. The launch of the Belt and Road Initiative is an important symbol of China's growing

Table 1.2 List of selected investments by Chinese companies in container ports in the BRI countries

Country	Container port	Chinese company	Shareholding ratio of Chinese company
Malaysia	Kuantan Port	Guangxi Beibu Gulf Port Group	40%
Singapore	Singapore Container Port	COSCO Pacific	49%
Myanmar	Kyaukphyu Port	China National Petroleum Corporation (CNPC)	50.9%
Sri Lanka	Colombo International Container Terminal	China Merchants Holdings (International)	85%
	Hambantota Container Port	China Harbour Engineering Corporation	65%
Pakistan	Gwadar Port	China Overseas Port Holding Company	40-year lease agreement for operating and managing port
Saudi Arabia	Container Terminal, Jeddah Islamic Port	COSCO Pacific	20%
Egypt	Safaga Port	COSCO Pacific	20%
UAE	Khalifa Port	COSCO Pacific	Building and operating a new container terminal
Djibouti	Djibouti Container Port	China Merchants Holdings (International)	23.5%
Peru	Port of Chancay	COSCO Pacific	60%
Israel	Haifa New Port	Shanghai International Port Group	25-year lease agreement for operating and managing port
Greece	Piraeus Container Port	COSCO Pacific	35-year lease agreement for operating and managing port
Italy	Naples Container Port	COSCO Pacific	50%
Belgium	Port of Antwerp	COSCO Pacific	25%

Source Compiled by the author based on public information available

influence in the region and even at the global level. The transformation of China's foreign policy began late in the era of Hu Jintao, the former Chinese President. Hence, China's foreign policy under the current leader is a reflection of continuity rather than radical change.

Nevertheless, like their predecessors, the new Chinese leaders need to show innovation in foreign policy by announcing new policies that will distinguish their leadership strategy and advance China's national interests abroad in the changing geopolitical environment in the region and throughout the world. The proactive foreign policy pursued by the Chinese government under Xi Jinping, China's President, is a clear departure from the low-profile foreign policy advocated since the 1980s by the then paramount Chinese leader Deng Xiaoping.

The Belt and Road Initiative demonstrates China's more assertive and proactive diplomacy on regional and global affairs. Rather than passively following international systems, China is now actively participating in the reform of global governance and the international institutional system. The ascendancy of China in the global arena and Xi's initiation of the BRI in such a short period of time after he took office have astonished both the region and onlookers in the West. The new Silk Road and AIIB proposals demonstrate China's capability to develop its own initiatives for financial and economic governance in the region. Allison (2015) rightly states:

> Nearly three years into his 10-year term, Xi has stunned colleagues at home and China watchers abroad with the speed at which he has moved and the audacity of his ambitions. …. Overseas, he has pursued a more active Chinese foreign policy that is increasingly assertive in advancing the country's interests.

China's foreign policy is now more centralised, proactive and assertive. President Xi has centralised foreign policy-making power under his own direction since he came to power in late 2012, chairing the Central Leading Group for Foreign Affairs, the highest authority for foreign policy decision-making in China, which demonstrates his strong man image and his ambitious vision.

The low-profile, passive approach to foreign policy previously adopted by China was understandable when it was a poor developing nation with many thorny domestic issues and limited financial resources. However, China is now far more powerful than in Deng Xiaoping's era and is able to project its power, regionally as well as globally. Xi views the change to China's foreign policy as necessary to match its ascendancy as the rising global power. Xi intends that China will one day become a rule-shaper in the global arena and regain a position of pre-eminence in the world. China's adoption of a more proactive foreign policy stance, following its rise as a global power after three decades of economic reform and opening up, reflects its aim to safeguard its domestic development and advance its national strategic and economic interests abroad.

China's foreign policy stance has been influenced by the increasing sense of national pride that has accompanied the emergence of China as a global power and the world's second-largest economy. The Chinese people and the youth population in particular (such as the post-1980s and 1990s generation) have become more confident about their nation (Breslin 2013). Meanwhile, the Chinese leaders have been increasingly responsive to this popular nationalism. Zhao (2013) argues that the Chinese government has become more accountable to popular nationalist calls since 2008 in terms of its muscular foreign policy, which he referred to as a "strident turn" for China.

China's share of the total world economy has risen in the past four decades from 1.7% in 1980 to 18.5% in 2021. In 2021, China's import and export volume of foreign goods was US$6.05 trillion, accounting for 13.5% of total world trade, and it is now the world's largest trader of goods, ahead of the United States and Germany. These figures reflect China's rise to become a major international power and its movement to the centre of the world stage.

As its economic and financial power accumulated, China began to engage in many multilateral regional cooperation platforms, including the BRICS grouping, Shanghai Cooperation Organization (SCO), ASEAN Plus China (10 + 1), China-ASEAN (Association of Southeast Asian Nations) Expo, Asia–Pacific Economic Cooperation (APEC), Conference on Interaction and Confidence-Building Measures in Asia (CICA), China International Fair for Investment and Trade, and Greater Mekong Sub-Region Economic Cooperation (GMS). Through its active role in relation to these cooperation mechanisms, China seeks to gain support from the respective countries in promoting the BRI.

Third, developing interconnectivity through infrastructure development forms a central pillar of the BRI. Developing infrastructure connectivity is becoming an important national strategy for China in its attempts to gain control over regional markets and industrial supply chains. BRI implementation gives China greater access to energy and other natural resources, from countries such as Saudi Arabia, Indonesia, Turkmenistan, Kazakhstan and Russia, and enormous markets along the Silk Road route to power sustained economic growth at home and advance its national economic interests abroad. The infrastructure development, trade and economic initiatives of the Silk Road strategy will reinforce China's geopolitical position in the world.

China is keen to use the BRI to help regional countries to modernise their infrastructure and improve cross-border transport and other crucial infrastructure facilities. This in turn will help China to forge strong bilateral trade and economic integration with the BRI countries. Connectivity through infrastructure provides the foundation for industrial and economic prosperity. Economic geography theorists (e.g. Kraft et al. 1971; Bougheas et al. 1999; Henderson et al. 2001) have long argued the importance of infrastructure development in overcoming backward geographical conditions and reducing high costs of production in landlocked countries. For example, the comparative cross-regional study by Calderón and Servén (2010) describes the significant contribution made by infrastructure development to economic growth in Sub-Saharan Africa.

Many developing countries have an urgent need to bring in related investment, production capacity and technology to accelerate industrialisation through improving their infrastructure. According to the Asian Development Bank's forecast of infrastructure investment needs for the Asian Pacific region (2017), by 2030, in order to realise their economic growth potential, the Asia–Pacific countries will need a total investment of $22.5 trillion in infrastructure development.

China is convinced that its BRI push will boost regional trade and economic development through interregional infrastructure improvement. Chinese enterprises and financial institutions have become among the most important financing and contracting parties in the infrastructure sector in the developing countries. The state-owned enterprises (SOEs) have been involved in most of China's global investment abroad under the BRI framework over the years. According to the statistics released by the State-owned Asset Supervision and Administration Commission, China's top watchdog for the SOEs, 81 China's centrally administrated SOEs had been involved in constructing 3400 BRI-related projects worldwide by January 2020.

China has embarked on very rapid and massive overseas lending since 2013 when it launched the BRI. It has emerged as a major lender and provided hundreds of billions in loans and credit to developing countries across all continents. Most of China's overseas lending has been directed at the energy, transport and other infrastructure sectors under the BRI framework. The Export–Import Bank of China and State Development Bank are the two major Chinese financial institutions for providing loans abroad for BRI-related projects. These two state-owned Chinese banks provided up to US$462 billion in total in financing overseas infrastructure development projects from 2008 to 2019, which was almost equivalent to the amount of development financing (US$472 billion) provided by the World Bank during the same period (Ray and Simmons 2020).

Hundreds of railways, roads, seaports, energy plants, telecommunications and other infrastructure projects built under the BRI framework have been welcomed by the recipient countries. China's push for the BRI cements its growing importance as an underwriter for infrastructure development for the developing countries. According to the Engineering News-Record's list of "2021 Top 250 Global Contractors", in the field of technological capacity and infrastructure construction, fourteen Chinese construction firms are listed among the top 20 largest infrastructure contractors in the world. These companies are ranked according to construction revenue, which were generated outside of each company's home country in 2020. Chinese firms are not merely the leading players; in fact, China structurally dominates the global infrastructure construction industry.

China has strong international competitiveness in infrastructure construction, equipment manufacturing, metallurgy, building materials and communication equipment. Around the world, from Cambodia, Indonesia and Saudi Arabia to Croatia, Serbia and Greece, from Egypt, Kenya and Ethiopia to Brazil, Chile and Mexico, Chinese infrastructure companies and engineers are involved in the construction of roads, railways, bridges, energy facilities, ports and terminals and airports.

In addition to the transport, energy, power and information and communication infrastructure projects that have already been completed and put into operation, many large-scale cross-border infrastructure projects are under construction, such as Phnom Penh Airport in Cambodia, the Jakarta-Bandung High-Speed Railway in Indonesia, the Hungarian-Serbian Railway Project and the Malaysia East Coast Railway Project.

The Belt and Road Initiative will have a long-term impact on infrastructure development, industrialisation and economic growth in countries along the route. According to a 2019 World Bank study entitled "The Economics of the Belt and Road: Opportunities and Risks of Transport Corridors", BRI transport projects can expand trade, increase foreign investment and reduce poverty by reducing trade costs. If fully implemented, BRI transport projects could increase global trade by 1.7–6.2% and global real income by 0.7–2.9% (Baniya et al. 2019).

The Belt and Road projects can help developing countries improve logistics and transportation capacity and efficiency, speed up the flow of people and enhance the economic competitiveness of countries along the route. The BRI unleashes the potential for economic growth and expanded trade through infrastructure development. In 2016, Chinese companies won the right to operate the port of Piraeus through a competitive bid and then invested in the modernisation of the port's container terminal and the renewal of terminal loading and unloading equipment, thereby improving the operational efficiency of the terminal. The renovated port of Piraeus has become the fourth-largest port in Europe and one of the most important transshipment ports in the Mediterranean. On the one hand, Chinese goods are more easily exported to the Balkans and Central and Eastern European countries through the port of Piraeus. On the other hand, Greece receives taxes through the transit of goods in the port, which drives the development of shipping, logistics and commerce in the area around the port, and provides more jobs for Greeks. China and Greece achieve mutual benefit and win–win results through the Piraeus Port project.

Over the past decade, according to statistics provided by China's Ministry of Commerce, China's direct investment in countries along the Belt and Road has shown a steady upward trend, from US$12.6 billion in 2013 to US$20.9 billion in 2022. The share of BRI countries in China's total outbound investment increased from 11.7% in 2013 to 17.9% in 2022 (Fig. 1.1). The BRI marks the change in the direction of China's trade, export and foreign investment from mainly developed countries toward a mix of developed countries, emerging countries and developing countries.

Despite the adverse impact of the global COVID-19 pandemic, China's investment in the BRI countries has continued to grow, and Chinese investment in the countries along the Belt and Road routes has not slowed down. From 2013 to the end of 2022, according to data provided by China's Ministry of Commerce, the accumulated direct investment of Chinese enterprises in the BRI countries reached US$177.2 billion.

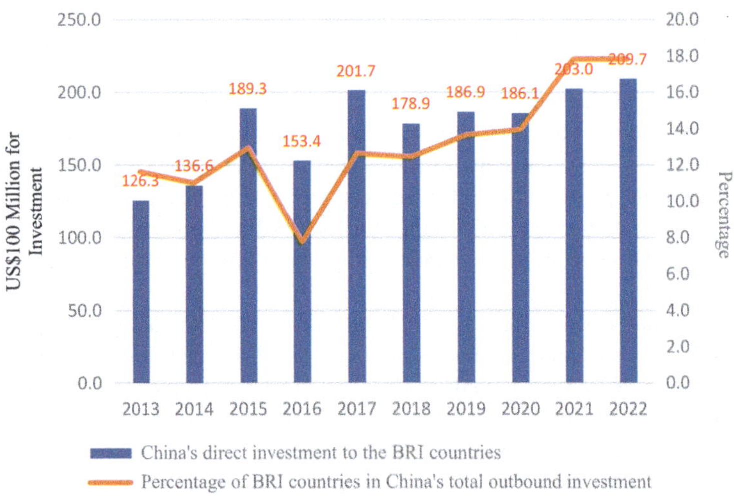

Fig. 1.1 China's direct investment to the BRI countries. *Source* Belt and Road Trade and Investment Development Report (2021, 2022), Ministry of Commerce of People's Republic of China

Relocating excessive production capacity to the BRI countries where there is a demand will be also beneficial to their economies and accelerate local industrialisation, through engaging in bilateral infrastructure, trade and investment cooperation and tapping into China's huge domestic markets. China also needs to engage with other fast emerging markets and to power sustainable domestic economic development.

With the advancement of the BRI infrastructure projects, the transportation infrastructure and interconnectivity between the BRI countries have been improved. China's trade volume with the Belt and Road countries has increased. For the countries involved, the BRI will not only help their respective countries attract more Chinese investment in the infrastructure sector, but also provide a platform for their products to easily enter the Chinese market. In 2013, China's exports and imports to the BRI countries amounted to US$569.19 billion and US$471.36 billion, respectively. By 2020, China's exports and imports to the BRI countries had risen to a record high of US$783.86 billion and US$569.91 billion, respectively (Fig. 1.2). In 2021, the BRI countries combined accounted for nearly 30% of China's total foreign trade.

From the historical perspective, the rationale behind China's BRI is to revive its historical Silk Road. In 1877, the German Geographer Ferdinand von Richthofen first coined the term "Silk Road" to describe the vibrant trade in many commodities, such as silk, porcelain, and spices, between China and the countries along the 11,000-km-long Silk Road routes.

The Silk Road initiatives echo the so-called China Dreams of the great revival of the Chinese nation, which was first announced by President Xi Jinping in November 2012 (The Economist 2013), and this has been reiterated by the Chinese leaders in

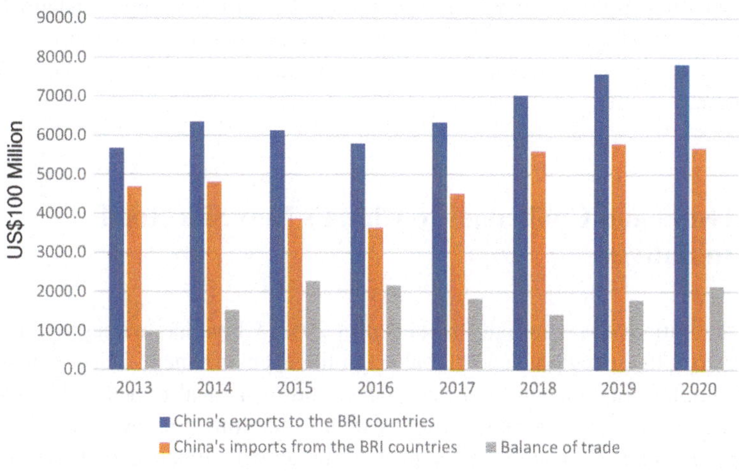

Fig. 1.2 China's merchandised trade with the BRI countries. *Source* China's Belt and Road Trade and Investment Development Report, 2021 Ministry of Commerce of the People's Republic of China

their speeches thereafter. The Chinese leadership sees the BRI as an important step on the road to reclaiming China's historical global position.

Moreover, Ye (2020) argues that the BRI could improve internal economic integration of China's vast inland western regions such as Xinjiang, Inner Mongolia, Heilongjiang, Guangxi and Yunnan and enable them to expand their participation in foreign trade. Improving the interregional connectivity of the landlocked western regions would allow them direct access to port facilities in neighbouring countries. As an example, Yunnan Province borders three ASEAN countries, Myanmar, Laos and Vietnam and is a short distance from India and Bangladesh in South Asia, Thailand and Cambodia in Southeast Asia. Its land connectivity with the ASEAN will be strengthened through cooperation on expressway and railways, and development of its ports and harbour-related and airport infrastructure (Li 2014). These cross-border links will enable Yunnan to serve as the international gateway or connector for China, Southeast Asia and South Asia and will bring much-needed rejuvenation to the region.

The rise of China and the BRI implementation is helping China to boost its soft power in the region and beyond. China wants to build the BRI into a new development model for international infrastructure financing, industrial investment and trade. BRI implementation marks China's transition from integrating into the world economy through reform and opening up to actively promoting globalisation and participating in the formulation of relevant international rules. China has reached consensus with 27 countries on infrastructure financing and financial institutions to support the development of infrastructure projects, in the form of the Guiding Principles for Belt and Road Infrastructure Financing. By getting countries along the route to become signatories to this document, China hopes to form a BRI standard for financial institutions to finance infrastructure projects, which will promote the BRI's standing in the international community. China is seeking to establish BRI standards with countries along the Belt and Road in a wide range of areas, including digital economy, energy development, tax collection and administration, and legal arbitration.

1.3 Issues and Challenges to China's New Silk Road Initiatives

Since the initiative was initially launched in 2013, China has witnessed profound changes to both the regional and global geopolitical environment. During the decade of BRI implementation, multifaceted and multidimensional issues and challenges have arisen. Many Chinese enterprises are facing mounting pressures and difficulties in carrying out business and investment activities abroad, affecting such as outbound investment, mergers and acquisitions, and building manufacturing plants (Yu 2019).

From the domestic perspective, intensifying local competition represents a concern for China. A lack of central-local coordination, in a system already dogged by red tape and bureaucracy, could not only delay implementation of the BRI but could also cause confusion in the participating countries as to who is in charge of the Silk Road plan and with whom they should negotiate. Wang (2011) points out, "Almost all institutions in the central leadership and local governments are involved in foreign relations to varying degrees, and it is virtually impossible for them to see China's national interest the same way or to speak with one voice. These differences confuse outsiders as well as the Chinese people". Such problems over unity and communication undermine China's efforts to promote its grand strategy.

Starting in July 2023, China's "Foreign Relations Law" came into enforcement (The National People's Congress of the People's Republic of China 2023), as the first law attempting to outline the objectives, tasks and responsibilities of Chinese central ministries and agencies in conducting diplomacy and foreign relations through such as the BRI. As written by Wang (2023), China's top diplomat and Director of the Central Foreign Affairs Commission Office, the Law also attempts to clarify the functions and tasks of local Chinese governments in China's overall foreign policy.

From the external perspective, the biggest challenge to China's Silk Road initiative relates to geopolitical factors. China hopes to use the initiative to forge close trade and economic cooperation with the Silk Road countries and boost their economic growth by improving infrastructure connectivity and increasing flow of trade and investment. However, due to their suspicion over China's real intention, the world's reactions to the BRI have been mixed. Meanwhile, China has failed to cultivate the necessary strategic and political trust among the respective parties over the BRI. However, China is eager to demonstrate the "win–win" philosophy as the upholding pillar for BRI implementation. Global perceptions of the BRI are becoming increasingly negative. Salient differences have emerged between foreign media coverage and the Chinese official narrative on the BRI. For instance, according to a survey report of the Southeast Asian countries published by the ISEAS-Yusof Ishak Institute in January 2020, ASEAN members' attitudes towards China have become increasingly complex and cautious. Most of the Southeast Asian elites surveyed believe that "China is a revisionist power and intends to turn Southeast Asia into its sphere of influence", with 63.6% of the respondents having little or no confidence in China's BRI.

By borrowing Chinese money to finance domestic infrastructure construction, many BRI countries are concerned that they might fall into the "debt trap" if their relations with China turn sour or they encounter severe domestic financial and economic crises. Beijing's Belt and Road Initiative was launched against the backdrop of rapid growth in public and corporate debt across the world. Public debt in emerging market economies continues to rise, reaching its highest level for the past four decades and thereby increasing fiscal risk and vulnerability.

As reflected in the case of Sri Lanka, the BRI is not a charitable programme, and the BRI's project financing is based on interest-bearing loans. Sir Lanka is facing its worst economic, political and social crisis in decades. It has been struggling to repay external loans and the interest associated with borrowing for infrastructure construction, partially deriving from BRI projects financed by Chinese firms and banks. On 31 March 2021, the Aid Data Lab at the William & Mary Global Research Institute released a report that examined 13,427 BRI-related projects worth US$843 billion across 165 countries between 2000 and 2017. The report revealed that over 40 countries have debt exposure to Beijing in excess of 10% of gross domestic product (GDP), and 35% of the projects have encountered problems such as corruption scandals, labour violations, environmental hazards and public protests. China has been accused of so-called debt trap diplomacy through its BRI. The critics argue that there is a significant risk that developing countries may not be able to repay their debts related to participating in the BRI. Given their debt obligation to China, these countries must align their foreign policy with Beijing by taking a pro-China stance.

As for the recipient countries, the borrowing costs from China to finance the BRI projects are relatively expensive and could create a significant long-term debt burden for these countries if their domestic economic and financial situations become dire. For example, as reflected from the case of the Philippines, the interest rates and tenor associated with the Chinese loans are relatively much tougher and harsher compared to the infrastructure-related borrowings from Japan and the Republic of Korea (see Table 1.3). The so-called concessional Chinese loans and grants under the BRI are not genuinely concessional or preferential.

Given the fact that almost all of China's global lending derives from the Chinese state and its various state-owned entities, China has become the world's largest official creditor, with outstanding claims in 2017 surpassing those of the IMF, World Bank, or those of all the 22 Paris Club governments combined. According to a study by Horn et al. (2019, 2023), low-income countries that have encountered huge debt burdens associated with China's BRI investment include Laos, Pakistan, Mongolia, Kyrgyzstan and Djibouti. According to a report published by the Beijing-based International Institute of Green Finance in January 2021, among the BRI countries,

Table 1.3 Comparison of terms of loans and grants among selected infrastructure projects in the Philippines

Project	Financing country	Total value of loan (in billion peso)	Interest rate (p.a.)	Tenor (in years)
Chico River Pump Irrigation Project	China	4.37	2.00	20
Kaliwa Dam	China	12.19	2.00	20
Panguil Bay Bridge	Republic of Korea	7.38	0.15	40
New Cebu International Container Port	Republic of Korea	9.96	0.15	40
Improvement of Sections along Pasig River from Delpan Bridge to Napindan Project	Japan	6.97	0.75	40
Cavite Industrial Area Flood Risk Management Project	Japan	9.89	0.30	30
Metro Manila Subway Phase I	Japan	356.97	0.10	40
North–South Commuter Railway Project	Japan	628.42	0.10	40

Source Department of Finance, Philippines (2023)

Pakistan (owed US$20.2 billion to China), Angola (owed US$15.0 billion), Kenya (US$7.5 billion), Ethiopia (US$6.5 billion) and Laos (US$5 billion) had become the five countries most indebted to China by 2019 (Yue and Wang 2021).

According to the International Monetary Fund's "World Economic Outlook", which was published in April 2023, many countries are still absorbing the shocking impacts brought about by Russia's war on Ukraine and the outbreak of new COVID-19 variants, these countries could experience slower growth and rising joblessness in 2023. Against this backdrop, the economic prospects for many BRI countries in the post-COVID-19 era look dismal. Many BRI developing countries have experienced severe domestic economic downturn, debt crises and social instability, and some countries, including Mongolia, Sri Lanka, Bangladesh, Pakistan, Kenya and Zambia, have experienced difficulties in repaying their foreign debts owed to China and other countries. For example, in January 2022, the Kenyan government said that due to the economic crisis in Kenya, it hoped to negotiate with China to delay the repayment of the loan owed to China for the construction of the Mombasa-Nairobi railway.

Nevertheless, labelling the BRI as a "debt trap" is both factually wrong and exaggerated. In fact, even before the launch of the BRI, some countries that joined the Initiative were already facing rising debt levels. Many developing countries have debt problems, but their debt problems have accumulated over a long period of time, and although their debt increased when the Chinese projects were implemented, these debts account for a relatively small proportion of the countries' total debt, compared to their debt borrowed from multilateral financial institutions and commercial creditors. There is no evidence to support the claim that China's BRI push either deliberately sets a debt trap to lure low-income BRI countries into financial crises, or forcefully attempts to take over their strategic assets. In fact, China has restructured its loan contracts with a few countries to help them to meet their loan repayment obligations more easily, for example, Sir Lanka, Pakistan and Laos.

Among the BRI countries, none of their domestic economic and debt crises have so far been caused by China; instead, they have been caused by internal fiscal mismanagement or external shocks, such as the global COVID-19 pandemic and the Ukraine war. Many low-income developing countries that receive BRI financing lack a comprehensive and robust fiscal framework. For example, while there was much hype about China plunging Sri Lanka into a debt trap, China has in fact provided loans that account for around 10% of Sri Lanka's total external debt. Sir Lanka's economic, political and social crises are rooted in the rampant corruption of its political elites, the government's poor economic management and the impacts of the global pandemic. Although the Chinese firm acquired the operation rights for the Hambantota Port, it does not enjoy conclusive authority.

BRI is not an aid programme or a charitable initiative. China views the BRI infrastructure projects as commercial endeavours with loans based on a market interest rate (or slightly lower). Even countries with low levels of debt must carefully weigh the pros and cons of BRI investments. Projects should conform to national development priorities. The BRI countries have full rights to either accept or refuse Chinese loans (Yu 2023).

China expects the BRI loans to be fully repaid since it did not force the developing countries to borrow from China, and it has no legal obligation to offer debt relief or a "haircut". Regarding countries struggling with domestic economic crises and debt repayment, China has accepted a rollover of payments and even offered some interest rate relief, but not a true haircut. The G20 Debt Relief Initiative and the Common Framework have initiated China's participation in multilateral debt coordination.

The strategic competition between China and the United States presents a major challenge to BRI implementation. U.S.-China relations have become increasingly confrontational and contentious in nature, and there is little space for bilateral cooperation. The United States and China compete fiercely in the multidimensional aspects of the global arena, and infrastructure financing and construction has become one of the important areas of contest. The U.S. fears that the BRI, cemented by the rise of China, poses a serious long-term threat to U.S. interests and national security. U.S. elites regard China as having both the will and resources to reshape the United States-led international order, rules and global governance system through the BRI platform. The intensified China-U.S. competition in infrastructure financing and the U.S.'s unveiling of the "Indo-Pacific Strategy" to counter the rising influence of China and its BRI will be discussed in detail in Chap. 11.

1.4 Concluding Remarks

China has been extremely keen to project its rising power and expand its global influence through implementing the BRI abroad, and to forge close trade and economic cooperation with the BRI countries. This marks a major departure from China's long-held international affairs policy of "hiding one's capabilities, biding one's time and focusing on domestic development", which was advocated by the former paramount leader, Deng Xiaoping.

The Belt and Road Initiative forms a cornerstone of China's new foreign policy under President Xi Jinping. By leveraging on its financial power and strong manufacturing and infrastructure development capacity, China is determined to push for the BRI's implementation overseas.

Many countries have aligned their development strategies with China's BRI and explored the opportunities brought by Chinese investment. Driven by domestic economic, geopolitical, interregional connectivity and historical considerations, the BRI has already generated profound impacts for the participating countries, and it is likely to continue to have far-reaching geoeconomic implications at home and abroad in years to come. China's rising global influence and the Belt and Road Initiative also have had a huge impact on the existing West-led global geopolitical and geoeconomic order.

The BRI goes far beyond investment cooperation and economic interests as it has clear geopolitical underpinnings. BRI implementation has advanced China's strategic, political and economic interests in the participating countries. The BRI has brought China to the world, and the world is approaching China. The BRI is also helping China to deal with the domestic problem of industrial overcapacity and speed up industrial restructuring and technological upgrading at home.

Nevertheless, compared to the time of its inception in 2013, the regional and international environment for BRI implementation is now increasingly complex and severe. Despite the initiative attracting huge international attention and China's efforts to increase its momentum, China's push for the BRI implementation is encountering serious internal and external challenges. The effective implementation of the BRI largely depends on the response of China's neighbours, large and small, and will require much more than simply rhetoric and goodwill. The BRI is still, by and large, a China-centric solo or bilateral initiative. China has thus so far been unable to project the BRI as a credible multilateral endeavour. The Chinese authorities have to focus on consultation in order to explain the Silk Road initiatives in detail to the BRI countries and convince them that this initiative will not be for the benefit of China alone.

References

Allison, Graham. 2015. The Thucydides Trap: Are the US and China Headed for War? *The Atlantic*. Available at: http://www.theatlantic.com/international/archive/2015/09/united-states-china-war-thucydides-trap/406756/. Accessed 14 Dec 2015.

Asian Development Bank. 2017. *Meeting Asia's Infrastructure Needs*, 1–106. The Philippines. Available at https://www.adb.org/sites/default/files/publication/227496/special-report-infrastructure.pdf. Accessed 17 Jan 2019.

Baniya, Suprabha, Nadia Rocha, and Michele Route. 2019. *Trade Effects of the New Silk Road: A Gravity Analysis*. World Bank Policy Research Working Paper No. 8694.

Bougheas, S., P.O. Demetriades, and E.L.W. Morgenroth. 1999. Infrastructure, Transport Costs and Trade. *Journal of International Economics* 47: 169–189.

Breslin, Shaun. 2013. China and the Global Order: Signaling Threat or Friendship? *International Affairs* 89 (3): 615–634.

Calderón, César, and Luis Servén. 2010. Infrastructure and Economic Development in Sub-Saharan Africa. *Journal of African Economies* 19 (AERC Supplement 1): i13–i87.

ENR's 2021 Top 250 Global Contractors. Engineering News-Record. Available at https://www.enr.com/toplists/2021-Top-250-Global-Contractors-Preview. Accessed 30 June 2022.

Foa, R.S., Mollat, M., Isha, H., Romero-Vidal, X., Evans, D., and Klassen, A.J. 2022. *A World Divided: Russia, China and the West*. Cambridge, United Kingdom: Centre for the Future of Democracy.

Henderson, J.V., Z. Shalizi, and A.J. Venables. 2001. Geography and Development. *Journal of Economic Geography* 1: 81–105.

Horn, Sebastian, Carmen M. Reinhart, and Christoph Trebesch. 2019. China's Overseas Lending. NBER Working Paper 26050. https://www.nber.org/system/files/working_papers/w26050/w26050.pdf.

Horn, Sebastian, Bradley Parks, Carmen M. Reinhart, and Christoph Trebesch. 2023. China as an International Lender of Last Resort. Kiel Working Paper No. 2244. https://www.ifw-kiel.de/fileadmin/Dateiverwaltung/IfW-Publications/-ifw/Kiel_Working_Paper/2023/KWP_2244_China_as_an_International_Lender_of_Last_Resort/KWP_2244.pdf.

International Monetary Fund. 2023. *World Economic Outlook: A Rocky Recovery*. Available at https://www.imf.org/en/Publications/WEO/Issues/2023/04/11/world-economic-outlook-april-2023.

Katigbak, Jovito Jose P. 2023. Unfavorable Terms of the Loan Agreement. Department of Finance of the Philippines, presentation given during the 2023 NEAT Working Group Meeting "Belt and Road Initiative: Partnership for Enhancing Regional Connectivity".

Kraft, G., J.R. Meyer, and J. Valette. 1971. *The Role of Transportation in Regional Economic Development*. London: D.C. Health and Company.

Li, Mingjiang. 2014. Local Liberalism: China's Provincial Approaches to Relations with Southeast Asia. *Journal of Contemporary China* 23 (86): 275–293.

Ministry of Commerce of People's Republic of China. 2021. *Belt and Road Trade and Investment Development Report*.

Ministry of Commerce of People's Republic of China. 2022. *Belt and Road Trade and Investment Development Report*.

Ministry of Foreign Affairs of the People's Republic of China. *Vision and Actions on Jointly Building Silk Road Economic Belt and 21st Century Maritime Silk Road*. Available at: http://www.fmprc.gov.cn/mfa_eng/zxxx_662805/t1249618.shtml. Accessed 2 Apr 2015.

Office of the Leading Group for Promoting the Belt and Road Initiative. 2019. *The Belt and Road Initiative: Progress, Contributions and Prospects*. Beijing: Foreign Languages Press. Available at https://www.yidaiyilu.gov.cn/wcm.files/upload/CMSydylgw/201904/201904220254037.pdf.

Ray, Rebecca, and B.A. Simmons. December 2020. *Tracking China's Overseas Development Finance*. https://www.bu.edu/gdp/2020/12/07/tracking-chinas-overseas-development-finance/. Accessed 9 Feb 2022.

Sparke, Matthew. 2007. Geopolitical fears, geoeconomic hopes, and the responsibilities of geography. *Annals of the Association of American Geographers* 97 (2): 339–340.

The Economist. 2013. *China's Future: Xi Jinping and the Chinese Dream*. Available at: http://www.economist.com/news/leaders/21577070-vision-chinas-new-president-should-serve-his-people-not-nationalist-state-xi-jinping. Accessed 20 Feb 2014.

The National People's Congress of the People's Republic of China. 2023. Foreign Relations Law of the People's Republic of China. In *Adopted at the third meeting of the Standing Committee of the Fourteenth National People's Congress on 28 June 2023*. Available at http://www.npc.gov.cn/npc/c30834/202306/d4a1d80fd2764a7ca3c57387cf17109d.shtml.

Wang, Jisi. 2011. China's Search for a Grand Strategy: A Rising Great Power Finds its Way. *Foreign Affairs* 90 (2).

World Economic Forum. 2022. *Promoting Green Development of the Belt and Road Initiative: Harnessing the Role of Finance and Technology to Advance Low-Carbon Infrastructure*. https://www3.weforum.org/docs/WEF_Advancing_the_Green_Development_of_the_Belt_and_Road_Initiative_2022_CN.pdf.

Ye, Min. 2020. *The Belt Road and Beyond: State-Mobilised Globalization in China (1998–2018)*. Cambridge: Cambridge University Press.

Yi, Wang. 2023. Implement the Law on Foreign Relations and Provide Strong Legal Guarantee for Major-Country Diplomacy with Chinese Characteristics in the New Era. *People's Daily*. Available at http://politics.people.com.cn/n1/2023/0629/c1001-40023485.html.

Yu, Hong. 2017a. *The Belt and Road Initiative, China's Rise and International Cooperation*. Beijing: World Knowledge Press.

Yu, H. 2017b. Motivation Behind China's 'One Belt, One Road' Initiative and Establishment of the Asian Infrastructure Investment Bank. *Journal of Contemporary China* 26 (105): 353–368.

Yu, Hong. 2019. Reflections on the Belt and Road Initiative. *China: An International Journal* 17 (4): 8–23.

Yu, Hong. 2023. Why China's BRI is Not a Debt Trap? *ThinkChina*. Available at https://www.thinkchina.sg/why-chinas-bri-not-debt-trap.

Yue, Mengdi, and Christoph Nedopil Wang. 2021. *Debt-For-Nature Swaps: A Triple-Win Solution for Debt Sustainability and Biodiversity Finance in the Belt and Road Initiative (BRI)?* Beijing: International Institute of Green Finance. https://iigf-china.com/wp-content/uploads/2022/03/Yue-2021_Debt-for-nature-swaps-BRI.pdf.

Zhao, Suisheng. 2013. Foreign Policy Implications of Chinese Nationalism Revisited: The Strident Turn. *Journal of Contemporary China* 22 (82): 535–553.

Chapter 2
BRI as China's Platform to Push for Economic Globalisation

2.1 Globalisation Characterised by Interconnection and Interconnectivity

Against the backdrop of global economic growth slowdown, rising unemployment and widening income disparities and de-industrialisation in some developed nations, in the West, there is growing resentment towards free trade and economic globalisation. In contrast, China has leveraged on the Belt and Road Initiative and other platforms to promote its approach and thinking on global economic development, free trade and economic globalisation.

Arguably, the ancient Silk Road was the first attempt at globalisation. People from different regions used the ancient Silk Road as a bridge for trading silk, china, tea, spices and porcelain and cultural exchange between the East and West.

The contemporary version of globalisation is characterised by trade facilitation, investment liberalisation and interconnection based on infrastructure connectivity improvement. In today's world, globalisation, based on interconnection and global industrial chains, is intensifying rapidly, and countries have become embedded in this process to varying degrees.

Never before have global economic activities been so highly interconnected and interdependent. As New York Times columnist Friedman (2020) said, "Our planet is now not only interconnected, but also interdependent, and even interconnected in many ways".

Since China opened its door to the outside world in the early 1980s, millions of Chinese workers have joined the global workforce to assemble and manufacture, firstly, toys, textiles, and garments, and later, home appliances, electronic and communication equipment, to name a few, for the global market. Since China's admission to the World Trade Organization, it has benefited more from global economic cooperation and free flow of investment and trade than any other major country.

An initial form of this Chapter was published as journal articles, please see Yu (2017a, b).

H. Yu, *Understanding China's Belt and Road Initiative*, Asia in Transition 26,
https://doi.org/10.1007/978-981-99-9633-9_2

China is keen to be a new champion for economic globalisation. During his speech at the World Economic Forum in Davos in January 2017, China's President Xi Jinping, made this point clearly. In a move to defend economic globalisation and oppose protectionism, Xi vowed to promote closer global economic integration through the implementation of the Belt and Road Initiative.

China's push for the improvement of interregional infrastructure connectivity via the BRI platform is based on its understanding that such connectivity is a crucial component boosting trade and driving economic globalisation. China's promotion of its infrastructure-centred BRI marks the nation's attempt to put its own stamp on globalisation.

China is a global champion for infrastructure construction and financing. For example, China has built the world's largest domestic high-speed rail network, which is longer than the high-speed railways in all other countries combined. High-speed rail has thus become a brand that China is now seeking to export overseas under the BRI (Yu 2014). The construction of Indonesia's Jakarta-Bandung high-speed railroad is based on Chinese technology and design, demonstrating that China's high-speed railway is "going global". It showcases China's ascendancy on indigenous technological innovation and projects its image as a modern and technologically oriented economy.

Export of China's transport and other infrastructure products overseas will not only create new business opportunities for infrastructure construction and related industrial companies at home and for Chinese policy banks such as the State Development Bank, but also, more importantly, it will help China to tackle its excessive domestic production overcapacity and allow it the space to move up the industrial value chain by pursuing domestic industrial upgrading and economic restructuring. By leveraging on its Silk Road initiative, China seeks to grasp the opportunities offered by the global economy.

China views the BRI as a long-term policy initiative and has the necessary patience to pursue the related strategic and economic goals. With its push for BRI implementation, China will continue to expand its global trading and investment ties to enhance its economic resilience and to gain wider market access. China anticipates that the push for BRI implementation will help to develop reliable alternative sources of demand in the Silk Road countries that can help to absorb many of China's exports and then to reduce its dependence on the traditional Western markets.

2.2 Driving Forces Behind China's Push for Economic Globalisation

From the Chinese perspective, many regional and global problems, such as the widening income disparities, de-industrialisation, illegal migration and the refugee crisis, and unemployment cannot be attributed to economic globalisation. The rising tide of anti-globalisation will not reverse or stop a trend of globalisation exemplified by free flow of capital, technology and people. Launching or threatening to launch a trade war, or putting up more trade and non-trade barriers will only result in a "lose-lose" outcome as this will invite more retaliation from both sides.

Nevertheless, globalisation in its present form is far from perfect. The next phase of economic globalisation should be based on a more balanced, inclusive and sustainable model. This would require national governments to implement more measures to cushion the various adverse effects and deal with the downsides of globalisation. For the international community, the most likely hit would be on the poor and vulnerable who lack the resources and necessary skills to take advantage of economic globalisation; this group of people requires protection in order to share more in the benefits of economic globalisation.

First, having already benefited much from globalisation through opening up its domestic economy, it fits China's own interests to push for free trade and economic globalisation. China's emergence as a major global economic power, in particular since its admission to the World Trade Organization (WTO) in 2001, is testimony of the power of free trade and globalisation. According to WTO data, in 1983, China's share in global merchandise trade was merely 1% or so, while in 2021, it accounted for 15.5% of global merchandise exports and 12.2% of global imports. The free trade and free flow of capital and technology offered by burgeoning globalisation have contributed enormously to the Chinese economic miracle of the past several decades. China's determination to play an even more proactive and important role in the next phase of economic globalisation is hence understandable.

The fragmentation of production processes due to technological innovation and the global pursuit of lower production bases has led to China's emergence as the world's major manufacturing plant and a key regional hub of the global supply chains. Its market-driven development experience over the last three decades has confirmed China's belief that globalisation has a vital role to play in its economic future.

For the past five years, the United States and China, the world's two largest economies, have been engaged in a tit-for-tat trade war. However, bilateral trade volume between the two countries increased from US$635.15 billion in 2017, the year prior to the trade war, to US$690.58 billion in 2022, an enormous figure that marks a historic new record (Fig. 2.1). The United States' trade deficit with China jumped to US$382.92 billion in 2022 from US$346.83 billion in 2016 (Fig. 2.2). It is apparent that the United States is importing more from China despite the tariffs imposed on the imported goods from China.

Both the former Trump and current Biden administration have attempted to rebalance trade with China and reduce the trade deficit through different measures. These measures have included imposing punishing tariffs on vital Chinese goods under President Trump, restricting high-tech exports to China (chip and semiconductor products made with the American technology and equipment) and pursuing diversified trade and resilience supply chain policies under President Biden. However, none of these measures have so far achieved trade rebalancing or deficit reduction with China.

Fig. 2.1 U.S.-China trade in goods. *Note* The figures are in billions of USD calculated on a nominal basis, not seasonally adjusted. *Source* United States Census Bureau (2023)

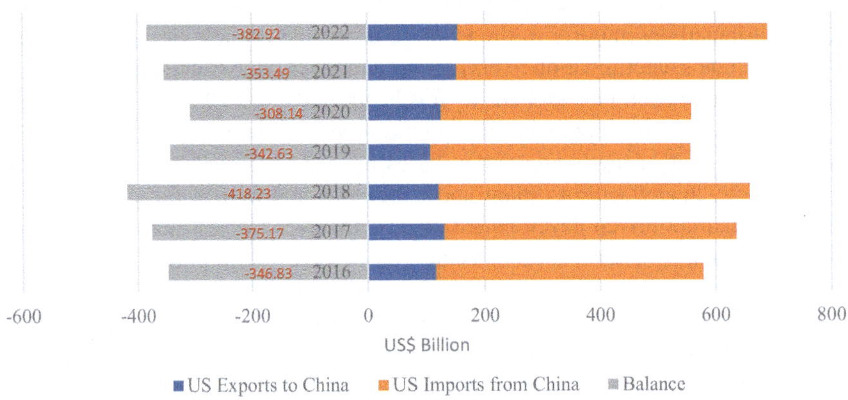

Fig. 2.2 U.S. trade deficit in goods with China. *Note* The figures are in billions of USD calculated on a nominal basis, not seasonally adjusted. *Source* United States Census Bureau (2023)

The much-discussed decline of China's export capacity has failed to materialise. Due to its comparative advantage in terms of manufacturing production capacity, its linkage of upstream and downstream industrial sectors, and productivity and efficiency of skilled Chinese labour, China has maintained its position as a key hub in the global supply chain and the world's major manufacturing base.

The United States' long-held argument is that countries can gain huge benefits through the globalisation of trade and capital, but now the rise of China poses a threat to the national security of the United States and its close allies, which has led both of the two most recent American administrations, the Trump administration and the present Biden administration, to use various policy and legal tools to limit China's influence and supress its development, including tariffs, investment reviews, and export controls. Senior US officials touted the benefits of "near-shoring" and "friend-shoring" and signalled to the multinational corporations that moving supply chains out of China would be wise.

Some policy experts and scholars in the United States (e.g. Boustany and Friedberg 2019) who have argued that China is unlikely to make concrete concessions or give in to the American pressures of tariffs on imports of Chinese goods have now gone even further by calling on the United States to adopt a strategy for partial disengagement with China, aiming to build leverage to address the perceived threats from China, to slow down Chinese technological advancement, as well as to retain the US supremacy in economic, military and technological power over China.

The US trade pressure and "economic decoupling" policy towards China have not served either the intended purposes of balancing the US-China trade relationship, excluding China from regional supply chains, de-sinicizing, or suppressing China's manufacturing and export capacity. The free market is simply adapting itself to find the cheapest way to offer goods to consumers. The policies of the Trump administration and the Biden administration in the United States have succeeded only in changing the routes of products entering the American market and have been unable to reduce the dependence on Chinese products in any meaningful way. For example, Vietnam and Mexico have become two prominent source countries for the US's imports of merchandised goods. Nevertheless, these countries are deepening their trade, investment and economic ties with China. For example, Mexico's imports of auto parts from China have doubled in the past five years, while Vietnam's imports of electronic intermediate goods, equipment and materials for textile and garment manufacturing have increased substantially over the past several years.

In some cases, the Chinese-made goods are simply repackaged and rebranded and then shipped to the United States through a third country like Vietnam. For example, according to the Economist's revaluation (2023a, b), at the end of 2022, the U.S. Department of Commerce found that four major solar suppliers located in Southeast Asia were effectively circumventing tariffs imposed by the United States on Chinese goods by doing small-scale processing of Chinese products.

China, with its well-developed infrastructure, large skilled workforce and efficient logistics, remains the cheapest supplier of manufacturing goods to the global markets. It would be difficult and extremely costly for another country to replace China as the world's largest manufacturing base. For many ordinary Americans, buying affordable and competitive consumer goods from China is still the primary choice. The US-imposed restrictions and anti-China policy measures might have the power to change the direction of US trade with China, but they cannot free the entire supply chain from Chinese influence.

The approach taken by the American government only promotes the transshipment of Chinese goods through third countries, while at the same time deepening the trade relationship between China and the transshipment countries (e.g. Vietnam and Mexico), making the global supply chain more complex and dangerous. Consequently, the global supply chains have become more complex and costly under the

US's pursuit of de-risking and de-link strategy, whereas China's influence has not been shaken.

Second, China's push for globalisation via the BRI platform is intended to facilitate Chinese outbound foreign investment and its pursuit of better returns on its investment. China has since 2008 been transformed from a key destination of inward foreign investment to a major global investor. Chinese construction companies have become engaged in infrastructure projects throughout the region and beyond. Meanwhile, the Chinese central and local governments have for the past two decades encouraged the Chinese firms to "go out" by investing abroad and to become globally competitive. Chinese companies and business people are cutting deals and looking for commercial opportunities the world over.

Many Chinese state-owned firms and private firms have become globally competitive, and adopted a "go global" strategy to gain market access and expand their business overseas. For example, Sinopec and PetroChina, two state-owned oil giants in China, achieved foreign sales of US$126 billion and US$123 billion, respectively, in 2021. Foreign sales accounted for 27% and 34% of Sinopec and PetroChina's respective total sales. The private-owned Chinese tech firms are also expanding their business abroad. For example, Huawei's foreign sales amounted to US$25 billion, accounting for 65% of the firm's total sales in 2021. Meanwhile, Lenovo's foreign sales reached US$19 billion and accounted for 57% of its total sales revenue (See Table 2.1).

Third, China's push for economic globalisation is intended to sustain its domestic economic growth and tackle the problem of excessive production overcapacity that afflicts many of its domestic industries. After nearly three decades of fast economic growth, China's economy has slowed down substantially for the past several years. The Chinese government therefore views the BRI as a new engine to boost its flagging economy and gain market access for Chinese companies in the BRI countries.

China's ongoing industrial transformation and economic restructuring from an export-led economy to one driven more by domestic investment and demands is an encouraging sign for the promotion of global economic rebalancing and offers potential to guide economic globalisation along a more inclusive and sustainable path.

Fourth, China's drive for economic globalisation is intended to meet the huge energy demand at home that has accompanied domestic industrial and economic development, and rapid urbanisation. To meet this growing domestic energy demand and diversify energy supply, China must use the BRI to improve energy facilities and other forms of infrastructure connectivity, which will involve establishing strategic partnerships in both upstream and downstream energy projects with participating countries. This goal can only be pursued through continuing the trend of free trade and economic globalisation.

Expanding its global trade and growing economic ties with the BRI countries will increase China's global economic reach. BRI implementation and the signing of Regional Comprehensive Economic Partnership agreement (RCEP) both demonstrate China's dedication to promoting closer regional and global economic integration as the means to accelerate the trend of economic globalisation.

Table 2.1 Foreign sales of selected Chinese firms

Company	Foreign sales (US$ billion)	Percentage of total sales (%)	Ownership	Headquarters	Sector
Sinopec (中国石化)	126	27	State-owned	Beijing	Energy
PetroChina (中国石油)	123	34	State-owned	Beijing	Energy
CNOOC (中海油)	15	33	State-owned	Beijing	Energy
Haier (海尔集团)	7	25	Private-owned	Qingdao	Household appliance
Alibaba (阿里巴巴)	1	12	Private-owned	Hangzhou	Internet
Huawei (华为)	25	65	Private-owned	Shenzhen	Telecommunication equipment
Lenovo (联想集团)	19	57	Private-owned	Beijing	Telecommunication
ZTE (中兴通讯)	6	53	State-owned	Shenzhen	Telecommunication equipment
Sany (三一集团)	2	30	Private-owned	Changsha	Diggers

Source Respective companies; the author's own estimation

China has emerged as the largest merchandise trading nation. China's share in world merchandise exports increased from 5.9% in 2003 to 15.5% in 2021 (Table 2.2). Meanwhile, China's share of world merchandise imports had jumped to 12.2% in 2021, compared to the corresponding figure of 5.4% in 2003 (Table 2.3). Admission to the WTO has helped to open up the Chinese domestic economy and allowed China to become a key global manufacturing hub, by leveraging on its supply of cheap but skilled labour and low production costs.

In contrast, other major trading nations' shares in world merchandise exports have been decreasing for the past decades. For example, the United States' share in world merchandise exports had dropped to 8.1% in 2021, compared to the corresponding figure of 12.6% in 1993. In addition, Germany's share in world merchandise exports had decreased to 7.5% in 2021 from 10.2% in 2003 and Japan's share had fallen to 3.5% in 2021, from 9.8% in 1993.

Through the boom in trade, China has achieved rapid economic growth based on its strong manufacturing and exporting capability. This has resulted in China's rise to become the world's second-largest economy and the largest trading nation.

There has been much media fanfare that other countries, such as Vietnam and India, could potentially replace China as the world's next manufacturing base and export hub, particularly since India has overtaken China to become the world's most

Table 2.2 World merchandise exports by region and selected major economies (percentage)

Region/Country	1948	1953	1963	1973	1983	1993	2003	2015	2021
World (US$ billion)	59	84	157	579	1838	3688	7382	15,985	21,678
World	100.0	100.0	100.0	100.0	100.0	100.0	100.0	100.0	100.0
North America	28.1	24.8	19.9	17.3	16.8	17.9	15.8	14.4	12.7
United States of America	21.6	14.6	14.3	12.2	11.2	12.6	9.8	9.4	8.1
South and Central America and the Caribbean	11.3	9.7	6.4	4.3	4.5	3.0	3.1	3.4	3.3
Europe	35.1	39.4	47.8	50.9	43.5	45.3	46.2	37.3	36.9
Germany	1.4	5.3	9.3	11.7	9.2	10.3	10.2	8.3	7.5
Netherlands	2.0	3.0	3.6	4.7	3.5	3.8	4.0	3.5	3.9
France	3.4	4.8	5.2	6.3	5.2	6.0	5.3	3.2	2.7
United Kingdom	11.3	9.0	7.8	5.1	5.0	4.9	4.2	2.9	2.2
Africa	7.3	6.5	5.7	4.8	4.5	2.5	2.4	2.4	2.6
Middle East	2.0	2.7	3.2	4.1	6.7	3.5	4.1	5.3	5.3
Asia	14.0	13.4	12.5	14.9	19.1	26.0	26.1	34.2	36.3
China	0.9	1.2	1.3	1.0	1.2	2.5	5.9	14.2	15.5
Japan	0.4	1.5	3.5	6.4	8.0	9.8	6.4	3.9	3.5
India	2.2	1.3	1.0	0.5	0.5	0.6	0.8	1.7	1.8
Six East Asian traders	3.4	3.0	2.5	3.6	5.8	9.6	9.6	9.9	9.9

Note The Six East Asian traders include Hong Kong SAR, Malaysia, Republic of Korea, Singapore, Taiwan, China and Thailand
Source World Trade Organization (2022)

populous nation in 2023 and has a huge reserve of young people. However, compared to the corresponding figure of 15.5% for China, India's share in world merchandise exports was only 1.8% in 2021 (Table 2.2).

Given China's efficient transport and logistics network, its well-established upstream and downstream industrial network and status as the hub of the global supply chain, India will be unable to knock China off its perch as the world's main manufacturing hub in the foreseeable future.

Table 2.3 World merchandise imports by region and selected major economies (percentage)

Region/Country	1948	1953	1963	1973	1983	1993	2003	2015	2021
World (US$ billion)	62	85	164	594	1883	3805	7599	16,299	22,034
World	100.0	100.0	100.0	100.0	100.0	100.0	100.0	100.0	100.0
North America	18.5	20.5	16.1	17.2	18.5	21.3	22.7	19.3	18.0
United States of America	13.0	13.9	11.4	12.4	14.3	15.9	17.1	14.2	13.3
South and Central America and the Caribbean	10.4	8.3	6.0	4.4	3.9	3.3	2.5	3.8	3.4
Europe	45.3	43.7	52.0	53.3	44.1	44.5	44.6	36.2	36.4
Germany	2.2	4.5	8.0	9.2	8.1	9.0	8.0	6.4	6.4
Netherlands	13.4	11.0	8.5	6.5	5.3	5.5	3.5	3.1	3.4
France	5.5	4.9	5.3	6.4	5.6	5.7	5.2	3.5	3.2
United Kingdom	3.4	3.3	4.4	4.8	3.3	3.3	5.2	3.8	3.1
Africa	8.1	7.0	5.2	3.9	4.6	2.6	2.2	3.4	2.9
Middle East	1.7	2.2	2.3	2.7	6.2	3.3	2.8	4.3	3.9
Asia	13.9	15.1	14.1	14.9	18.5	23.5	23.8	30.8	33.4
China	0.6	1.6	0.9	0.9	1.1	2.7	5.4	10.3	12.2
Japan	1.1	2.8	4.1	6.5	6.7	6.4	5.0	4.0	3.5
India	2.3	1.4	1.5	0.5	0.7	0.6	1.0	2.4	2.6
Six East Asian traders	3.5	3.7	3.2	3.9	6.1	10.2	8.7	9.1	9.4

Note The Six East Asian traders include Hong Kong SAR, Malaysia, Republic of Korea, Singapore, Taiwan, China and Thailand
Source World Trade Organization (2022)

2.3 Infrastructure Development and Connectivity in the BRI Countries

Infrastructure connectivity plays a crucial role in bridging different areas and regions and enabling them to reap the full socioeconomic benefits of economic cooperation and globalisation. Geographical economic theories suggest that long distance between two locations increases transport costs, which then negatively impacts on bilateral trade flows (e.g. Brakman et al. 2001; Overman et al. 2003). Modern infrastructure facilities are regarded as an important factor in accelerating economic growth. Sapir's paper (1990) on South Korea illustrates how public investment in infrastructure construction helped this country to transition from a poor nation to a developed country.

Conversely, infrastructure underdevelopment can deter firms from investing in landlocked countries and impede these countries' economic growth. Hence, high transportation costs act as a key barrier to the growth of trade flows and local industrial and economic take-off. Infrastructure development not only is the key to unleashing untapped trade and economic growth potential, but also it lays the foundation for economic globalisation by allowing the multinational corporations to source resources and set up manufacturing assembling plants across different nations based on their comparative advantages and resource endowments.

Geographical economic theorists have produced a number of studies identifying the contribution of transportation improvements in increasing bilateral trade and mutual investment (e.g. Redding and Venables 2001; Yu 2011; Amiti and Javorcik 2008). As demonstrated from the Chinese case, infrastructure investment also helps to promote regional economic integration through redistribution of industrial and economic activities (Qin 2016). Drawing on its own development experience, China believes that enhancing interregional connectivity, and in particular transport development, will boost regional economic growth and promote closer regional integration.

Physical infrastructure connectivity has hard and soft components, which both contribute to realisation of efficient and smooth flow of goods, service, capital, technology and people. Hard infrastructure refers to a comprehensive network of expressways, railroads, ports, airport, power plants, energy supply, and electricity infrastructure and ICT adoption (information and communications technology), while soft infrastructure refers to institutional quality, trade facilitation mechanisms, efficient and speedy custom procedures, and border controls. Hard and soft infrastructure are thus both vital to effectiveness and reliability of regional connectivity. As Brooks' study (2016, p. 191) emphasises:

> The competitiveness of each country's production depends on the other countries in a production network as well as on the efficiency of the trading links among them. They thus have a strong incentive to cooperate with each other, particularly on improving physical and soft infrastructure to reduce the costs of trading between them.

Infrastructure underdevelopment and poor connectivity are daunting challenges that are faced by many BRI countries. Due to domestic economic and fiscal constraints, and the shortage of external channels for infrastructure funding, many BRI countries are ranked poorly on global infrastructure competitiveness (see the global infrastructure competitiveness rankings of the selected BRI countries in Table 2.4) in terms of transport and utility infrastructure, as well as ICT communication infrastructure.

As shown in the Global Competitiveness Index published by the World Economic Forum, while Singapore has world-class infrastructure, many BRI countries score very poorly on international infrastructure performance, including Angola, Democratic Republic of Congo, Kenya, Tanzania, Nepal, Pakistan, Bangladesh, Kyrgyz Republic, Vietnam, Cambodia and the Philippines.

In relation to infrastructure connectivity, these countries are facing the serious challenges of inadequate and inefficient highways and railroads, outdated or uncompleted seaport and airport facilities, as well as lack of cross-regional road and railroad links or a reliable power supply. These difficulties have impeded the growth of trade

Table 2.4 Global ranking of infrastructure competitiveness of the selected BRI countries (Rank/141 countries/economies)

Country	Overall rank on infrastructure	1. Transport infrastructure	2 Utility infrastructure	3 ICT adoption
Angola	126	116	129	123
Argentina	68	78	57	68
Bangladesh	114	100	113	108
Brunei Darussalam	58	77	45	26
Cambodia	106	96	107	71
China	36	24	65	18
Congo Democratic Republic	140	138	139	138
Egypt	52	44	64	106
Ethiopia	123	121	120	137
Greece	37	39	35	52
Hungary	27	30	29	54
Indonesia	72	55	89	72
Iran	80	82	76	84
Kazakhstan	67	73	60	44
Kenya	110	81	115	116
Kuwait	66	79	52	37
Kyrgyz Republic	103	129	88	65
Laos	93	87	97	102
Malaysia	35	29	51	33
Mongolia	101	119	91	96
Nepal	112	91	116	109
New Zealand	46	57	30	21
Nigeria	130	130	124	118
Pakistan	105	69	114	131
Philippines	96	102	96	88
Peru	88	97	79	98
Russia	50	49	50	22
Serbia	51	46	54	77
Singapore	1	1	5	5
South Africa	69	45	92	89
Sri Lanka	61	50	82	107
Tajikistan	91	111	80	121

(continued)

Table 2.4 (continued)

Country	Overall rank on infrastructure	1. Transport infrastructure	2 Utility infrastructure	3 ICT adoption
Tanzania	121	110	122	133
Thailand	71	53	90	62
Vietnam	77	66	87	41
Saudi Arabia	34	34	47	38

Notes (1) The transport infrastructure index comprises the following eight elements: road connectivity, quality of road infrastructure, railroad density, efficiency of train services, airport connectivity, efficiency of air transport services, liner shipping connectivity and efficiency of seaport services. (2) The utility infrastructure index comprises the following four components: electricity access % of population, electricity supply quality % of output, exposure to unsafe drinking water % of population, and reliability of water supply. (3) The ICT adoption index uses the following measures: mobile-cellular telephone subscriptions per 100 population, mobile-broadband subscriptions per 100 population, fixed-broadband Internet subscriptions per 100 population, fibre Internet subscriptions per 100 population, and Internet users as % of adult population
Source World Economic Forum (2019)

flows across countries and stunted local economic growth potential. The BRI countries urgently need external financing to accelerate domestic and regional infrastructure construction. As estimated by the Asian Development Bank (2017), Asia and the Pacific countries will require over US$26.1 trillion for climate-adjusted infrastructure development up to 2030, with average annual investment of US$1.74 trillion.

From the soft infrastructure aspect, the BRI countries are almost all located in regions with underdevelopment of soft infrastructure in terms of border compliance, as reflected in relatively long waiting times to export and high cost to export. The World Bank's "Doing Business Archive" records the time and cost (excluding tariffs) associated with three sets of procedures, including documentary compliance, border compliance and domestic transport, within the overall process of importing and exporting a shipment of goods.

Compared to the corresponding figures for the OECD high-income countries, scores for East Asia and the Pacific, Central Asia, South Asia, Latin America & Caribbean, Middle East and African regions on trading across borders were much lower. This is an indication of underdevelopment of soft infrastructure facilities. In terms of cost and time to export, Sub-Saharan Africa's scores were almost twice as high as those of the OCED countries (Table 2.5). The OECD economies came out quite well on simplification of custom procedures and compliance with export and import requirements compared to regions which have high concentrations of low-income and developing countries. In South Asia, the Middle East, and Africa, much improvement is still needed in relation to port efficiency and elimination of red-tape bureaucracy in customs clearance.

For the BRI countries, enhancing connectivity by improving both hard and soft infrastructure issue is the key determinant for unleashing full growth potential and pursuing industrial take-off. However, this constitutes the most difficult part as it requires enormous amounts of long-term investment. Given that many BRI countries

Table 2.5 Trading across borders scores by region

Region	Trading across borders score	Time to export: border compliance (hours)	Cost to export: border compliance (US$)
East Asia and Pacific	71.6	57.5	381.1
Europe and Central Asia	87.3	16.1	150.0
Latin America and Caribbean	69.1	55.3	516.3
Middle East and North Africa	61.8	52.5	441.8
OCED high-income countries	94.3	12.7	136.8
South Asia	65.3	53.4	310.6
Sub-Saharan Africa	53.6	97.1	603.1

Note The ranking of regions on the ease of trading across borders is determined by their scores for trading across borders. These are the average scores for border compliance on imports and exports. The data collection was completed in May 2019. The scores are presented on a scale between 0 and 100, where 0 represents the lowest and 100 represents the best performance
Source The World Bank May (2019)

remain among the world's least developed countries, they have to source different channels to meet their huge infrastructure financing needs, including government budgets, regional cooperation funds, commercial banks, private investment in the form of public–private partnerships (PPP), and multilateral development institutions and capital market initiatives.

In his remarks at the 19th ASEAN plus Three Summit held in Vientiane in September 2016, Li Keqiang, China's then Premier, reaffirmed that: "China will work with other parties to make full use of such financing platforms as the AIIB and the Silk Road Fund to secure greater financial support for connectivity projects in Asia, especially in ASEAN countries" (State Council of the People's Republic of China 2016). China has provided huge investment abroad for BRI-affiliated infrastructure projects since 2013. According to the Chinese official data released by the Ministry of Commerce, the stock of Chinese direct investment in the BRI countries between 2013 and 2022 was worth US$177.2 billion.

Meanwhile, the American Enterprise Institute's "Worldwide Chinese investments & construction" data from 2013 to 2022 estimated that the Chinese BRI-related investments and contracts were worth as much as US$369.1 billion. Regardless of the discrepancy between these two sets of figures, they both report enormous BRI-related capital investment in infrastructure financing and construction which is an indication of China's emergence as a significant player in global infrastructure industry.

2.4 Limitations of China's Push for Economic Globalisation

The success of China's efforts to drive forward globalisation remains a matter for conjecture, as taking on a leadership role in the new wave of economic globalisation is no easy task. China's power has its limits, and it may not be able to replace the West in leading globalisation in the short term. The United States combined with Europe and Japan still account for over half of the world's merchandise trade, far exceeding China's contribution. The West is still the world's primary and dominant market for trading merchandised goods. Hence, it is not feasible for China to steer and maintain the dynamism of global trade and economic globalisation on its own.

In addition, China still has a long way to go in promoting the open economy at home. Although Chinese leaders have publicly committed to further opening up of the Chinese economy and industries to foreign investment, the reality indicates quite the opposite. The domestic economic reforms on critical areas have been sluggish and without any real breakthrough for the past decade.

The reform of state-owned enterprises in China is such a case in point. For example, despite the Chinese government's rhetoric, since 2013, reform of the state-owned enterprises (SOEs) has been disappointingly slow. Due to the lack of real progress, much of the once-held optimism at home and abroad has faded. Aims to increase competition and promote better market access for the private sector, as well as to raise corporate efficiency and profit-making capacity, are yet to be realised. It is largely business as usual for the SOEs, as they continue to enjoy privileged treatment in terms of exclusive market access, market protection, bank credit and state policies.

The situation on protection of SOEs' privileges has hardly changed, and there has been little sign of the SOEs retreating from the non-strategic and competitive sectors as pledged by the Chinese authority in 2013. Yu (2019) points out that the increasing encroachment of the state through its creation of larger and more powerful SOEs is antithetical to the Chinese authority's commitment to deregulation and development of a market-based competitive domestic economy.

The dominance of SOEs in the Chinese economy has strengthened, despite the nation's implementation of "reform and opening up" and promotion of the market economy since the late 1970s (Yu 2014). Far from being in retreat, the state is marching in and the market is retreating. The inadequacy of the SOE reform process appears to contradict the state's proclaimed commitment to deregulation and development of a market-based competitive economy in China by allowing "the market to play a decisive role". Despite the private entrepreneurial sector being the key to unleashing China's economic potential, the state sector is still seen by the CCP as crucial to maintaining its domestic economic, political and social control. The ongoing SOE reforms under President Xi Jinping are seen as causing conflict with the market-oriented direction of development and reform in China to which the Chinese authority has expressed commitment, and as perpetuating the blockade on fair and genuine competition between the state and non-state sectors.

Powerful vested interests within the state sector and central ministries, such as the State-owned Assets Supervision and Administration Commission of China

(SASAC), have resisted any reform proposals that might reduce their dominance of the Chinese economy. In September 2015, the Central Committee of the Chinese Communist Party (CCP) and State Council of China jointly issued the "Guiding Opinion on Deepening Reform of the State-Owned Enterprises" document (termed the Plan hereafter). In this Plan, the Chinese government outlined many ambitious and bold measures for SOE reform, including the retreat of the SOEs from the competitive sectors such as the real estate industry (The State-owned Assets Supervision and Administration Commission of China 2015). Nevertheless, the powerful state conglomerates only paid lip service to this latest round of state reform plans and there is no sign of SOEs retreating from the real estate sector.

China has to take bold actions to reform its SOEs, in order to introduce more competition and set a level playing field for state and non-state sectors. Its strict regulations and rules need to be eased in order to allow domestic and foreign private investors greater access to strategic industrial sectors ranging from petrochemicals, resources, telecommunications and infrastructure to public utilities and other service industries. The existing laws and regulations have impeded or prevented entry of private investors into many strategic market sectors by limiting their access to bank loans, state funds and favourable state policies.

Concrete actions taken so far contradict the CCP's stated commitment to allow broader participation of private companies in the domestic economy and reduce government interference. This wave of state-directed SOE reforms may claim to be market-driven, but in practice it reflects the Chinese leaders' determination to retain the state sector's dominance over domestic industries and increasingly to use the SOEs as a powerful instrument for achieving the various political and social goals of the Party-state (Yu 2019).

China has long been criticised for forcing foreign companies to transfer technological know-how to their Chinese counterparts in exchange for greater access to the Chinese market. This strategy has restricted the involvement of foreign companies and foreign technologies in the domestic markets. Many foreign countries have also accused China of adopting "an aggressive mercantilist policy" on trade through offering unfair subsidies to its SOEs to undermine competitors and thereby restricting foreign access to a wide range of domestic industries.

Domestic and foreign private enterprises have increasingly complained of the adverse effects of the tightening of the regulatory and investment environment in the Chinese market over the last decade. The deterioration in market conditions has indeed either swallowed up or squeezed out many domestic and foreign privately owned companies.

Thus, the SOEs present a test of the willingness of the Chinese leader to implement a genuine market-oriented reform agenda that increases access for private companies to domestic industries. Moreover, China can only claim a leadership role in championing globalisation by fulfilling its commitment to opening up the domestic economy.

2.5 The Systemic Risks of Globalisation and Call for National Resilience

Today, people, goods, money and services can easily cross-national borders, which also facilitates the cross-border spread of viruses and global epidemics of infectious diseases. China was the country where the COVID-19 pandemic first broke out, and it quickly spread beyond China's borders. The coronavirus pandemic has highlighted further the risks and vulnerabilities of globalisation.

As of writing this chapter, the global pandemic has caused 7 million deaths, and many more could have been uncounted in the least developed countries. Billions in economic output and millions of jobs have been lost due to the severe impacts of the pandemic, which has changed the world forever.

Goldin and Mariathasan (2015) point out in his coauthored book, "The Butterfly Defect: How Globalization Creates Systemic Risks, and What to Do About It", that globalisation brings not only economic development opportunities, but also sudden and significant systemic risks, including infectious diseases, financial crises and terrorism. Goldin analysed that the impact of the crisis will sweep the world in a nonlinear, unpredictable way. His predictions are undoubtedly forward-looking in terms of the significant systemic risk effects of the COVID-19 pandemic that are sweeping the world.

In the context of globalisation, the public health challenges faced by citizens are not limited to the domestic environment but may also come from abroad. Therefore, at the early stages of an outbreak of an infectious disease in a country, it is essential to alert the international community immediately. One important lesson learnt from the global COVID-19 pandemic is that individual countries must also take precautionary measures quickly to effectively block the cross-border spread of the virus.

Cutting off the cross-border spread of the virus is the most effective measure to stop the global spread of infectious diseases. If measures to prevent and control the spread of the virus are not put in place in a timely manner, the infectious disease disaster in one country is very likely to evolve into a global public health disaster, affecting every country and everyone.

The international community live in an era of globalisation characterised by interconnection, while, unfortunately, there are no global governance systems or institutions in place that can deal with such fast-changing emergencies. A sound global governance system is needed to facilitate economic integration among countries while, at the same time, a regulatory system is required to prevent and mitigate the major systemic risks brought by globalisation. However, despite being the multilateral organisation leading global public health throughout the world, the World Health Organization (WHO) has insufficient human, financial and technical resources. The WHO is not tasked with coordinating national responses or providing technical support to lead the fight against global spread of a pandemic. Indeed, the onset of the COVID-19 pandemic has highlighted the weak leadership of such international organisations.

Therefore, in the face of infectious disease pandemics, the resilience of sovereign states has become particularly important. The COVID-19 pandemic will prompt countries to rethink and comprehensively assess the benefits and risks of globalisation. If it is unconstrained and lacks safeguards to manage risks, is it in the interest of all countries, especially poor countries with weak resilience, to continue with globalisation, characterised by interconnectivity? Can the economic and trade gains of globalisation offset the potential systemic risks? How can countries pursue economic growth and efficiency while protecting the health of their own citizens? Globalisation advocates the removal of restrictions on the movement of people across borders and the opening of borders. But in the absence of effective regulatory safeguards, this is not a viable approach and can exacerbate the global spread of viruses.

The pandemic has made us realise the fragility of globalisation, and that globalisation is not as solid and irreversible as imagined. It is an indisputable fact that both states and international organisations lack awareness of the negative effects of globalisation and underestimate the major risks it poses. The pandemic will eventually pass. However, the COVID-19 pandemic will permanently change the landscape of globalisation. After the pandemic, the process of globalisation will slow down, and the "era of national sovereign economy" may prevail again.

Globalisation promotes competition and efficiency, but ignores individual national resilience. When infectious disease pandemics arrive, countries with less resilience, especially those with weak public health systems, find that their public health systems are overwhelmed by a sudden flood of patients. The once-in-a-century global pandemic has tested the resilience of every country, in relation to its public healthcare system, economic stability, administrative system efficiency, manufacturing capacity and social cohesion.

In order to curb the spread of the virus, countries announced various lockdown measures: banning foreigners, vehicles, ships and planes from entering the country. The global situation under the pandemic was called the "Great Lockdown" by the International Monetary Fund (2020). The three-year-long coronavirus pandemic had forced governments to adopt policies of "unilateralism and isolationism" in order to protect themselves. This is a reality of globalisation in the twenty-first century, and it has also presented a great irony since the pandemic brought back to a globalised world the prototype of a "closed and self-contained" society. Many countries not only adopted closed-door measures one after another, but also acted separately. Some countries even competed with each other for limited medical supplies, food and industrial resources.

Apart from making empty promises and broad vision statements, international organisations, including the United Nations, have failed to come up with a meaningful global response plan. In the era of globalisation, the international community's expectation of countries to cooperate with each other to deal with crises has become nothing more than a beautiful fairy tale. Major powers such as China and the United States have accused each other of scolding the others while shirking their own responsibilities during the pandemic.

While mankind is facing a global public health crisis, unfortunately, international organisations such as the United Nations and major countries have not shown the global leadership or international coordination needed to fight emergencies such as a pandemic. The world has never been more uncertain than it is today, and anxiety and fear are enveloping humanity.

2.6 The Era of Globalisation Calls for a New Type of Global Governance System

The pandemic has highlighted the huge risks arising from the facilitation of cross-border movement of people, and the global governance and regulatory systems lag far behind globalisation characterised by interconnection. Globalisation in this form is uncontrolled and unsustainable; hence, the pandemic may prove a turning point in that "anti-globalisation" may become the mainstream voice.

However, it should be emphasised that in the twenty-first century it would be impossible and misguided to return to an era of self-isolation. The globalisation of interconnection has brought opportunities for economic growth and industrialisation in developing countries and has also helped to eradicate poverty in these countries. Insularity will only limit trade and investment, impede the proper functioning of economies and industries, push more people into poverty, and even lead to war. During the G20 Leaders' Virtual Summit held in March 2020, Singapore's Prime Minister Lee Hsien Loong argued:

> Naturally, countries will now want more safeguards against the risks of globalization, and to strengthen national capabilities to reduce dependence on others. Stronger assurances of supply chain reliability and safer human mobility will be needed. A more hard-headed, pragmatic internationalism may arise. But we should resist the urge to turn inwards and discard globalization completely, because autarky will result in a poorer world for all. The pandemic is proof of our interdependence, not an indictment of globalization. (Prime Minister's Office Singapore 2020)

A virus does not respect borders, neither does it discriminate on the basis of race, region or country. Countries in the "global village" era must find ways to strengthen cooperation, unite to fight the pandemic, and stabilise the world economic situation. The international community must also take concerted and firm measures to gradually address the risks posed by globalisation. In future, countries throughout the world should not only pursue economic growth and industrial efficiency through globalisation, but also the globalisation of the future must strike an effective balance between achieving economic growth potential and maintaining national economic security.

References

Amiti, M., and B.S. Javorcik. 2008. Trade Costs and Location of Foreign Firms in China. *Journal of Development Economics* 85 (1–2): 129–149. https://doi.org/10.1016/j.jdeveco.2006.06.001.

Asian Development Bank. 2017. *Meeting Asia's Infrastructure Needs*. https://www.adb.org/sites/default/files/publication/227496/special-report-infrastructure.pdf. Accessed 5 May 2023.

Boustany Jr., Charles W., and Friedberg, Aaron L. 2019. *Partial Disengagement: A New U.S. Strategy for Economic Competition with China*, 1–26. NBR Special Report #82, November 2019, The National Bureau of Asian Research.

Brakman, S., H. Garretsen, and C. Van Marrewijk. 2001. *An Introduction to Geographical Economics: Trade, Location and Growth*. Cambridge: Cambridge University Press.

Brooks, D.H. 2016. Connectivity in East Asia. *Asian Economic Policy Review* 11 (2): 176–194. https://doi.org/10.1111/aepr.12132.

Friedman, Thomas. 2020. Our New Historical Divide: B.C. and A.C.—The World Before Corona and the World After. *The New York Times*. https://www.nytimes.com/2020/03/17/opinion/coronavirus-trends.html.

Goldin, Ian, and Mike Mariathasan. 2015. *The Butterfly Defect: How Globalization Creates Systemic Risks, and What to Do About It*. Princeton University Press: Princeton.

International Monetary Fund. 2020. *World Economic Outlook: The Great Lockdown*. https://www.imf.org/en/Publications/WEO/Issues/2020/04/14/weo-april-2020.

Overman, H.G., S. Redding, and A. Venables. 2003. The Economic Geography of Trade, Production and Income: A Survey of Empirics. In *Handbook of International Trade*, eds. E.K. Choi, and J. Harrigan, 353–387. Oxford: Blackwell Publishing. https://doi.org/10.1002/9780470756461.ch12.

Prime Minister's Office Singapore. 2020. *Written Statement by PM Lee Hsien Loong at the Extraordinary Virtual G20 Leaders' Summit*. https://www.pmo.gov.sg/Newsroom/Written-Statement-by-PM-Lee-Hsien-Loong-at-Extraordinary-Virtual-G20-Leaders-Summit-March-2020.

Qin, Y. 2016. China's Transport Infrastructure Investment: Past, Present, and Future. *Asian Economic Policy Review* 11 (2): 199–217. https://doi.org/10.1111/aepr.12135.

Redding, S., and A.J. Venables. 2001. *Economic Geography and International Inequality*. London: Centre for Economic Performance.

Sapir, A. 1990. Discussion. In *Unity with Diversity in the European Economy: The Community's Southern Frontier*, ed. C. Bliss and J.B. de Macedo, 76–77. Cambridge: Cambridge University Press.

State Council of the People's Republic of China. 2016. *Remarks by Li Keqiang at the 11th East Asia Summit*. China: English.gov.cn. http://english.gov.cn/premier/speeches/2016/09/10/content_281475438626268.htm.

The Economist. 12 August 2023a. *Costly and Dangerous-Why Biden's China Strategy is Not Working?*. Available at https://www.economist.com/weeklyedition/2023-08-12.

The Economist. 10 August 2023b. *Joe Biden's China Strategy is Not Working*. Available at https://www.economist.com/leaders/2023/08/10/joe-bidens-china-strategy-is-not-working.

The State-Owned Assets Supervision and Administration Commission. 2015. Guiding Opinion on Deepening Reform of the State-Owned Enterprises. http://www.sasac.gov.cn/n85881/n85901/c2051975/content.html. Accessed 15 Sept 2015.

United States Census Bureau. 2023. *Trade in Goods with China*. https://www.census.gov/foreign-trade/balance/c5700.html.

World Bank. 2019. *Doing Business Archive*. https://archive.doingbusiness.org/en/data/exploretopics/trading-across-borders.

World Economic Forum. 2019. *The Global Competitiveness Report 2019*, 1–648. https://www3.weforum.org/docs/WEF_TheGlobalCompetitivenessReport2019.pdf.

World Trade Organization. 2022. *World Trade Statistical Review 2022*. https://www.wto.org/english/res_e/publications_e/wtsr_2022_e.htm.

Yu, Hong. 2011. *Economic Development and Inequality in China: The Case of Guangdong*. Routledge: London and New York.

Yu, Hong. 2014. China's Eagerness to Export Its High-Speed Rail Expertise to the ASEAN. *The Copenhagen Journal of Asian Studies* 32 (2): 13–36.

Yu, Hong. 2014. The Ascendancy of State-Owned Enterprises in China: Development, Controversy and Problems. *Journal of Contemporary China* 23 (85): 161–182.
Yu, Hong. 2017a. China' Belt and Road Initiative: The Push for Economic Globalization. *East Asian Policy* 69–75.
Yu, Hong. 2017b. Infrastructure Connectivity and Regional Economic Integration in East Asia: Progress and Challenges. *Journal of Infrastructure, Policy and Development* 1 (1): 44–63.
Yu, Hong. 2019. Reform of State-Owned Enterprises in China: The Chinese Communist Party Strikes Back. *Asian Studies Review* 43 (2): 332–351.

Chapter 3
China-ASEAN Cooperation Under the BRI

3.1 Southeast Asia and ASEAN

Southeast Asia has historically been a loose, pluralistic and non-uniform region that has never had a single name or a single geographical identity. Different people of the region have different perceptions and different interpretations. People across Southeast Asia have only ascribed the term "Southeast Asia" to the part of the region they understand or are interested in and have never identified with the whole. According to the historian Wang Gungwu (2021), "Southeast Asia" today, as a geographical whole, is a concept defined by British colonisers to separate this region from China and India and protect British interests in this former colony. As he claims:

> The name Southeast Asia was originally absent in history, and the name originated from World War II, when the British used Southeast Asia as the code name of the war zone in this region. After that, it became customary in the international community to become the new region of Southeast Asia in their minds, so Southeast Asia was a geographical area concept that only existed after World War II.

Southeast Asia is a highly differentiated region, as reflected in the diversity of topography and geomorphology; geographically, about one-third of Southeast Asia is continental, and two-thirds are islands. Geographically and topographically, Association of Southeast Asian Nations (ASEAN) member countries can be divided into continental (Laos, Cambodia, Myanmar, Thailand, Vietnam) and maritime countries (Indonesia, Philippines, Singapore, Malaysia, Brunei).

Southeast Asia has both mainland and island characteristics, and different geographical conditions have nurtured different ethnic groups, cultures, languages, lifestyles and religious traditions in what is a highly diverse region. For example, the Thai culture is based on Buddhist culture. Buddhism was introduced to Thailand from India in the third century BC. In the mid-thirteenth century, after the establishment of the Sukhothai Kingdom, in order to establish a culture compatible with political independence, Ramakhanhen not only unified the written language, but also vigorously promoted Buddhism, introduced Theravada Buddhism, as transformed by Ceylon,

H. Yu, *Understanding China's Belt and Road Initiative*, Asia in Transition 26,
https://doi.org/10.1007/978-981-99-9633-9_3

and combined it with the original religion, which quickly spread across Thailand. Today, 95% of the country's people follow Buddhism, in a "country of yellow-robed Buddhas". Buddhism therefore influences many aspects of society, politics, culture and daily life in Thailand.

In addition, the countries in Southeast Asia vary greatly in their level of development, politically, economically and socially. On the one hand, this diversity reflects the huge development potential of this region. On the other hand, it reflects the difficulty of governing ASEAN and the great challenges facing its development.

While the ASEAN is a political concept, its establishment will strengthen the overall identity and political independence of the countries and peoples of the Southeast Asia region. Bordered by the Pacific Ocean to the east and the Indian Ocean to the south, ASEAN is at the crossroads between Asia, Oceania, the Pacific Ocean and the Indian Ocean. ASEAN member countries guard the Strait of Malacca, which is the world's busiest shipping route and therefore of great strategic importance to the region.

Before the founding of ASEAN, Southeast Asia was in turmoil, its countries stricken by domestic and interregional conflicts. For example, in 1963, the former Federation of Malaya joined forces with former British colonies Singapore, Sabah and Sarawak to form Malaysia. This was opposed by Indonesia based on claims of British neo-imperialism, while the Philippines opposed it due to a dispute over the sovereignty of Sabah. Even within the Federation of Malaysia, the situation was unstable, intensified by racial contradictions between the Chinese and Malays. Tensions between the federal government of Malaysia and the state government of Singapore reached a peak in 1965, leading to Singapore being expelled from Malaysia by the federal government in August 1965 and having to seek independence.

In August 1967, Indonesia, Thailand, Singapore, the Philippines and Malaysia jointly issued the "Declaration on the Establishment of the Association of Southeast Asian Nations" in Bangkok, Thailand, officially announcing the establishment of ASEAN. Brunei then joined in 1984, Vietnam in 1995, Laos in 1997, Myanmar in 1997 and Cambodia in 1999. ASEAN is now an influential regional organisation with ten member countries (Please see Map 3.1 for geographical location). In 2022, the ASEAN Leaders' Summit expressed "agreement in principle" to admit Timor-Leste as its newest member, granting it observer status and allowing it to participate in all ASEAN meetings. Hence, the ASEAN could soon have 11 full member countries.

Based on accession date, ASEAN members can be divided according to the first six ASEAN countries (Indonesia, Thailand, Singapore, the Philippines, Malaysia and Brunei) and the new four member countries (Vietnam, Laos, Cambodia and Myanmar). The differences among the ASEAN countries, between the continental and maritime, or the first six member countries and the four new countries, are not only conceptual, but also reflected in differences in their economic development level, foreign policy, stance on regional economic and trade agreements, geopolitics and regional free trade.

Through ASEAN, as a political organisation, the ten member countries collectively exercise power based on consensus, to determine the destiny of Southeast Asia, find their own place in the great power competition, and strive to maximise the

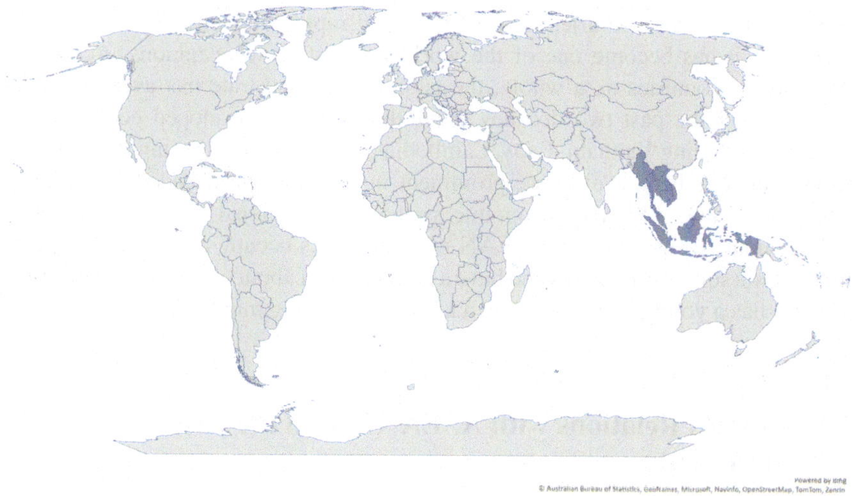

Map 3.1 Location of the ASEAN countries

region's development while minimising geopolitical risks. The unity of the Southeast Asian countries is key to their taking control of their own destiny and avoiding being forced into the sphere of influence of major powers. The economies of ASEAN's member countries are small and single they have no say in the international arena.

Only when acting as a unified whole can ASEAN have the strength to influence international affairs. The basic idea adhered to by the Southeast Asian countries is that in this complex globalised economy, small countries cannot survive independently, and must be unified, at least in some aspects, to speak with a common voice, to have the right to speak and fight for international living space, which was the starting point of their contract. "The ASEAN Charter", which was signed in Singapore in November 2007, is ASEAN's first universally legal and binding document since its establishment in 1967 and needs to be adhered to by all member countries. This Charter, which came into force in December 2008, sets out the direction and objectives for building the ASEAN Community. The strength of the ASEAN community lies in it being able as a whole to exert its influence in the international arena.

Building the ASEAN Economic Community requires creating a unified market within the ASEAN and a competitive region that is integrated into the global economy and industrial chains. The ASEAN Economic Community will also help its members achieve more balanced development and narrow the development gaps between the different countries.

The establishment of ASEAN heralded the countries of the Southeast Asian region's intent to become capable of determining their own destiny and finding their place and room for manoeuvre among the major powers. Based on geopolitical relations and establishment of various regional dialogue mechanisms such as "10 + 1", "10 + 3" and "10 + 6", ASEAN has become an important force, capable not only of influencing but also taking a lead in regional and international affairs.

Southeast Asia's countries have experienced rapid economic growth in recent years, and it has become one of the world's fastest-growing regions. Across the ten ASEAN countries as a whole, the economic growth rate has averaged 5.7% per year over the past two decades. Regarding the less developed economies of ASEAN (including Vietnam, Laos, Cambodia and Myanmar), the annual economic growth rate has been even more prominent in the past two decades, reaching an average of 7.8%. ASEAN's economic strength and regional influence cannot be underestimated, since the ten ASEAN member states occupy a total area of about 4.44 million square kilometres and have a population of about 650 million. Moreover, ASEAN has a young population and a large and growing middle class.

3.2 China's Relations with ASEAN: From the Past to Present

The Southeast Asian countries are China's immediate neighbours. China and Southeast Asia are connected by land and sea and lie within the East Asian region. China's Yunnan Province and Guangxi are bordered by Laos, Vietnam and Myanmar. The 4900-km-long Mekong River flows through five ASEAN countries: China, Laos, Myanmar, Thailand, Cambodia and Vietnam. In addition, China and some ASEAN countries are adjacent to the South China Sea. China's southbound sea passage to the Indian Ocean, the South Pacific region, Europe and Africa is through Southeast Asia. The ASEAN countries' geographical proximity to China makes it keen to develop strong ties with these countries. Given its geographical proximity, Southeast Asia will always be important to China.

China has a long history of interaction with Southeast Asia. The ancient Silk Road, Zheng He's voyage to Southeast Asia during the Ming Dynasty, and the historically tributary systems (Annam, Sumatra, Java, Siam, etc.) all contributed to forging links between this region and China. Meanwhile, due to its vast geographical and population size, as well as its economic prowess and military might, China has always been impossible for its smaller Southeast Asian neighbours to ignore.

The Chinese authorities describe Southeast Asia as an important commercial hub along the maritime Silk Road route, with an indispensable role in expanding China's external trade with the outside world. In the past, China sold its silk, and porcelain products to this region in exchange for foreign commodities. In the early fifteenth century, under the command of Admiral Zheng He, the Ming emperor dispatched a series of naval expeditions and treasure ships to foreign countries, reaching as far as the South China Sea, Indian Ocean and the African continent (Waugh 2010; Page 2013). Hence, the trade links between China and its neighbouring littoral states in the region can be traced back to ancient times.

However, the Chinese government's version of the significance of Zheng He's voyages to the Southeast Asia during the Ming Dynasty should be treated with caution as it contains some myths. Zheng He's main mission was not to promote trade and build friendly relations with countries and regions along the route, but instead to demonstrate China's sea power and the formidable imperial rule of Emperor Yongle (Wang 1970).

In fact, most of the maritime trade across the Silk Road routes was not initiated by the Chinese, and imperial China's trade with the Southeast Asian littoral states was limited, as was its maritime prowess. The historian Wang Gungwu's studies (2008; 2009) show that expansion of the Chinese empire had been consistently landwards and Chinese rulers were consistently passive about forging maritime contact with the outside world, despite sporadic maritime trade links with Southeast Asian ports during Emperor Yongle's era. After his death, his successors showed little interest in maritime trade with the outside world. The Dutch and Portuguese played an important role in maritime trade with Southeast Asia along the Silk Road, while by the eighteenth century the British had started to play a dominant role in the maritime routes in the region.

In 1991, China and ASEAN formally established dialogue relations. In July 1991, then Chinese Foreign Minister Qian Qichen attended the 24th ASEAN Foreign Ministers' Meeting, which was a diplomatic move by China to try to break its isolation and economic blockade by the West and also to mark the opening of a new chapter in China-ASEAN relations. In 1996, China became a comprehensive dialogue partner of ASEAN. In 2003, China took the lead in signing the "Treaty of Amity and Cooperation in Southeast Asia" with ASEAN and a bilateral strategic partnership was established.

The bilateral cooperation between China and ASEAN has breadth, depth and intensity. China and ASEAN are each other's most important economic and trade partners. China was the first foreign country with which the ASEAN established a strategic partnership, and the China-ASEAN Free Trade Area is also the first bilateral free trade area established by ASEAN. Cooperation between China and ASEAN countries includes bilateral cooperation at the national level as well as multilateral and subregional cooperation.

Comprehensive cooperation between China and ASEAN has become well-established. China has been proactively participating in the multilateral cooperation mechanisms, which are initiated or organised by the ASEAN since the 1991. Major bilateral cooperation mechanisms include the China-ASEAN Summit ("10 + 1" cooperation mechanism), China-ASEAN Free Trade Area, China-ASEAN Expo, the BRI and China-ASEAN maritime cooperation mechanism. In addition, China has made efforts to forge strong bilateral ties with individual ASEAN countries over the years. Under the framework of multilateral cooperation, China and Southeast Asian countries have also established multilevel, all-field and institutionalised bilateral cooperation in fields such as diplomacy, economy and trade, health, tourism, cultural exchanges, military, law enforcement agencies, infrastructure and water resources management.

Since China is one of the world's largest consumer markets, ASEAN countries expect greater market access and to expand their business operations and investment space in China. In terms of breadth and depth, China's economic ties with ASEAN are stronger today than ever before. The rise of China, leveraged on its position as the world's second-largest economy and the largest trading nation, has exerted a powerful pull on the ASEAN economies. China is among the most important trade, investment and economic partners for all Southeast Asian countries. Meanwhile, due to the increasing importance of ASEAN to its foreign policy interests, China is keen to deepen its political, economic and people-to-people ties with the ASEAN countries.

China accounts for over 18% of the global economy. It is also the world's largest buyer of resources since it needs resources to achieve sustainable economic growth and industrial development and has insufficient resources of its own to meet demand. However, ASEAN is rich in energy and other mineral resources. For example, some ASEAN countries are among the world's leading producers of natural rubber. According to the International Rubber Research Organization, the global total natural rubber production in 2019 was 13.76 million tonnes, and Thailand, Indonesia and Vietnam were the world's top three natural rubber producers, accounting for 5.09 million tonnes, 3.16 million tonnes and 1.23 million tonnes, respectively. China is the world's largest consumer of natural rubber, accounting for 40% of global natural rubber consumption. Moreover, China's natural rubber imports account for 75% of its total domestic consumption.

China has also become one of the important foreign investors in ASEAN. ASEAN countries have huge potential in the consumer market and steady economic growth. The middle-class population in the region is expanding and the population is relatively young and energetic. As a result, the region is attracting more and more attention from Chinese companies and other multinational companies. China's direct investment in ASEAN countries increased from US$2.06 billion in 2009 to US$13.02 billion in 2019, with Singapore, Indonesia and Vietnam attracting the most Chinese investment, amounting to US$4.82 billion, US$2.22 billion and US$1.64 billion, respectively, in 2019 (See Table 3.1).

As of the end of December 2019, the stock of two-way investment between China and ASEAN was US$236.9 billion. China had invested a total of US$113.3 billion in ASEAN, while ASEAN's cumulative investment in China was US$124.6 billion. Chinese enterprises and business people are very active in Southeast Asia, and Chinese companies are involved in many large-scale infrastructure construction projects in the region. Imports from China also play an important role in the Southeast Asian countries' domestic consumption. "Made in China" products range from consumer goods and food, household appliances, to high-end train locomotives, smartphones and telecommunication equipment.

The ASEAN is accelerating its internal economic integration and building a unified regional market to achieve the free flow of goods, services, people, investment and technology. These efforts will inevitably bring new business opportunities for Chinese companies and increase direct investment in ASEAN. Many Chinese enterprises, such as Huawei, ZTE, TCL, Midea, and BYD, have already set up factories and regional headquarters in Southeast Asia. Improvements in interregional connectivity infrastructure, as well as reductions in non-tariff barriers brought about by the implementation of the Regional Comprehensive Partnership (RCEP) from January 2022, and additional measures to enhance trade and investment facilitation will encourage

Table 3.1 China's FDI in ASEAN, 2009–2019 (in US$100 million)

Country	2009	2010	2011	2012	2013	2014	2015	2016	2017	2018	2019
Singapore	10.49	6.99	54.66	59.70	25.08	41.67	39.91	43.71	66.80	37.61	48.25
Indonesia	3.59	3.53	2.15	3.35	5.91	10.68	3.23	3.54	19.94	21.42	22.23
Vietnam	1.11	1.15	3.82	1.90	9.48	2.09	3.81	9.69	8.52	10.77	16.48
Laos	0.36	0.45	2.78	N/A	N/A	6.14	6.65	7.10	13.13	10.45	11.49
Cambodia	0.97	1.27	1.79	3.67	2.86	5.54	5.37	5.01	6.18	7.98	7.46
Thailand	1.69	6.33	0.21	5.98	9.39	– 2.21	2.38	10.72	0.07	6.62	13.71
Philippines	– 0.03	0	– 0.04	– 0.01	0.06	0.46	0.59	0.17	0.29	1.98	– 0.04
Malaysia	– 1.21	– 0.06	– 0.15	0.33	0.94	3.02	3.23	14.07	15.88	1.77	11.09
Myanmar	3.70	15.21	6.70	4.80	7.90	0.71	0.52	2.05	5.54	0.75	– 0.42
Brunei	0	0	0	0	0	0	0	0	0	0.02	– 0.04
Total	20.67	33.87	71.92	79.72	42.84	68.10	65.69	96.06	136.35	99.37	130.21

Source ASEAN Secretariat database

Chinese companies to further expand their direct investment in Southeast Asian countries.

In 2022, China's leading electric vehicle company, BYD announced that it will set up an electric vehicle factory in Thailand, which is expected to reach an annual production capacity of 150,000 electric vehicles in 2024 to supply the market in Thailand and other ASEAN countries. The Thailand plant will be BYD's first electric vehicle manufacturing plant in Southeast Asia and the company's first passenger car plant overseas. Based on its optimism about the foundations of Thailand's local auto industry, rich human resources and technical reserves, BYD is targeting Thailand's new energy vehicle market and also values the export potential of Thailand's auto industry. BYD's investment is not only conducive to the development of Thailand's new energy vehicle industry and strengthening Thailand's position as a Southeast Asian automobile manufacturing hub, but also helping Chinese enterprises to benefit from relevant technological advantages, increase foreign investment and expand ASEAN's market opportunities, thereby helping to deepen cooperation between China and ASEAN in the field of manufacturing.

Thailand has traditionally been the largest automobile manufacturing centre and car sales market in Southeast Asia. With the new trend towards developing green new energy vehicles and the growth of the global new energy vehicle market, the Thai government has issued support policies for the production and sale of green energy vehicles, to boost production to 30% (or 750,000 vehicles) of the total domestic automobile production by 2030, develop Thailand as an important new energy vehicle market centre in Southeast Asia and also to build a mature supply chain system.

In the face of the global trend of renewable energy transition and the rapid rise of electric vehicles in recent years, Thailand, as a major automobile manufacturing centre in Southeast Asia, is seeking new investment to achieve sustainable development and diversification of the automotive industry.

Thailand has consequently become one of the most active countries in the whole of Southeast Asia in terms of electrification transition. It is not only embracing new energy, as represented by pure electric vehicles, at the local market level, but also vigorously driving this transformation through policies, including battery production and other industrial chains. In addition, the Thai government's policy incentives cover the production and sales of electric vehicles, including tax breaks, subsidies, supporting facilities construction, etc., to attract foreign car companies to invest in Thailand and improve local consumption power.

Chinese car companies, such as BYD and Great Wall, have entered the Southeast Asian market, which is geographically close to China, has lower labour and land costs, and where preferential state policies are in place, such as tax reduction subsidies and tariff exemptions. Hence, many Chinese carmakers choose to buy factories or build manufacturing plants locally.

3.3 China-ASEAN Free Trade Area

The China-ASEAN Free Trade Area (CAFTA) covers about 2.04 billion people, accounting for 26.8% of the global population. The CAFTA has a combined economy of over US$23 trillion, accounting for about 20% of the global economy. China and the ASEAN countries have their own industrial structures, strong industrial complementarity and obvious advantages that offer great potential for bilateral production capacity cooperation. China and ASEAN have reached a bilateral free trade area agreement to make it easier for domestic enterprises to enter each other's markets as a result of significantly reduced tariffs.

The CAFTA promotes bilateral trade and investment exchanges and also enables the two sides to participate more closely and play stronger roles in the regional industrial supply chain. Under the framework of the bilateral free trade area, more than 90% of the goods and products now have zero tariffs, which has effectively reduced the cost of the trade system, making it easier to allocate production factors across the region and achieve efficiency improvement.

ASEAN is an export-oriented economy that is highly dependent on foreign trade and investment. The establishment of the CAFTA will help ASEAN countries expand exports of advantageous products (such as agricultural products, resources and electronic products) to the Chinese market. It will also help Chinese companies export electronic products and machinery to ASEAN countries at a lower cost. China's share of ASEAN countries' total exports increased from 11.4% in 2012 to 16.4% in 2021. For example, China is Vietnam's largest export market for agricultural and aquatic products and aquatic exports to China account for more than 16% of Vietnam's total seafood exports. Growth in the Chinese population's consumption power has led to huge demand for imported seafood in China. Hence, the Chinese market is one of the main drivers of development of the aquaculture industry globally, as well as in Vietnam.

Accelerated industrialisation and urbanisation are taking place in many ASEAN countries. These countries have a huge need for external capital, technology and talent. China, on the other hand, has surplus capital and other advantages in many industrial sectors. Under the framework of the China-ASEAN Free Trade Area, there is room for complementarity between the industries of China and ASEAN countries.

The establishment of the CAFTA in 2010 led to rapid growth in the scale of bilateral trade. Since 2009, China has maintained its position as ASEAN's largest trading partner. Since 2020, ASEAN has been China's largest trading partner, and ASEAN is also China's second-largest source of foreign investment. The COVID-19 pandemic has not affected bilateral trade and the ASEAN has maintained its position as China's largest trading partner, with bilateral economic and trade ties becoming even closer during the COVID years.

China is actively promoting trade liberalisation and seeking to reach free trade agreements with more countries/regions, with the aim of expanding its share in regional markets and global trade. This was the original intention of China's promotion of the FTA with ASEAN and its participation in the RCEP. China's domestic economy will benefit under the framework of the bilateral free trade area through Chinese enterprises being able to expand their overseas business space and find new markets for China's exports of goods and services. Meanwhile, close economic and trade ties with ASEAN based on bilateral free trade areas will also help China expand its geostrategic space and strengthen its influence on regional integration.

Trade between China and ASEAN countries has a deep historical foundation, and the two sides have developed close economic and trade partnerships with breadth, depth and resilience. Since the implementation of the CAFTA, bilateral trade increased from US$41.6 billion in 2001 to US$970 billion in 2022 (Table 3.2), during which time bilateral trade increased by more than 23 times. China has remained ASEAN's largest trading partner for 13 consecutive years, and ASEAN has remained China's largest trading partner for three consecutive years. In particular, in 2022, the bilateral trade total was US$970 billion, but it bucked the trend and increased by 5.7% during the pandemic years, with ASEAN accounting for 15% of China's total foreign trade.

Nevertheless, there are several increasingly acute problems and complex challenges facing economic and trade cooperation between China and ASEAN countries. First, China and some ASEAN countries have similar industrial structures and similar export destinations, so they still compete fiercely in overseas export markets. There are high levels of overlap in the structure of China and some ASEAN countries' export commodities, causing homogeneity in competition. In the industrial sectors where competition is intense, the impact on China is relatively small (about 12.8%), as China's industrial structure is more diversified, while 40% of the total exports of ASEAN countries come from these sectors.

China and ASEAN both have fast-developing emerging economies, dependent on export trade, and located at the middle and low end of the value chain/supply

Table 3.2 China-ASEAN bilateral trade, 1991–2022 (in US$100 million)

Year	Total trade	China's exports to ASEAN	China imports from ASEAN	Balance of trade
1991	84.0	44.6	39.4	5.2
1992	90.8	46.7	44.1	2.6
1993	116.4	53.4	63.0	− 9.6
1994	143.3	71.6	71.7	− 0.1
1995	203.7	104.7	99.0	5.7
1996	211.6	103.1	108.5	− 5.4
1997	251.6	127.0	124.6	2.4
1998	231.0	110.3	120.7	− 10.4
1999	270.4	121.7	148.7	− 27.0
2000	395.2	173.4	221.8	− 48.4
2001	416.2	183.9	232.3	− 48.4
2002	547.7	235.7	312.0	− 76.3
2003	782.5	309.3	473.3	− 164.0
2004	1058.8	429.0	629.8	− 200.8
2005	1303.7	553.7	750.9	− 196.3
2006	1608.4	713.1	895.3	− 182.2
2007	2025.5	941.8	1083.7	− 141.9
2008	2311.2	1141.4	1169.7	− 28.3
2009	2130.1	1062.9	1067.1	− 4.2
2010	2927.8	1382.2	1545.6	− 163.4
2011	3630.8	1700.7	1930.2	− 229.5
2012	4000.9	2042.7	1958.2	84.5
2013	4436.0	2440.4	2003.4	437.0
2014	4803.9	2720.7	2083.2	637.5
2015	4721.6	2777.0	1944.6	832.4
2016	4518.0	2555.7	1962.2	593.5
2017	5147.7	2790.7	2356.9	433.8
2018	5878.7	3192.4	2686.3	506.1
2019	6414.6	3594.2	2820.4	773.8
2020	6845.9	3837.2	3008.7	828.5
2021	8782.0	4836.9	3945.1	891.8
2022	9700.0	5600.0	4100.0	1500.0

Source China Customs; Ministry of Commerce of China

chain under economic globalisation. Due to the high degree of similarity in their export commodities and export markets, competition in terms of export commodities and export destinations is inevitable. For example, China competes with Vietnam, Cambodia, Indonesia and Laos in the textile and garment industries and with Vietnam in wood manufacturing, leather and footwear. However, due to China's rising production costs and industrial transfer strategy, ASEAN has become increasingly competitive in low-end labour-intensive manufacturing based on lower production costs, cheap labour and natural resource advantages. Competition between China and ASEAN in this area is slowing down.

Nevertheless, industrial competition between China and ASEAN also exists in industries such as electronic information, automobile manufacturing, petrochemical, machinery and equipment manufacturing, and office equipment manufacturing, with medium- and high-end added value. As China accelerates its industrial upgrading, the degree of competition between the two sides in these industrial fields has increased. For example, China and Vietnam compete in the electronics industry and smartphone manufacturing, while China competes with Thailand and Malaysia in the field of automobile manufacturing.

China's competitive advantage lies in its large number of skilled and hardworking industrial workers, improved transportation and power infrastructure, upstream and downstream supporting supply chains, stable domestic political situation and huge consumer market. Since the launch of the CAFTA, Chinese-made goods have had a greater impact on the home markets of ASEAN countries, especially Vietnam, the Philippines and Indonesia, because of their relatively low cost and scale advantages. The influx of large numbers of Chinese-made goods into the markets of ASEAN countries has caused great pressure on local enterprises, resulting in bankruptcy due to the inability to compete and rising unemployment among local workers.

Second, many ASEAN countries, such as Vietnam, the Philippines, Indonesia and Thailand, have widening trade deficits with China. This is not conducive to the sustainable development of bilateral economic and trade cooperation in the long run. Especially since the implementation of the CAFTA in 2010, with the expansion of bilateral trade, there has been much faster growth in China's exports to ASEAN than in imports from ASEAN, resulting in ASEAN going from surplus to deficit in bilateral trade, which has expanded year by year. China's trade surplus with ASEAN soared from US$8.45 billion in 2012 to US$150 billion in 2022 (see Table 3.2).

ASEAN's bilateral trade with China was already in deficit before the signing of the CAFTA agreement, but since the CAFTA came to enforcement in 2010, the bilateral trade imbalance between China and ASEAN has gradually expanded. China has transitioned from being a trade deficit country to a surplus country. The widening of the trade deficit, which reached a new high in 2022, will ultimately be detrimental to industrialisation of ASEAN countries.

The main reasons for the imbalance between trade between China and ASEAN are, first, the Chinese goods are more cost-effective to produce and are able to meet the current consumption needs of ASEAN people. Second, in ASEAN countries there is great demand for intermediate products produced in China, which are processed and assembled in ASEAN and sold to developed markets in Europe and the United States.

Third, regarding institutional factors, the Chinese market is not open enough, and strict market access thresholds restrict ASEAN products from entering the Chinese market. This uneven playing field has exacerbated the trade imbalance.

These three factors have led to bilateral trade imbalances in China's favour that will intensify bilateral economic and trade frictions between China and ASEAN. This huge trade deficit is the biggest obstacle to further development of bilateral economic and trade relations and cooperation between the two sides.

However, as China's economic transformation and industrial upgrading accelerate, some of the low-value-added manufacturing industries will be transferred to ASEAN countries with relatively low production costs, which will drive Chinese investment in ASEAN and provide new opportunities for industrial development in the ASEAN countries. In addition, updating and expanding the content and scope of the CAFTA Agreement, to improve interregional connectivity and transportation infrastructure, as well as to reduce non-tariff barriers and introduce more trade and investment facilitation measures will enable Chinese enterprises to expand their direct investment in ASEAN. At the same time, ASEAN is accelerating internal economic integration and building a large regional unified market to achieve the free flow of goods, services, people, investment and technology. These efforts are bound to increase the need for investment in infrastructure and other industries. This will bring new business opportunities for Chinese companies and direct investment in ASEAN.

In November 2021, China and ASEAN held a summit commemorating the 30th anniversary of the establishment of dialogue relations. Chinese President Xi Jinping has proposed the development of a China-ASEAN Free Trade Area Version 3.0 to further enhance investment liberalisation and facilitation and expand bilateral cooperation in new fields such as digital economy.

3.4 The Impacts of China-US Rivalry on ASEAN

Southeast Asia is open for business, and it has developed multiple external links. The economic and trade development of Southeast Asian countries can, however, be easily affected by external factors. The situation regarding the United States is the most important external variable affecting the development of China-Southeast Asian relations, and the spillover effects of the great Sino-US power competition are increasingly affecting bilateral relations.

The Sino-US trade war has impacted regional and even global supply chains/industrial chains. The Sino-US trade dispute has so far had a polarising impact on Southeast Asian countries. The impact of the Sino-US trade war will depend on the industrial development levels of the different ASEAN countries and their respective positions in the regional/global industrial chain.

Due to the rise in China's production costs in recent years, the trend of dispersion and restructuring of regional industrial chains, and the Sino-US trade war, the regional industrial chain has tended to relocate from China, particularly in the case of labour-intensive industries. The primary destinations for these labour-intensive industries are Southeast Asian countries adjacent to China, especially Vietnam. China's outward direct investment and exports of intermediate semifinished products triggered by China's relocation of industrial chains have become the leading forces driving the growth of bilateral trade between China and ASEAN.

Due to the impact of the Sino-US trade war and the tariffs imposed by the United States on Chinese exports, a large number of Chinese enterprises have been driven to export Chinese goods to ASEAN countries for simple processing, OEM and customs declaration locally, before exporting the finished products to the United States. ASEAN developing countries such as Vietnam and Indonesia enjoy low tariff treatment in trade with the U.S. under the most-favoured-nation (MFN) agreement. This encourages Chinese companies to avoid the high tariffs by obtaining local certificates of origin for their products.

In recent years, the rise in production costs has forced some foreign and Chinese companies to transfer their labour-intensive industry and some processing and manufacturing activities to relatively low-cost areas. Southeast Asia, which is geographically close to China and has strong economic growth momentum, has become the preferred destination for industrial relocation by China.

Multinational and Chinese companies are increasingly looking to Southeast Asia as a new regional manufacturing base. Due to the abundance in natural resources and low production costs, Southeast Asian countries are fully equipped to play a more important role in the global industrial chain. Taking the Chinese company Xiaomi as an example, in order to reduce logistics and transportation costs and improve supply efficiency, in 2020, it began construction of a foundry in Vietnam to produce smartphones, data transmission equipment and circuit boards, its products being mainly supplied to the local market in Vietnam and other ASEAN countries.

Nevertheless, the industrial chain/supply chain in Southeast Asia is incomplete, the supporting industries are incomplete, and for a large number of raw materials and intermediate manufactured goods ASEAN is reliant on imports. In contrast, China has a complete industrial chain and is one of the few countries in the world engaging in all industrial activities in the United Nations Industrial Classification. Based on ASEAN's imperfect supply chain, infrastructure bottlenecks, and insufficient labour, it will be difficult in the short term for Southeast Asia to fully accommodate the production capacity transferred by China to become the next world factory.

From the perspective of long-run development, Southeast Asian countries generally have a high degree of economic dependence on China and the United States, so the Sino-US trade war will inevitably have a negative impact on the economic growth of these countries. As World Bank Vice President Mari Elka Pangestu said at the 2019 Summer Davos Forum: "China and the United States are two fighting elephants, and we don't want to be trampled to death". She believes that while the Sino-US trade war has led to the transfer of production capacity out of China, which seems to benefit Southeast Asian countries, the latter are actually being put at long-term risk; the order in this region will be dominated in the longer term by the intensifying Sino-US competition.

3.5 The Belt and Road Initiative in Southeast Asia

China's grand diplomacy, especially its neighbourhood diplomacy, is strongly focused on ASEAN. The ASEAN countries are the core regions for China to promote the construction of the Belt and Road Initiative. BRI implementation depends on the support and participation of the countries involved, and the ASEAN countries are particularly vital to the initiative.

ASEAN countries are geographically close to China, it was the first region to sign an agreement to participate in the joint construction of the BRI, and the ASEAN countries, as a group, were founding members of the China-founded Asian Infrastructure Investment Bank. Therefore, Yu (2017b) argues that ASEAN's response and support for the Belt and Road Initiative is an important litmus test for the Initiative's success internationally.

Poor infrastructure and inadequate logistics capacity hinder rapid economic growth in many ASEAN countries. According to a study published by the Asian Development Bank in 2017, in order to achieve the annual average economic growth target of more than 5% and address the challenges posed by climate change, Southeast Asia alone will need a total of US$2.75 trillion by 2030. The regional countries must urgently address the thorny issues of inefficient and insufficient infrastructure in order to unleash their economic growth potential.

To improve local infrastructure, the Southeast Asian countries urgently need investment. The ASEAN countries' governments believe that the BRI will help to attract Chinese infrastructure investment and address their infrastructure development needs. Many countries have aligned their development strategies with the BRI, such as Indonesia's "Global Marine Fulcrum" development strategy, Cambodia's "Four Corners" Strategy, Laos' "Land-linked Countries" development plan, and Vietnam's "Two Corridors and One Circle" development strategy.

For the developing countries in the ASEAN, infrastructure shortages and inefficient logistics and transportation are major obstacles to realising their regional economic potential through regional integration. Meanwhile, China has demonstrated strong international competitiveness in infrastructure construction, equipment manufacturing, metallurgy, and manufacturing building materials and communication equipment. Under the framework of the Belt and Road Initiative, China is supporting the construction of the ASEAN Community through development of connectivity by providing substantial financing for infrastructure projects, especially in the ASEAN's less developed countries such as Laos and Cambodia. It is, however, worth noting that the ASEAN countries collectively had made some headway on promoting connectivity even before the launch of the BRI in 2013. For example, the regional countries initiated the Master Plan for ASEAN Connectivity back in 2010, in pursuit of regional integration.

By providing loans and setting up special cooperation funds, as well as working with multilateral development institutions, including the Asian Development Bank and the Asian Infrastructure Investment Bank, China is stepping up efforts to help regional countries improve their infrastructure and logistics and transportation efficiency. Chinese enterprises have provided large-scale overseas operations and investments, becoming important players in improving infrastructure in Southeast Asia. The China-Laos Railway, Indonesia's Jakarta-Bandung High-Speed Railway, Cambodia's Sihanoukville Port Upgrade, and the Phnom Penh-Sihanoukville Expressway Project are some large-scale infrastructure projects financed and built by China under the BRI in the region. The construction of these infrastructure projects is of great significance in terms of strengthening connectivity between countries in the region and improving the socio-economic situation and local people's livelihoods. Beijing is very keen to see the decline of American hegemony and dominance in the Southeast Asia through its push for the BRI.

BRI implementation in the region remains on track, despite the impacts generated by changes in the regional and geopolitical environment and the global COVID-19 pandemic. Among the 358 BRI projects launched in Southeast Asia between 2013 and 2021, 210 (58.6%) have already been completed. Another 90 projects are currently under construction, while 54 projects are in the planning stage. In contrast, only four (around 1%) of the projects have been cancelled or terminated. The two countries hosting the most BRI projects are Indonesia and Cambodia, with 63 and 47 projects, respectively. The BRI is expected to have a long-term impact on infrastructure development, industrialisation and economic growth in Southeast Asia.

Setting aside for the moment the geostrategic and geoeconomic considerations behind China's push for the initiative, there is evidence of the pervasiveness of economic benefits derived from the BRI by the ASEAN countries. ASEAN is the key region for China's outbound investment under the BRI umbrella. According to the "China Global Investment Tracker" statistics, the accumulated value of Chinese investments and contracts in the ASEAN under the BRI umbrella rose to US$125.26 billion between 2013 and 2022, accounting for 34% of China's investments and contracts under the BRI during the same period. Singapore, Indonesia and Malaysia were the three top recipients of Chinese investment in ASEAN countries, with US$32.57 billion, US$29.97 billion and US$18.67 billion, respectively (Fig. 3.1).

One of the landmark projects of the BRI in Southeast Asia is the railway connecting China and Laos (China-Laos Railway). Laos is surrounded by mountains and is the only landlocked country in Southeast Asia. For a long time, roads have been the main mode of transportation in Laos and the backward transportation conditions and high costs have restricted Laos' domestic economic growth. The first railway in Laos was built by France in 1920, is about 7 km long, and connects the islands of Dongde and Dong Khong in the South of Laos. From 1983 to 1949, the railway was narrow gauge (600/1000 mm) only. Another railway in Laos, funded by Thailand in 2009, is located in the border area between Laos and Thailand, and is only 3.5 km long. These two railways are incapable of meeting Laos' freight demand.

The 1035-km China-Laos Railway, funded and built by China, connects Kunming, Yunnan Province, China, with Vientiane, the capital of Laos. This railway is also connected to China's domestic railway network. The official operation of the China-Laos Railway has effectively reduced the logistics and transportation costs in Laos

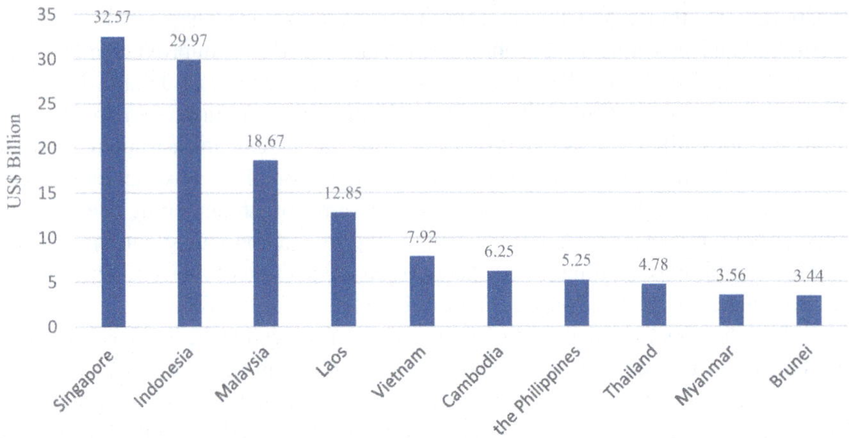

Fig. 3.1 Chinese investments and contracts in ASEAN countries under the BRI umbrella. *Source* American Enterprise Institute (2023)

and across the border between China and Laos, promoted the development of logistics and transportation, commerce and tourism industries along the Laos, and provided employment opportunities for many Lao people.

The Laotian government has endorsed the railway project as part of its national strategy to boost infrastructure development and drive economic growth. The railway is regarded by the Lao government as the key to Laos' transformation from a "land-locked country" to a "land-linked country" development strategy since it will fully exploit Laos' advantageous geographical location between China and the Southeast Asian mainland. In December 2021, Chinese President Xi Jinping and Lao President Thonglun jointly attended the official opening ceremony of the China-Laos Railway online, witnessing the completion and opening of this flagship project of the "Belt and Road" in Southeast Asia.

Since its opening at the end of 2021, the China-Laos Railway had transported nearly 3 million tonnes of cross-border goods by February 2023 (National Development and Reform Commission of the People's Republic of China 2023), making bilateral trade between China and Laos more convenient and faster, and increasing the scale of trade between the two countries. Through this railway, more Chinese products, such as fertilisers, electronic communication products and auto parts, will be exported to Laos. In addition, more advantageous agricultural products from Laos, such as rubber, rice and cassava, will be exported to the Chinese market. Cross-border passenger transport was opened in April 2023, after the ending of COVID-19 pandemic restrictions, and the number of passengers transported by the China-Laos railway reached 13,310 people in May 2023 alone (Xinhua News 2023).

According to a study released by the World Bank in 2020, the opening of the China-Laos Railway will reduce domestic transportation costs in Laos by 20–40%, and cross-border cargo transportation costs between China and Laos by 40–50%. The benefits of the railway in terms of improving logistics and transportation efficiency and reducing the time and cost of cargo transportation are becoming increasingly apparent.

The construction of the 142-km Jakarta-Bandung High-Speed Railway by Chinese companies is another landmark project of the Belt and Road Initiative in Southeast Asia. When completed, the Jakarta-Bandung railroad will be the first high-speed railway in Indonesia and the entire Southeast Asian region. For a long time, the inadequacy of its transportation infrastructure has seriously restricted Indonesia's domestic economic development and, therefore, local living standards. Jakarta, the capital city and main centre of industry and commerce, has a population of more than 10 million and is blighted by traffic congestion. It is expected that the opening of the Jakarta-Bandung high-speed railway in 2023 will greatly alleviate Jakarta's urban traffic congestion problem and generate new growth points in urban service industry and business development. The high-speed railway will thus become a symbol of Indonesia's rise as an emerging regional power.

This high-speed railway, from project exploration and design, engineering construction, raw material procurement, engineering equipment manufacturing to project operation and management, will be entirely based on Chinese standards and technical solutions. The Jakarta-Bandung high-speed railway, which will reach an operating speed of 350 km/h, marks the first project in which a Chinese company has undertaken to build a complete high-speed railway network overseas. The construction machinery, rails, rolling stock, communication signals and train operation control equipment used in the construction of the railway are all being manufactured and produced by Chinese enterprises (Yu 2021).

Under the framework of the Belt and Road Initiative, China and ASEAN countries have cooperated in areas such as modern agriculture, information technology industry, infrastructure, energy, finance, logistics, law, accounting, culture and tourism, human resources development, environmental protection and public health. These areas also provide important business opportunities for Chinese enterprises to expand their outbound investment and exports.

In addition, under China's push for the Digital Silk Road (DSR), China and ASEAN countries are also exploring ways to expand cooperation in the field of digital economy, especially e-commerce, artificial intelligence, smart city construction and cloud computing. Leveraging on its booming digital economy, China seeks to create synergy between traditional infrastructure facilities and digital infrastructure and technologies (e.g. telecommunication equipment, cloud computing and artificial intelligence) under the DSR umbrella.

China's digital economy[1] has developed rapidly over the past decade, accounting for almost 40% of GDP in 2020. The number of Chinese netizens has grown to 989 million. The scale and speed of its 5G telecommunication network are among the best in the world, with the total number of 5G terminals reaching over 200 million. China's digital economy is focused on data-related industries and technologies,

[1] Digital economy refers to the e-commerce platform economy, manufacturing and services related to digital devices, application of digital and data technology in non-digital sectors, such as finance and agriculture.

including e-commerce, smart city, big data, Internet of Things, cloud computing, 5G telecommunication network and artificial intelligence.

The ASEAN countries have a total population of 650 million, among whom more than 440 million are Internet users with growing demand for various digital services. Chinese-made smartphones, such as Huawei, Vivo, Xiaomi, and OPPO, have already become popular in many Southeast Asian countries. In 2021, the size of the digital economy in the Southeast Asian countries was about US$174 billion and is expected to reach $1 trillion by 2030 (Temasek 2021).

Over the past several years, various ASEAN countries have successively formulated and implemented blueprints for digital economy development, anticipating to accelerate economic restructuring by improving digital connectivity. Examples include Singapore's Smart Nation 2025 Plan of 2014, Malaysia's national industry 4.0 policy framework (2018) and "Digital Malaysia Blueprint" (2021), Indonesia's Indonesia Manufacturing 4.0 Strategy (2018), and Cambodia's Digital Economy and Digital Society Policy Framework (2021–2035), proposed in 2021.

Both China and the ASEAN countries view the digital economy as the focal point of future development. There is a great desire for China and ASEAN countries to collaborate and cooperate in digital sectors, such as cross-border e-commerce, big data, smart cities and artificial intelligence. In 2021, during the commemorative summit for the 30th anniversary of the establishment of China-ASEAN dialogue relations, the two sides vowed to strengthen cooperation in the field of digital economy by exploring the synergy between ASEAN's Master Plan on ASEAN Connectivity 2025 and China's Belt and Road Initiative.

Leveraging on its competitive digital economy, Chinese tech firms have targeted Southeast Asia as a key market to invest, operate and seek business collaboration via investment, partnership with local firms and acquisitions. In many Southeast Asian countries, the digital economy is at a nascent stage when compared to China. Moreover, there is a huge gap between the more developed member countries (e.g. Singapore) and the least developed member countries (e.g. Myanmar, Cambodia and Laos) in terms of digital infrastructure. Chinese capital, technology and talents could help boost digital economy development in the region. The huge potential for expanding the scale and momentum of Southeast Asia's digital economy has attracted the attention of Chinese high-tech enterprises, and Chinese companies such as Tencent, Alibaba, Huawei and ZTE have moved into Southeast Asian countries.

It is fair to say that the entire Southeast Asian e-commerce sector has basically been wrapped up by Chinese companies. Almost all of the e-commerce giants in the region are somehow linked with Chinese e-commerce firms or actually funded by Chinese capital, such as Shopee, J&T Express, Lazada, Tokopedia, TikTok, Shein and Tmall Global. Shopee's parent company is Donghai Group, and Donghai Group's largest shareholder is Tencent. Although Tokopedia was founded by an Indonesian native and its largest shareholder is Japan's SoftBank, its second-largest shareholder is Alibaba, and it can also be regarded as Alibaba's e-commerce platform. TikTok is a leading social media network dedicated to short-form video, developed and owned by the Chinese technology firm ByteDance, and mainly engaged in live streaming e-commerce, and Shein's business originated in Guangzhou, China.

Founded in 2015, J&T Express is the world's fastest-growing logistics company, in operation for 6 years, and in the first quarter of 2021, it was the top-ranked logistics service in Southeast Asia. Jitu Express is also widespread across Indonesia, Malaysia, Singapore, the Philippines, Thailand, Vietnam, Cambodia and other Southeast Asian countries.

Under the framework of the RCEP, China and Southeast Asian countries can work together to strengthen cooperation in the digital economy, especially in the fields of e-commerce and mobile payment. In addition, China has formally applied to join the Digital Economy Partnership Agreement, which will bring new opportunities for China to expand its participation in the development of the digital economy and rule-making in the region.

3.6 Challenges for BRI Implementation in Southeast Asia

Given the sheer size of the Chinese economy and the scope and coverage of the BRI initiative, China could become the dominant force in shaping the future economic landscape of Southeast Asia (Yu 2017b). However, although the participating countries along the Belt and Road routes welcome the increased investment and infrastructure improvements brought about by the BRI, many countries have doubts about China's strategic considerations behind the initiative.

With the implementation of the initiative, Chinese enterprises are facing increasing challenges in carrying out economic and trade activities such as outbound investment, mergers and acquisitions, and industrial transfer to overseas markets. Compared with 2013, when the Belt and Road Initiative was launched, the regional and international geopolitical environment facing China is undergoing profound changes (Yu 2019). From a geopolitical point of view, despite the close bilateral economic and trade cooperation, there is insufficient mutual trust between Southeast Asia and China. On the one hand, although Southeast Asian countries believe that the BRI will accelerate their infrastructure development, which will improve their economies and people's livelihoods, some countries are also concerned about the high cost, low practicality and internal corruption linked with the BRI infrastructure projects.

For example, the Export–Import Bank of China has provided loans of around 80% loan for the construction of the China-Laos railway (construction cost estimated at around US$5.9 billion). Laos has subsequently experienced a sharp increase in external debt which can be attributed to the BRI project. Moreover, China is by far its largest sovereign creditor, with Laos' debt to China accounting for nearly 50% of its total debts. Moody's Investors Service, the ratings agency, downgraded Laos's credit rating to Caa3, due to the combined factors of high debt burden, poor economic management, and insufficient foreign exchange reserves to cover maturing external debt. According to Moody's estimation, Laos is on the brink of default (Springfield 2022).

It remains to be seen how economically viable the railway will be and how much economic benefit it will generate for the Laotian government and Laotian people.

The success of the railway will depend on its achievement of smooth and efficient customs clearance and timeliness of shipments. In addition, most of the raw materials and equipment for the railway's construction will need to be sourced from China, as Laos' domestic manufacturing industries lack the capability to supply these. Laos also has little experience in building large railway projects on its soil and has very few skilled rail engineers and construction workers.

On the other hand, Southeast Asian countries also have voiced concern that China will use the promotion of the Belt and Road Initiative to gain geostrategic advantages and strengthen its influence in the region. They are concerned that the initiative will also pull Southeast Asia into China's development track, and eventually Southeast Asian countries will lose autonomy over their development. Both maritime and mainland Southeast Asian nations have always been aware of an asymmetrical relationship that might swing in China's favour. As Womack (2017) argues, compared with any single ASEAN country, China has absolute advantages in terms of economic strength and national power:

> As the center of Asia, China's status and power put it in an asymmetrical relationship with other countries. If not properly controlled, this can also be a source of anxiety and tension in other countries. Because of China's unequal size and power with each of its neighbors, China is always the less risky party in its bilateral relations with its neighbors and has more leverage to use.

There is concern that Southeast Asia will be drawn into a China-centric form of regional integration architecture, weakening the ASEAN's role in the regional integration process. According to the 2021 State of Southeast Asia Survey Report, which was released by the ISEAS-Yusof Ishak Institute (2021), more than 45% of respondents in Southeast Asia believe that China is a "revisionist country" that intends to change the current international order and try to draw Southeast Asia into its sphere of influence, especially in Vietnam, the Philippines and Singapore. The report also shows that 51.5% of respondents in Southeast Asian countries distrust China more than any other major country. The report reflects that the "China threat theory" is widespread and has considerable public support in Southeast Asian countries.

The maritime and territorial disputes in the South China Sea have affected bilateral relations between China, and several ASEAN countries, including the Philippines and Vietnam. The ASEAN claimant states are alarmed by China's shift in policy and its aggressive stance towards them in the South China Sea disputes. The BRI could be seen as a serving China's aim to project its growing sea power and naval capabilities globally. Some scholars (e.g. Crisp 2010) believe that the main purpose of the maritime Silk Road proposal is to safeguard China's maritime trade route along the South China Sea which is vital to its importation of energy and resources.

There have been increased numbers of clashes and confrontations involving Chinese coastal guards and fishing boats and coastal guards from the Philippines and Vietnam over the past several years. For example, in May 2014, the Philippines condemned China's action on land reclamation to build new facilities on a SCS reef that is the subject of a dispute between the two countries (Reuters 2014). On 11 May 2014, several large-scale rallies and protests took place in Vietnam's major cities, where people vented their anger over a deepwater oil drilling operation conducted by a state-owned Chinese company in disputed waters of the SCS (South China Sea) (Wall Street Journal 2014). These protests, which were reportedly the largest anti-China protests in Vietnam in recent years, then escalated into rioting and looting, with the rioters setting fire to up to 15 foreign business premises in southern Vietnam. Some of these companies were even forced to halt production and evacuate their employees from Vietnam for safety reasons. The Vietnamese leader accused China's oil drilling operation of "dangerous and serious violations" (New York Times 2014).

China's assertiveness in territorial and maritime disputes in the SCS since 2009 has been an alarm bell for many ASEAN countries. All or part of the Paracel/Xisha and Spratly/Nansha Islands, as well as their surrounding waters and resources in the SCS, are claimed by China, Vietnam, the Philippines, Brunei and Malaysia individually. China has massively stepped up its efforts in land reclamation and infrastructure construction activities in the SCS in the past few years, and its increasing assertiveness in the SCS is a signal to the ASEAN that China will not hesitate to safeguard its territorial sovereignty and protect its maritime interests, taking unilateral action if necessary (Yu 2017a). The ASEAN countries have consequently become very wary of any move made by China in the region. China's perceived aggressive behaviour has not helped its attempts to establish cooperative relations with its neighbours in the region.

From the ASEAN perspective, China's growing military power is widely perceived as a threat to free movement of cargo and a form of deterrence to endorse its sovereignty claim over the SCS. As one scholar points out, China's vast size, huge market potential, and growing military capabilities have presented both opportunities and threats to the ASEAN (Ho 2001). With the rise of China as a global power, these Asian countries are concerned that China will become more aggressive and eventually use or threaten to use force to solve its territorial disputes with neighbouring countries. The neighbouring Asian countries fear that China will reestablish the "Chinese empire" by imposing a Sino-centric order and a new tributary system in the region, while China views the actions and maritime claims by the Philippines and Vietnam in the SCS as a challenge to its territorial integrity and "core interests".

The Chinese government has insisted on dealing with SCS territorial disputes with the ASEAN member states on an individual bilateral basis and rejected intervention by a multilateral ASEAN negotiating framework. Meanwhile, the ASEAN countries are cautious about the potential implications of Chinese-financed infrastructure projects for their national security.

Consequently, mutual trust between the ASEAN countries involved and China has been eroded. Concern over China's actions in the South China Sea disputes could impede China's push for the BRI in Southeast Asia, because the development of large-scale infrastructure projects under the initiative requires both political commitment and strategic trust from the ASEAN governments.

There is no sign of the South China Sea issue being resolved in the near future, and the tensions surrounding the South China Sea are likely to persist and even escalate. It is imperative for Chinese authorities to work closely with their ASEAN counterparts to regain mutual trust and manage their disputes peacefully by keeping the lines of communication open.

The construction of dams in the upper reaches of the Mekong River by the Chinese enterprises has become another contentious issue between China and the Southeast Asian countries along the Mekong River. The Chinese-constructed dams have impacted negatively on the local environment, water resources and livelihoods of the riparian states located lower down the Mekong.

Lower Mekong countries depend on Mekong water for their agriculture and fisheries development, and the livelihoods of farmers and fishermen along its banks depend on Mekong water. In recent years, fish catches in the Mekong basin have declined, water use for agricultural irrigation has declined, and climate change has brought about rapid changes in water flows. Downstream ASEAN countries see this as related to China's new hydropower projects upstream along the coast, where dam storage reduces downstream volume. China has built and operated 11 controversial hydropower dams in the upper reaches of the Mekong River. From China's point of view, the construction of hydropower plants will help to use the abundant hydropower resources of the Mekong River basin to generate electricity, thereby alleviating the shortage of electricity in China's southwestern provinces like Sichuan and Yunnan.

However, from the perspective of Southeastern countries located in the lower Mekong River basin, China's damming actions are unilateral and self-serving, ignoring the water needs of downstream countries, the latter arguing that China's construction of hydropower plants in the upper Mekong River basin has reduced the amount of water in the basin, resulting in water scarcity, drought, environmental damage and depletion of fishery resources in downstream countries.

In addition, many ASEAN countries are concerned that their economic dependence on China through the BRI's implementation could cause them eventually to lose autonomy over their foreign policy by being forced to adopt pro-China diplomacy. China's political and economic influence loom large in the region and beyond through the BRI platform. There is a widely shared perception among the governments, academia and media in Southeast Asia that the BRI also carries geopolitical implications in terms of China's strengthening military buildup.

Southeast Asia becoming a privileged sphere of influence for China would be a nightmare scenario for the regional countries. Hence, to avoid the emergence of a China-centric regional order, the Southeast Asian countries are keen to maintain a geostrategic balance among the major powers, without tilting too far towards either China or the United States.

Safeguarding national security by deploying a "balance of power" strategy to keep China's growing influence in check has been an indispensable element of Southeast Asian nations' relations with China. Maintaining close relations with China under the BRI is important for the ASEAN countries and they want to maintain a pragmatic approach towards China. Meanwhile, building on relations with other powers including the United States, Europe, Japan, India and Australia is equally crucial. The "balance of power" hedging strategy is the best option for the ASEAN countries to respond to the pressure created by the intensifying China-U.S. rivalry. By adopting this hedging strategy, the Southeast Asian countries are placing their national interests above those of either China or the United States.

To counterbalance China's rising influence, ASEAN countries are looking for infrastructure investment from other major powers, for example, Japan's High-Quality Infrastructure Development Plan with a value of more than US$100 billion, and the Korea-ASEAN Strategic Initiative proposed by the Yoon Suk Yeol administration. Both Japanese and Korean construction firms are active in expanding their business operations in the lucrative infrastructure sectors of the ASEAN countries.

Japan and Republic of Korea have paid increasing attention to strengthening their relations with the ASEAN countries during recent years. With the implementation of the New Southern Policy by then South Korean President Moon Jae-in in 2017, Republic of Korea has started to focus on enhancing economic, investment and trade cooperation with the ASEAN countries.

The year 2023 marks the Golden Jubilee of Japan-ASEAN Friendship and Cooperation. The Kishida administration will host the Japan-ASEAN summit with the ASEAN countries' leaders in Tokyo in late 2023. Japan's Prime Minister Kishida is expected during the summit to renew the Japanese commitment to forge close ties with the ASEAN countries and to pledge more ODA (official development assistance) and grants to support the infrastructure development of the less developed Southeast Asian countries.

Southeast Asia has moved to the forefront in the power rivalry between China and the United States, the world's two largest economies and systemic rivals (Shambaugh 2018, 2020). China is ASEAN's largest trading partner for merchandised goods. According to the "ASEAN Statistical Yearbook 2022", which was published by the ASEAM Secretariat, in 2021, China's trade with ASEAN was almost twice higher than that with the US. Nevertheless, the United States is the largest foreign investor for the ASEAN countries, and the European Union is the second largest. The stock of US investment in ASEAN is substantially larger than China's. Both China and the United States are competing for influence in ASEAN countries.

Third, BRI implementation has been weak in terms of compliance with internationally recognised standards on such as transparency and opening bidding, and labour and environmental protection safeguards. After the completion of many BRI projects, the environmental and social impacts are becoming visible.

Indonesia is rich in laterite nickel ore reserves and production, but its weak infrastructure, backward technology, insufficient talents and engineers are among factors that have restricted the development of its local nickel ore processing industry. The China Tsingshan Holding Group, whose main business is stainless steel production, entered Indonesia in 2009. In October 2013, a contract was signed to start construction of the Morowali Park project. While the park's activities will mainly be related to infrastructure construction, it will also attract Chinese ferronickel smelting enterprises with complementary industrial chains, which will invest together, share risks and develop in groups. According to statistics for 2021, China's Tsingshan Group, which mainly relies on nickel ore resources from Indonesia, was ranked among the top companies in the world on annual output of stainless-steel crude steel and nickel products.

Boosted by Chinese investors, Indonesia has become one of the world's major stainless-steel producers. Nickel is not only an essential raw material for the manufacture of stainless steel in traditional industries, but also an important component of the manufacture of nickel-metal hydride batteries in new energy industries. Since 2017, Tsingshan has joined up with China Enterprise Huayou Cobalt and Grammy to carry out a new energy battery ternary precursor material manufacturing project in the two parks of Morowali and Weidabei for the development of the electric vehicle industry. These parks currently employ more than 100,000 Indonesian workers, and the rapid development of the parks has also boosted the development of commercial facilities and surrounding employment, thereby promoting local economic and social development.

The China-Indonesia Industrial Park Castle Peak Park (operational since 2013) is located in Morowali District, Central Sulawesi and Castle Peak Weidabe Park (operational since 2018) is located in Vida County, North Maluku Province. As claimed by China, investment in these industrial parks by Chinese firms has brought economic benefits for all parties. On Indonesia's part, its natural resources have been effectively utilised and value added, and its manufacturing industry has achieved a breakthrough in industrial upgrading. Meanwhile, Chinese enterprises entering the park are exempted from the costs of preliminary investigation and research, and the nickel ore resources required for production are immediately available. The developers of the parks, Tsingshan, also share the rewards deriving from these enterprises' development and growth.

Nevertheless, the critics argue that the Chinese-invested industrial parks in Indonesia were to be blamed for causing local environmental pollution and threatened the health of local Indonesians. A damning investigative report was written by Timmerman (2022), titled "The Dirty Road to Clean Energy: how China's electric vehicle boom is damaging the environment" found this,

> The report mentioned that due to the global development of new energy vehicles, especially China's new energy vehicle industry, the Chinese-funded nickel industry has a dominant position in Indonesia, but a number of Chinese-funded nickel industrial parks located in Tsingshan Industrial Park (IMIP) in Morowali County, Sulawesi Island and Wakedabe Industrial Park (IWIP) on Maluku Island have also seriously impacted the local natural and social environment, often causing large-scale destruction of ecological vegetation around the park, loss of habitat for rich biological species, and dusty roads on the road. A large amount of coal was burned in the industrial park, causing respiratory diseases among nearby villagers, especially children; It also causes the disappearance of fish in nearby rivers and seas. The compensation paid for local land requisition is too low, and ordinary villagers are unable to rely on their livelihoods.

The pollution and human health risks for the locals brought by the industrial parks in Indonesia are causing irreversible ecological and public health damage. The environmental pollution of Chinese-invested BRI industrial projects in Indonesia has triggered local anger and protests, which has put pressure on China to adopt a greener approach to BRI implementation.

Infrastructure projects have long development cycles and high risks due to national sovereignty, economic and strategic security implications; therefore, many countries are wary of China's efforts to expand its influence through the Belt and Road Initiative, regarding both China's motivations behind the initiative and the debt traps caused by borrowing for BRI projects.

In addition, the COVID-19 pandemic has had a huge impact on the domestic economic and financial situation of many developing countries, and, due to financing difficulties, construction of some BRI projects cannot continue according to the terms of the original contract. According to the Global Economic Prospects report released by the International Monetary Fund, 60% of low-income countries and 30% of emerging market countries are on or near the point of national debt crises due to the impact of the new crown pneumonia epidemic and the world energy crisis caused by the conflict between Russia and Ukraine.

In this context, many BRI developing countries, including the ASEAN countries, have experienced severe domestic economic recession, debt crises and social instability, while some countries have experienced difficulties in repaying their foreign debts, particularly debts owed to China.

References

American Enterprise Institute. 2023. The China Global Investment Tracker. Updated on 16 May 2023. https://www.aei.org/china-global-investment-tracker/

Beijing Pays a Price for Assertiveness in South China Sea. *Wall Street Journal*, 13 May 2014. Available at: http://online.wsj.com/news/articles/SB10001424052702303627504579558913140862896. Accessed 15 May 2014.

Crisp, Michael. 2010. The Great Chinese Sea Power Debate: A Review Essay. *Journal of Contemporary China* 19 (63): 201–212.

Ho, Khai Leong. 2001. Rituals, Risks and Rivalries: China and ASEAN in the Coming Decades. *Journal of Contemporary China* 10 (29): 683–694.

ISEAS-Yusof Ishak Institute. 2021. The State of Southeast Asia: 2021, 10 February 2021. Available at https://www.iseas.edu.sg/wp-content/uploads/2021/01/The-State-of-SEA-2021-v2.pdf.

National Development and Reform Commission of the People's Republic of China. 2023. *China-Laos Railway Freight Volume Increased Significantly, Cumulative Shipments Exceeded 15 million tons*, 30 Mar 2023. https://www.ndrc.gov.cn/xwdt/ztzl/zltl/202303/t20230330_1352748.html.

Page, Jeremy. 2013. Chinese Territorial Strife Hits Archaeology. *The Wall Street Journal*. Available at: http://online.wsj.com/news/articles/SB10001424052702304470504579164873258159410. Accessed 19 Feb 2014.

Philippines Says China Appears to Be Building an Airstrip on Disputed Reef. *Reuters*, 13 May 2014. Available at: http://www.reuters.com/article/2014/05/14/us-philippines-china-reef-idUSBREA4D00K20140514. Accessed on 15 May 2014.

Shambaugh, David. 2020. *Where Great Powers Meet: America & China in Southeast Asia*. Oxford: Oxford University Press.

Shambaugh, David. 2018. U.S.-China Rivalry in Southeast Asia: Power Shift or Competitive Coexistence? *International Security* 42 (4): 85–127.

Springfield, Cary. 2022. Can The Laos Economy Be Rescued From The Brink of Default? *International Banker*, 21 July 2022. Available at https://internationalbanker.com/finance/can-the-laos-economy-be-rescued-from-the-brink-of-default/.

Temasek. *Economy SEA 2021 Soaring 20s: The SEA Digital Decade.*

Timmerman, Antonia. 2022. The Dirty Road to Clean Energy: How China's Electric Vehicle Boom Is Ravaging the Environment. *Rest of World*, 28 November 2022. Available at https://www.business-humanrights.org/en/latest-news/the-dirty-road-to-clean-energy-how-chinas-electric-vehicle-boom-is-ravaging-the-environment/. Accessed 17 July 2023.

Vietnam Fails to Rally Partners in China Dispute. *New York Times*, 11 May 2014. Available at: http://www.nytimes.com/2014/05/12/world/asia/vietnam.html?_r=0. Accessed 15 May 2014.

Wang, Gungwu. 1970. China and South-East Asia 1402–1424. In *Studies in the Social History of China and South-East Asia*, 375–405, eds. J. Ch'en, and N. Tarling. Cambridge: Cambridge University Press.

Wang, Gungwu. 2008. The China Seas: Becoming an Enlarged Mediterranean. In *The East Asian 'Mediterranean: Maritime Crossroads of Culture, Commerce and Human Migration*, ed. Angela Schottenhammer, 7–22. Wiesbaden: Harrassowitz Verlag.

Wang, Gungwu. 2009. Southeast Asia: Imperial Themes. *New Zealand Journal of Asian Studies* 11 (1): 36–48.

Wang, Gungwu. 2021. China, ASEAN and the New Maritime Silk Road. *ThinkChina*. https://www.thinkchina.sg/wang-gungwu-china-asean-and-new-maritime-silk-road.

Waugh, Daniel C. 2010. The Silk Roads in History. *Expedition* 52 (3): 9–22.

Womack, Brantly. 2017. Repositioning China, ASEAN and Asian Centers. *World Economy and Politics* (7).

World Bank. 2020. *From Landlocked to Land-Linked: Unlocking the Potential of Lao-China Rail Connectivity*. Available at https://doi.org/10.1596/33891.

Xinhua News Agency. 2023. *China-Laos Railways International Passenger Transport in the First Month of Opening*, 15 May 2023. http://www.news.cn/world/2023-05/15/c_1129614725.htm.

Yu, Hong. 2017a. Motivation Behind China's 'One Belt, One Road' Initiatives and Establishment of the Asian Infrastructure Investment Bank. *Journal of Contemporary China* 26 (105): 353–368.

Yu, Hong. 2017b. China's Belt and Road Initiative and Its Implications for Southeast Asia. *Asia Policy*, 24: 117–122.

Yu, Hong. 2019. Reflections on the Belt and Road Initiative. *China: An International Journal* 17 (4): 8–23.

Yu, Hong. 2021. *The China-Laos Railway: A 'Game Changer' for Laos?* EAI Commentary No. 44, 16 Dec 2021.

Chapter 4
Vietnam's Mixed Reactions to China and the BRI

4.1 Overview of the China-Vietnam Economic Relations

Vietnam is China's largest neighbour in Southeast Asia and has historically been deeply influenced by Chinese culture. Vietnam has been implementing the policy of "innovation and opening up" since 1986, opening up the market, vigorously attracting foreign investment and developing an export-oriented economy. Vietnam's economic growth rate has exceeded 7% since the outbreak of the global financial crisis in 2008, and among Southeast Asian countries its economic performance is outstanding.

Vietnam is also one of the most successful countries in Asia in terms of attracting foreign investment. Significantly, Vietnam is the only ASEAN economy to continue to achieve positive economic growth under the impact of the COVID-19 pandemic. Vietnam's economic growth rates in 2020 and 2021 were 2.91% and 2.58%, respectively. In 2021, while the coronavirus pandemic was raging through the country, Vietnam imposed massive lockdowns and factory shutdowns as infection containment measures. However, Vietnam's economy still grew by more than 8% in 2022, the fastest growth rate in a decade and the highest economic growth rate among ASEAN countries.

The growth of foreign trade has been the main contributor to Vietnam's maintenance of overall economic growth. Vietnam's foreign trade exports reached US$371.8 billion in 2022, representing a 10.6% year-on-year increase, while the value of imports rose by 26%. Vietnam attracted US$31.1 billion in foreign investment in 2021, an increase of 9.2%, whereas in 2022, its actual utilisation of foreign capital amounted to US$22.4 billion, a year-on-year increase of 13.5%. These data show that foreign investors and multinational companies remain optimistic about Vietnam's development potential.

Vietnam has become an investment hotspot. The Republic of Korea is Vietnam's largest source of foreign direct investment. By 2022, Korean accumulated investment to Vietnam was US$81 billion. To date, 9000 Korean firms are operating in Vietnam, including Samsung Electronics, LG and Hyundai. There are currently about 180,000

H. Yu, *Understanding China's Belt and Road Initiative*, Asia in Transition 26,
https://doi.org/10.1007/978-981-99-9633-9_4

Koreans residing in Vietnam, which has the largest South Korean community in Southeast Asia (Kang 2023).

These Korean firms account for 30% of Vietnam's total exports and offer 0.7 million jobs in Vietnam. Vietnam is emerging as a crucial export-oriented production base for the Republic of Korea. In light of the Sino-US strategic competition, restructuring of the global supply chain, and its increasing trade deficit with China, the Republic of Korea has been keen in recent years to reduce its trade and economic dependence on China and to pursue trade and economic diversification strategy.

As part of their "China + 1" strategy, Korean companies view Vietnam as a primary destination to diversify their supply chains outside China and to reduce the dependence on China. This has helped to create a boom in Vietnam's export-driven manufacturing industries and presents many opportunities for Korean companies. Although China is less competitive than before, it still has well-developed infrastructure, efficient logistics and high-quality labour force.

China has been Vietnam's largest trading partner since 2004. Moreover, Vietnam's importance in terms of China's economic and trade relations with Southeast Asia continues to rise. Vietnam has surpassed Malaysia as China's largest trading partner in Southeast Asia and become China's eighth-largest trading partner worldwide. The trade volume between the two countries increased by more than 10 times, from US$21.4 billion in 2009 to US$230.1 billion in 2021 (Fig. 4.1).

Vietnam is also an important destination for Chinese enterprises' investment abroad. According to the Chinese official statistics, China's direct investment to Vietnam jumped to US$2.21 billion in 2021 from US$0.31 billion in 2010 (Fig. 4.2). Stock of China's accumulated investment in Vietnam exceeded US$11 billion between 2010 and 2021, representing the fourth-largest source of foreign investment in Vietnam.

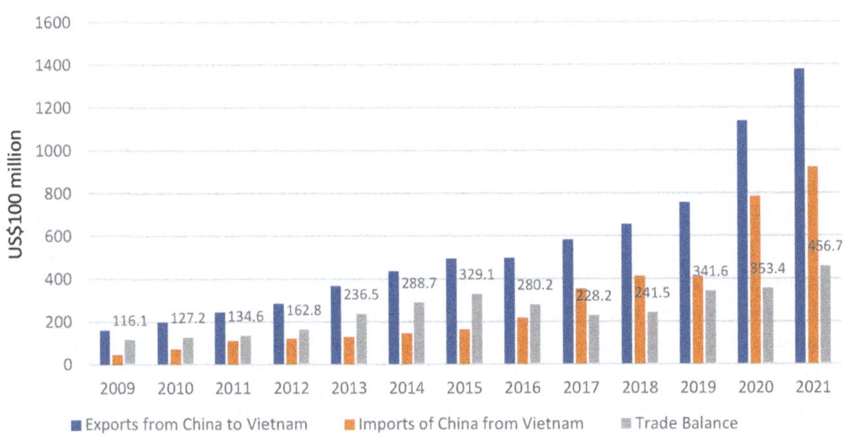

Fig. 4.1 Bilateral merchandised trade between China and Vietnam. *Sources* China Customs; Ministry of Commerce of People's Republic of China

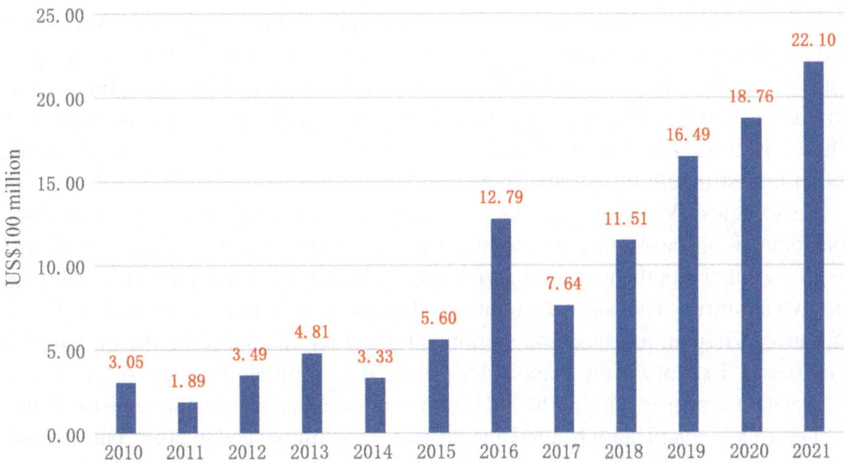

Fig. 4.2 China's outbound investment to Vietnam. *Source* Ministry of Commerce of People's Republic of China

China and Vietnam are immediate neighbours and share a long land border of over 1200 km. The two countries also share the same political system and ideology, both being socialist countries led by Communist parties. Vietnam has been able to learn from China's development experience while pursuing its own development path.

4.2 The Belt and Road Initiative in Vietnam

Vietnam knows it needs Chinese investment in its domestic infrastructure in order to achieve industrial take-off and sustained economic growth. According to the World Bank's 2019 study, The Economics of the Belt and Road: Opportunities and Risks in Transport Corridors, BRI transport projects can expand trade, increase foreign investment, and reduce poverty by reducing trade costs. If fully implemented, the project could increase global trade by 1.7–6.2% and global real income by 0.7–2.9%.

From the domestic infrastructure perspective, there is huge demand for investment in Vietnam's infrastructure sector. Due to its lack of financial and technological strength, Vietnam needs to attract foreign capital and foreign infrastructure enterprises, including Chinese capital and construction firms, to develop the domestic infrastructure required to achieve sustainable economic growth. Against this backdrop, Vietnam has endorsed and supported the BRI since 2017. In November 2015, Chinese President Xi Jinping visited Vietnam for signing of the MOU on promoting collaboration and forging synergy between China's BRI and Vietnam's "Two Corridors, One Belt" strategy. Both leaders are intent on strengthening economic and trade cooperation between local provinces of the two countries.

For the Chinese, Vietnam is an important node for promotion of China's Belt and Road Initiative. Participation in the BRI will not only help Vietnam attract more Chinese investment in the infrastructure sector, but also provide a platform for its products to enter the Chinese market more conveniently. Vietnam generally welcomes China's Belt and Road Initiative and is one of the founding members of the China-led Asian Infrastructure Investment Bank.

Nevertheless, Vietnam's approach on the ground to seeking investment from China for domestic infrastructure development has been more cautious than that adopted by many other Southeast Asian countries, such as Laos and Cambodia. Although the two countries have signed a memorandum of cooperation on the Belt and Road Initiative, Vietnam has made no significant progress on advancing the initiative on the ground. Except for the Hanoi Metro Line (Cat Linh-Ha Dong) project, no new infrastructure projects under the BRI framework are currently under construction.

The 13 km-long Hanoi Metro Line project was commenced in 2008, but was only completed in 2020, with a substantial cost overrun. The considerable length of time taken by the China Railway Sixth Group, the Chinese contractor tasked with the construction of the Hanoi metro line, to complete the project was due to issues such as land reclamation and compensation, construction safety, installation of dispute mechanism, funding and the impacts of the COVID-19 pandemic. The case of the Hanoi Metro Line project indicates that Vietnam has adopted a cautious, wait-and-see attitude towards implementing the Belt and Road Initiative.

Vietnam's caution has historical origins as, in the late 1970s, the two countries were engaged in a border war. Moreover, China and Vietnam have long had disputes over maritime rights and sovereignty in the South China Sea, resulting in mutual distrust. Hence, Vietnam has a very defensive attitude towards China, its giant neighbour in the North.

While Vietnam and China enjoy close bilateral economic and trade cooperation, there is a trust deficit between the two sides. Given the perceived aggressive behaviour of its giant neighbour, Vietnam is constantly reminded of its asymmetric relations with China, and that the power imbalance between China and Vietnam could pose a threat to its national security and sovereignty. In his book titled "China and Vietnam: The Politics of Asymmetry", Womack (2006) claims:

> One thing that has remained constant in China's relationship with Vietnam since the unification of the Chinese Empire in 221 BC is that China has been that much larger partner. Whether a relationship is hostile, good, or somewhere in between, it is asymmetrical. China is a far more important force for Vietnam than Vietnam is for China, and Vietnam has a keener understanding of the risks and opportunities presented by Sino-Vietnamese relations.

Many Vietnamese have a particularly deep memory of China's ancient tributary system. In addition, the dispute between China and Vietnam over sovereignty in the South China Sea and China's very presence in the South China Sea are sensitive topics in Vietnam that tend to stir up nationalist sentiment in Vietnam. According to the 2020 survey report by the ISEAS-Yusof Ishak Institute (2020) in Singapore, 43.4% of Vietnamese respondents have no confidence in the fairness or transparency of BRI projects, compared to just 1.3% of Vietnamese respondents who are confident about their fairness. According to the 2022 survey by the ISEAS-Yusof Ishak Institute (2022), 72.8% of Vietnamese respondents are concerned about China's expanding economic influence in the region, and only 27.2% of respondents from Vietnam welcomed China's rising economic influence.

The case of Vietnam is not unique. In fact, negative perceptions over the rise in Chinese economic influence are increasing and can be seen in the Philippines and Cambodia. Seizing the opportunities presented by the Chinese market and Chinese investment is indeed important to promote ASEAN's economic growth. Nevertheless, the coronavirus pandemic has been a wake-up call for ASEAN. From the perspective of many people in Southeast Asia, there is a huge risk of transitioning to dependence on China and China-centric industrial chains in the pursuit of regional economic growth. Attitudes of Southeast Asian countries towards China have hence become increasingly complex and cautious.

Although the BRI will accelerate infrastructure development in Vietnam and bring improvements to the economy and people's livelihoods, some Chinese enterprises' investment projects have caused local environmental pollution and ecological damage. Chinese enterprises, rather than paying due attention to environmental factors, take advantage of loopholes in the laws and regulations of Vietnam. This has led to a negative perception of Chinese enterprises and investment among the elites and many ordinary Vietnamese people, which has also affected the development of bilateral relations. For example, China's coal-fired power projects use relatively energy-efficient technologies that bring considerable environmental benefits to the host countries that they might not otherwise be able to afford. While China has introduced new stringent environmental monitoring standards for domestic power plants, these do not apply to projects in overseas countries such as Vietnam.

Many Vietnamese are concerned that the BRI will also pull Vietnam into China's orbit of development, which will eventually cause the country to lose autonomy over its development and foreign policy. There is also strongly voiced concern in Vietnam that China will use the BRI to gain geostrategic advantages and strengthen its influence in the region. In June 2018, the National Assembly of Vietnam deliberated on the Law proposed by the government on Special Administrative and Economic Units of Phu Quoc, which is intended to attract foreign investment to Vietnam and promote domestic economic growth and industrial development. According to the draft bill, the Vietnamese government plans to set up three special economic zones in the north and south of Phu Quoc Island to attract foreign investors through preferential policies such as allowing investors to rent land for 99 years.

People in several Vietnamese cities have protested against the bill and pointed the finger at China. Many people in Vietnam believe that the introduction of this bill will facilitate Chinese enterprises to seize Vietnamese land and infringe on Vietnam's territorial sovereignty and internal affairs. Due to strong domestic opposition, the Vietnamese government was forced to postpone the vote on the bill. Domestic demonstrations over the bill reflect deep-seated suspicion and rejection of China among Vietnamese citizens. This poses potential risks to the local investment and business activities of Chinese enterprises.

In exchanges and discussion with Vietnamese scholars, the author formed the impression that Vietnamese academia generally believe that China's Belt and Road Initiative has strong geostrategic and military significance, and is not merely an economic and trade cooperation initiative. Vietnam's biggest concern about the Belt and Road Initiative is that the advancement of the Belt and Road Initiative will strengthen China's sovereignty claims in the South China Sea and strengthen its presence in the region. This is a scenario that Vietnam is desperate to avoid. Meanwhile, many Vietnamese scholars believe that China's actual operation of the BRI lacks transparency, and countries along the route are not clear about whether or how to participate.

There are several acute issues and challenges in the economic and trade cooperation between China and Vietnam. First, both countries have similar industrial structures and similar export destinations in the West, so they compete fiercely in overseas export markets. Chinese and Vietnamese firms compete in medium and high value-added industries such as the electronics industry and office equipment and smartphone manufacturing, while also competing in many low value-added industries, ranging from toys and textiles to clothing and furniture manufacturing.

China, Vietnam and some other ASEAN countries are fast-developing emerging economies, dependent on export trade, and at the middle and low ends of the value chain/supply chain under economic globalisation, so there is a high degree of similarity between the two places in terms of export commodities and export markets, and competition in the structure of export commodities and export destinations is inevitable. However, amid China's rising production costs and consequent transfer of labour-intensive industry, ASEAN countries, such as Vietnam, have been increasingly competitive in low-end labour-intensive manufacturing based on their lower production costs (e.g. land and labour).

Another outstanding issue between China and Vietnam is the huge bilateral trade deficit, which is not conducive to the sustainable development of bilateral economic and trade cooperation in the long run. Since the launch of the CAFTA, Chinese-made goods have had a greater impact on the original markets of ASEAN countries with relatively low cost and scale advantages, especially Vietnam, the Philippines and Indonesia. In 2022, ASEAN countries ran up a record US$150 billion in goods trade with China. Among the Southeast Asian countries, Vietnam has the largest trade deficit with China.

Vietnam's trade deficit accounts for more than one-third of ASEAN's total trade deficit with China. There are strong voices of dissatisfaction in Vietnam, claiming that it has benefited too little from the economic and trade exchanges with China, and China is an unfair and unilateral winner. Vietnam's trade deficit with China reached a record high of US$45.67 billion in 2021, compared to the corresponding figure of US$11.61 billion in 2009.

China is Vietnam's largest source of imports. Vietnam is reliant on China for imports of electronic machinery, industrial equipment, high-tech products and ordinary consumer goods. Relatively speaking, Vietnam's exports to China still mainly comprise agricultural products, timber and other resource products. China is the largest export market for Vietnamese fruits (accounting for about 45% of the export share) and the third-largest export market for Vietnamese aquatic products.

Vietnam has encountered difficulties in gaining access to the Chinese market for many of its agricultural and aquatic products, due to the existence of non-tariff barriers, including quality inspection. The Chinese market lacks openness regarding institutional factors, and strict market access thresholds restrict Vietnamese products from entering the Chinese market.

Meanwhile, Vietnam has huge demand for machinery and electronic information goods produced in China, and intermediate products exported from China to Vietnam are processed and assembled and then sold to developed markets in the European countries and the United States.

The trade in goods between China and Vietnam was affected by the outbreak of the COVID-19 pandemic in Vietnam in 2021. At that time, China adopted strict inspection and isolation measures for cargo trucks and drivers from Vietnam based on its policy to prevent import of the COVID-19 virus from overseas. All goods imported from Vietnam were subjected to strict testing. These strict measures led to cumbersome or even stagnant customs clearance of goods, obstruction of customs clearance of goods and personnel, and serious traffic congestion.

China is one of the most important foreign trade markets for Vietnam, and the obstruction of customs clearance at China-Vietnam border ports has had a great impact on Vietnam's export enterprises and foreign trade. According to statistics from the General Administration of Customs of Vietnam, for example, from January to April 2022, the total value of import and export goods handled at China-Vietnam land ports was US$4.15 billion, down 64.5% compared with the same period in 2021. In addition, Vietnam's exports to China amounted to US$510 million, down 87.3% compared to the same period in 2021.

Trucks transporting large quantities of Vietnamese fruits and agricultural products were stranded on the Vietnamese side of the China-Vietnam border crossing, waiting for the completion of Chinese customs quarantine and customs clearance. Agricultural products are very time-sensitive, and long waiting time can cause deterioration and rot. In December 2021, hundreds of Vietnamese trucks were stranded at the Youyi, Puzhai-Tan Thanh and Aidian-Chi Ma crossings in northern Vietnam's Lang Son province on the border with Guangxi, China. However, since China's ending of its zero-COVID-19 policy on 8 January 2023, import and export trade and personnel clearance have begun to resume at many border ports.

Vietnam faces dual challenges in the field of foreign economic cooperation and trade. On the one hand, it has a huge trade deficit with China, While, on the other hand, there is the issue of how to achieve diversification of its export market and upgrading of its export structure. Some Vietnamese scholars believe that in the short term, the CPTPP can play only a limited role in reforming Vietnam's foreign trade structure and boosting the national economy. Trade with China has always played an important role in Vietnam's foreign trade and factors relating to the Chinese economy will continue to influence Vietnam's economic development.

For many years, China has been Vietnam's largest trading partner and largest source of imports. Trade with China accounts for nearly 20% of Vietnam's total foreign trade. In 2019, imports from China accounted for more than 28% of Vietnam's total imports, which included intermediate products mainly used for assembly and foundry in domestic manufacturing. Textile and garments and electronic information equipment are two major export industries for Vietnam, but 60% and 50%, respectively, of the raw materials and intermediate products of these two industries come from China.

In the face of escalating competition between the United States and China, Vietnam, like other countries in the region, has adopted a strategy of "balance of great powers" and does not openly steer to any side. Vietnam hopes to retain space to manoeuvre and further its national interests through diplomacy based on maintaining friendly relations with various major powers. On the one hand, Vietnam supports and participates in the BRI to attract Chinese investment, accelerate domestic industrial development and economic growth. On the other hand, in the long run, Vietnam believes that it is necessary to gradually reduce its economic dependence on China in order to avoid being diplomatically and strategically constrained by its northern neighbours.

The Vietnamese government has been trying to counteract China's economic influence in Vietnam by expanding bilateral economic and trade ties with other countries (European Union, United Kingdom, Japan, India, South Korea and the United States). The Vietnam-EU Free Trade Agreement (came into force in 2020) and the Vietnam-UK Free Trade Agreement (2021) have been signed and implemented. As of January 2022, Vietnam had signed a total of 15 free trade agreements. In addition, Vietnam has been actively participating in regional multilateral organisations, such as the Comprehensive and Progressive Agreement for Trans-Pacific Partnership (CPTPP), and adopting a market diversification strategy.

Vietnam officially joined the CPTPP in November 2018. Vietnam hopes to use the CPTPP and the Vietnam-EU Free Trade Agreement to broaden its export channels and channels, as well as to balance China's geoeconomic influence, accelerate diversification of the trade market and reduce over-dependence on the Chinese market. According to the forecast of Vietnam's Ministry of Industry and Trade, the CPTPP agreement will help to increase exports from Vietnam by 4% and GDP by 1.3% by 2030 and by 1.32% and 4.04%, respectively, by 2035. In the long run, the CPTPP will help Vietnam develop an export-oriented economy and accelerate its industrialisation.

The CPTPP has been in force since January 2019, and its member states have pledged to eliminate tariffs on Vietnamese products, especially textiles, footwear, agricultural products and seafood. Of course, in order to fulfil its commitments and meet the CPTPP accession criteria, Vietnam must also significantly reform its existing domestic laws and regulations on foreign trade, customs, state-owned enterprises, competition rules, trade unions, intellectual property rights and domestic procurement. Implementing these reforms will be challenging and painful, but in the long run, they are expected to enhance Vietnam's overall competitiveness.

4.3 The Impacts of the China-US Trade War on Vietnam

In the context of the escalation of the Sino-US trade dispute and the high tariffs imposed by the United States on Chinese imports, many multinational corporations and local Chinese companies with factories in China seek to avoid tariffs on their products, so consider moving production lines to regions with lower production costs outside China, with Vietnam receiving particular global interest regarding industrial transfer. The International Monetary Fund predicts that if the United States imposes a 25% tariff on all exports from China, Vietnam will be the Asian country that benefits the most by providing a new base for Chinese exports to the United States.

According to official United States statistics, bilateral trade between Vietnam and the United States reached US$60 billion in 2018, making Vietnam the United States' 16th-largest trading partner. US imports from Vietnam accounted for US$49.2 billion of this amount, with Vietnam ranking 12th among the major sources of US imports. In 2020, Vietnam rose to become tenth-largest trading partner of the United States, with bilateral trade volume of US$89.6 billion, with the United States' imports from Vietnam accounting for US$79.6 billion, and Vietnam ranking 6th among the major sources of US imports.

In the past several years, the rising production costs in China, domestic economic transformation and tariffs imposed under the Sino-US trade war have led a considerable number of multinational enterprises to transfer part of their production capacity and supply chain support out of China in pursuit of "China + 1" supply chain diversification strategy. The COVID-19 pandemic has only reinforced the necessity and urgency of restructuring the global supply chains.

Vietnam is aspiring to become the next emerging "factory of the world" after China. According to the Global Competitiveness Report 2019 released by the World Economic Forum, Vietnam's ranking on global competitiveness had risen by ten places compared to 2018, making it one of the fastest-rising economies. Vietnam's geographical proximity to China and its relatively low labour costs, relatively young population and relatively abundant workforce make it attractive to foreign companies as a replacement production base for Chinese exports to the United States.

Vietnam's total population is close to 100 million, of which a quarter are under the age of 25, and 70% of the total working-age population are under the age of 25. Vietnam has an abundant labour supply, able to meet the demand of labour-intensive manufacturing. Its other advantages include a long coastline, deep-sea ports, in good condition, and superior geographical location.

Based on its low production costs (e.g. Vietnam's labour costs are about half of those in China's Pearl River Delta region), Vietnam is highly successful in attracting foreign investment and is becoming one of the most competitive manufacturing bases in the Asia–Pacific region. In addition, Vietnam and some other Southeast Asian countries receive preferential treatment in terms of low tariffs on export products from Western countries due to their low level of economic development.

As China's rising labour costs and the U.S. tariffs on Chinese goods have led to the gradual relocation of some U.S. factories from China, shifting capacity to Southeast

Asia has become the preferred option. Taking the Korean firms as an example, after closing production plants in Shenzhen and Tianjin in 2018 and Huizhou, Guangdong province in October 2019, South Korea's Samsung Electronics completed the transfer of its supply chain out of China. At present, Samsung has two large-scale manufacturing and assembly plants in Vietnam.

Vietnam hopes to take advantage of the Sino-US trade war and the restructuring of the global industrial chain through the transfer of manufacturing industry from China. Industrial chain transfers from China to Vietnam have included not only Western multinational companies, but also local Chinese enterprises. There has been a concentrated shift of electronic equipment manufacturing, textiles, garments and furniture industries from China to Vietnam. In order to circumvent the punitive tariffs on Chinese exports to the United States, Chinese companies have increased their investment in Vietnam and set up new production bases and assembly plants (order transfer effect).

Before the outbreak of the trade war between China and the United States, many labour-intensive, low-value-added industries and factories in China's coastal areas had already moved to Vietnam. In the case of the sports products company Adidas, 40% of its footwear is produced by foundries based in Vietnam. Taking the international sportswear company LULULEMON as an example, in 2009, 75% of LULULEMON's products were OEM products from China, and 8% of its products were OEM products from Southeast Asian countries. By 2020, Only 9% of LULULEMON products were made in China, compared to 53% made in Southeast Asia (33% in Vietnam and 20% in Cambodia) and 38% in South Asia and elsewhere. Vietnam is Nike's number one producer. In 2010, Vietnam surpassed China on Nike footwear production, and in 2020, Vietnam surpassed China on clothing production. According to Nike's 2021 annual report, Vietnam's Nike shoe production accounted for 51% of output in 2021, while China's production accounted for 21%. In 2020, Vietnam surpassed China to become the largest producer of Nike clothing products, accounting for about 30% of production.

As a result of rising costs of various manufacturing elements, China's position as an "assembly foundry" in the global production chain has been challenged by Southeast Asian countries such as Vietnam. Many Chinese and multinational companies have moved low-end labour-intensive production to Vietnam. The growth of foreign trade has led to industrialisation in Vietnam, increasing its participation and market share in the global supply chain/production chain.

A common view of the international community and China's domestic media is that, first, Vietnam is the biggest beneficiary of the Sino-US trade war, and second, Vietnam is able to cope with the transfer of China's manufacturing against the dual background of Sino-US power competition and global supply chain restructuring and transfer. It could become the next "global manufacturing base" after China; however, some Vietnamese scholars are sceptical about Vietnam's ability to seize this opportunity to attract sufficient numbers of foreign manufacturers to set up factories in Vietnam.

On the one hand, Vietnam will face competition from countries such as Bangladesh, Indonesia and Cambodia with lower production costs. On the other hand, although Vietnam is similar to China in terms of economic structure and political system, its economy is only small to medium-sized, and it has problems such as backward infrastructure development, low urbanisation rate, and insufficient skilled labour and land resources. Therefore, it will be difficult for Vietnam to cope with large-scale transfer of production lines from China.

The wide media report that "Vietnam has become the biggest winner in the Sino-US trade war" is exaggerated. The trade war between China and the United States, the world's two largest economies, has had a negative impact on global economic growth, investment and trade exchanges. Since Vietnam's economic development is dependent on foreign trade, it cannot help but be affected by the Sino-U.S. trade war.

In addition, many media outlets and academics ignore or underestimate China's important role in Vietnam's exports to the United States. "Made in Vietnam" products are largely reassembled and repackaged as "Made in China" products, for eventual export to the United States and other Western markets under the "Made in Vietnam" label. Since 2018, Vietnam's exports to the United States, especially electronic products, have increased significantly, while most of the production equipment, intermediate goods and raw materials needed by Vietnam are imported from China, and China's export trade volume to Vietnam has more than doubled since 2017. This also explains the rapid rise in Vietnam's trade deficit with China in recent years.

In terms of the skilled labour required to develop its manufacturing industry, at most, Vietnam has only 15 million people available to participate in manufacturing development. Meanwhile, despite its ageing population, China still has more than 200 million skilled workers, its industrial chain/supply chain is well established and resilient, with sufficient supplies of domestic spare parts and other intermediate goods, and it has low dependence on foreign enterprises. Vietnam will find it difficult to emulate, let alone replace, China as the "world's factory".

China has obvious advantages regarding its production capacity, and absolute competitive advantages regarding its manufacturing capacity. Since joining the World Trade Organization in 2001, China has established strong comparative advantages in the global industrial chain that include its large number of skilled and hard-working industrial workers, its transportation and power infrastructure, upstream and downstream supporting supply chains, stable domestic political situation and huge domestic consumption market.

In contrast, Vietnam does not have the domestic transportation, power and other infrastructure required to become the world's factory. According to the "Global Competitiveness Report 2018" by the World Economic Forum, Vietnam ranked 75th among 142 countries/economies on infrastructure development (Table 4.1). With the influx of foreign capital and the completion of processing and assembly bases, the reality of the labour shortage in Vietnam has begun to emerge. Industrial land resources in Vietnam are becoming increasingly scarce, and local land prices are also rising.

Although labour costs in Vietnam and other Southeast Asian countries are cheaper than in China, productivity and technical proficiency are lower than in China. This factor will largely offset the cost advantage. China still retains its industrial

Table 4.1 Comparison of competitiveness between China and ASEAN countries

Country	GDP per capita (US$)	Overall competitiveness ranking	Institutions				
			Burden of government regulation	Efficiency of legal framework in setting disputes	Incidence of corruption	Intellectual property protection	Quality of land administration
Brunei Darussalam	29,711	62	85	58	29	57	52
Cambodia	1389	110	61	101	134	123	118
China	8643	28	18	47	66	49	51
Indonesia	3875	45	26	46	80	44	95
Laos	2542	112	47	49	113	87	99
Malaysia	9812	25	5	15	55	24	6
Philippines	2976	56	91	100	95	52	83
Singapore	57,713	2	1	1	6	3	1
Thailand	6590	38	58	48	80	99	52
Vietnam	2353	77	96	88	91	105	78

(continued)

Table 4.1 (continued)

Infrastructure	Skills		Product market		Labour market	
	Skillset of graduates	Ease of finding skilled employees	Prevalence of non-tariff barriers	Efficiency of the clearance process	Hiring and firing practices	Pay and productivity
54	49	108	82	72	71	77
112	111	121	84	109	45	55
29	37	44	57	31	23	27
71	33	35	73	61	19	18
99	74	96	91	73	90	50
32	6	4	16	44	9	5
92	27	20	42	85	41	10
1	5	9	1	6	4	3
60	61	88	61	36	33	36
75	128	104	124	42	46	66

Source World Economic Forum (2019)

advantages of complete industrial chain, high maturity and good resilience. Meanwhile, China's strong logistics and transportation capacity enhances the international competitiveness of its import and export trade. In terms of port handling capacity, the total container throughput in Southeast Asia's ports is less than one-third of that of Chinese ports.

It is not an easy task for multinational enterprises with long industrial chains to rearrange and set up new processing and assembly plants, involving the training and employment of industrial workers, complete support facilities for the plant, completeness of the supply chain and procurement costs. Based on ASEAN's imperfect supply chain, infrastructure bottlenecks and insufficient labour, it will be difficult in the short term for Southeast Asia to fully handle the production capacity transferred by China. Meanwhile, China is making every effort to achieve domestic industrial upgrading and economic transformation, from low-end value chains, reliant on labour, to medium and high-end value production chains, based on technological innovation and productivity.

4.4 The Case of Vietnam's Electronics Industry

Since joining the World Trade Organization in 2007, Vietnam has gradually integrated into the regional and global industrial chain, and its electronic information industry has developed rapidly. Vietnam has now become the third-largest exporter of electronic products in ASEAN and one of the world's important exporters of electronic information products. Nevertheless, most of Vietnam's exports of electronics and related spare parts come from the production plants of multinational companies (such as Japanese and Korean electronics companies) located in their countries. Foreign electronics enterprises enjoy special tax exemption or low tax rates from the Vietnamese government (Pham et al. 2020).

However, Vietnam's domestic electronics industry has developed slowly, has limited interaction and cooperation with foreign enterprises, a low degree of participation in the global industrial chain, and is at the low end of the industrial chain. Taking South Korea's Samsung as an example, only seven of the 93 suppliers providing intermediate goods and related professional services to its Vietnam-based production plants are local Vietnamese companies. These small, limited-capacity Vietnamese companies are struggling to integrate into the global electronics value chain led by large multinational companies. Greater participation of Vietnam's local electronics industry in the industrial chain is impeded by the difficulty in obtaining advanced technology from multinational electronics companies' investment and production centres in Vietnam.

Essentially, the rapid growth of Vietnam's electronics industry can be attributed to the establishment of production facilities of multinational enterprises in Vietnam. The emergence of these foreign-owned production facilities in Vietnam has created isolation between foreign players in the electronics industry and Vietnam's domestically owned firms.

Backward and forward linkages represent the ways in which economies participate in global value chains (GVCs). The proportion of total output outside China in terms of value-added is called backward participation. Backward participation represents the role of buyer (demander) in a global value chain and the relationship between a country and an upstream supplier. The share of domestic value-added exported to third countries is called forward participation. Forward participation represents a country's role as a seller (supplier) in the global value chain, through linkages with downstream producers.

According to the empirical research by Lin and Ye (2022), Vietnam's electronic communication industry is reliant on low value-added links for integration into the global industrial chain, and despite gradually strengthening its position, it is currently in a "low-end lock-in" situation. Vietnam's industry has far less forward than backward participation in the global electronic communication industry, so it is in a weak position overall, and it derives limited added value from the assembly and foundry links.

At present, Vietnam is mainly reliant on the small profits derived from electronic communication product assembly foundry, importing intermediate goods and raw materials from China, Japan and South Korea and other countries, and then, after simple assembly, selling on the goods to European and American sellers and customers.

4.5 Conclusion

While Vietnam may welcome the vision of the BRI, like many Southeast Asian countries it is unclear about key elements such as specific plans and details, or how to participate in the initiative. Vietnam is worried that the benefits from the Belt and Road Initiative unilaterally favour China. In order for Chinese enterprises to successfully go global and go forward, they need to have international operation capabilities and must at the same time be recognised and supported by the different countries' governments, society and people. Chinese enterprises need to pay equal attention to the three goals of economic efficiency, local society and environment, in order to achieve balance and win–win results in the four aspects of business operation, government, local community and environmental protection.

Moreover, Chinese enterprises need to accept and adapt to global standards and international rules, to establish sustainable development principles and take on the role of "responsible investors" in order to go global. Chinese President Xi Jinping said: "The Belt and Road should benefit the local people"; therefore, China needs to better share the benefits of the initiative with Southeast Asian countries, rather than overemphasising its own interests. The joint communiqué reached at the Second Belt and Road Summit clearly stated: "High-quality infrastructure should ensure that it is feasible, affordable, inclusive and widely beneficial throughout the cycle, contributing to the sustainable development of participating countries and the industrialization of developing countries".

The unilateral benefit model is not sustainable and will not be supported by countries along the route. The Chinese project development model of "Chinese design, Chinese equipment, Chinese construction, Chinese operation, and Chinese maintenance" needs to be adjusted. China could considerably allay regional countries' concerns about the "China centricity" of the Belt and Road Initiative by expanding the participation of host countries and deepening the "localisation" of its projects.

A rising China must understand that, as a major power, it has to shoulder international obligations in terms of maintaining regional stability and promoting multilateralism. Only in this way can China truly win the trust and respect of the international community, especially neighbouring countries like Vietnam. The depth of cooperation achieved between China, Vietnam and other Southeast Asian countries under the BRI will be a litmus test of the smooth implementation and even the success of the Belt and Road Initiative.

References

ISEAS-Yusof Ishak Institute. 2020. *State of Southeast Asia Survey Report 2020.*

ISEAS-Yusof Ishak Institute. 2022. *State of Southeast Asia Survey Report 2022.*

Kang, Gwiyoung. 2023. South Korea Looks to Vietnam to Reduce Reliance on China. *ThinkChina*, 22 August 2023. Available at https://www.thinkchina.sg/big-read-south-korea-looks-vietnam-reduce-reliance-china?utm_source=newsletter&utm_medium=email&utm_campaign=weekly_newsletter. Accessed 22 Aug 2023.

Lin, Mei, and Hao Ye. 2022. A Comparative Study on the Participation of Chinese and Vietnamese Electronics and Communication Equipment Manufacturing Industries in the Global Value Chain. *Southeast Asian Studies* 3.

Pham, Hanh Song Thi, Anh Ngoc Nguyen, and Andrew Johnston. 2020. Economic Policies and Technological Development of Vietnam's Electronics Industry. *Journal of the Asia Pacific Economy* 248–269.

Womack, Brantly. 2006. *China and Vietnam: The Politics of Asymmetry*. Cambridge: Cambridge University Press.

World Economic Forum. 2019. *The Global Competitiveness Report 2018.*

Chapter 5
The China-Singapore Chongqing Connectivity Project: A Cornerstone for Bilateral Relations

5.1 Literature Review on the Chinese Provinces' Ties with ASEAN

As part of a country's overall diplomatic strategy, Hocking (1993) argues that its central government can effectively use local external cooperation to break down sensitive and difficult political issues to the local level, thereby helping to reduce external pressures on the central government and helping state institutions to reduce the burden of complex policy implementations. Van der Pluijm (2007) argues that self-interest is the main driver of local engagement in diplomacy and that participation of local governments in diplomatic activities can benefit the local area in two ways. On the one hand, the place can attract tourists, foreign companies and host international events by participating in external activities. On the other, local governments can export services and knowledge through their external activities or sign cooperation treaties with local authorities in foreign countries. He believes that the traditional structure of diplomatic engagement must be changed to include non-state governments in order to defend local interests.

China's local governments are not passive implementers of central policy or simple participants in foreign affairs. Local officials can enhance their performance via their participation in international cooperation and this can increase their enthusiasm for participating in international affairs (Su 2010). Chen (2014) proposed that China's local participation in international affairs can provide the means and channels for the implementation of national strategies. Chen (2018) identified the concept of "city diplomacy" as playing a role in China's overall diplomacy strategy. Through urban diplomacy, the social foundation of relations between major countries can be consolidated from the bottom up. Li (2014) studied the role of local governments in China-ASEAN relations and proposed "local liberalism". He claimed that local authorities in China are not only central policy implementers, but also actively formulate their own foreign policy plans and bilateral cooperation initiatives, and, in so doing, seek the support of the central government. Yang (2018) stated that ASEAN

H. Yu, *Understanding China's Belt and Road Initiative*, Asia in Transition 26,
https://doi.org/10.1007/978-981-99-9633-9_5

countries have become important external economic partners of China. Chinese local governments that participate in China-ASEAN cooperation go through three stages: passive implementation of policies (1991–2003), active action (2004–2013), and acceleration of central-local cooperation (since 2014), which are characterized by diversity, non-balance, competition and multifaceted influence.

The participation of Chinese provinces and cities in foreign affairs and international cooperation will help local governments to promote local economic development by using the international arena to obtain external funds, information and talents. International exchanges and economic growth are related to local interests and are also important weight indicators that determine the promotion of local officials. Local governments in China are oriented towards economic development and formally or informally participate in foreign affairs and strengthen international connectivity and external ties, with the goal of pursuing local interests. At the same time, these local endeavours help China achieve its overall foreign policy goals.

Economic globalisation and China's deep integration into the world economy have pushed Chinese provinces into the trend of internationalisation and strengthening international ties. Through China's economic development and the expansion of foreign relations, its provinces and cities have increasingly gained the strength to participate in international cooperation and local diplomatic affairs to further expand the market space for economic development. China has 17 provinces and regions whose economic output exceeds that of South Africa and Argentina, respectively, which are G20 countries with respective economic output of around US$419 billion and US$450 billion.

However, when engaging in foreign exchange and cooperation activities with foreign countries, local governments are inevitably influenced by China's current foreign policy and the relationship between the central and local governments. Under the current institutional framework, the central government grants local governments the authority to carry out such activities. From an institutional point of view, the lack of legal authorization has made China's participation in foreign affairs and foreign exchanges ambiguous and uncertain.

China's local diplomatic activities and participation in international cooperation practice are beset by problems of unclear powers and responsibilities and ambiguous boundaries for authorization of the relations between the central and local governments, between ministries and commissions, and between local and foreign countries. Hence, foreign countries and international organisations tend to have doubts about engaging in exchanges and cooperation with the Chinese local governments.

Therefore, the participation of local provinces and municipalities in international cooperation requires both the authorization of the central government and the establishment of a coordination mechanism between the central and local governments. In the process of local participation in international cooperation, there are contradictions between the handling of legal mandates and the granting of transactional mandates by the state, comprising a contradiction between centralization and decentralisation and another between central policy and the local governments' need to obtain central approval, which limit the actual external autonomy obtained.

In foreign relations, the factors considered by local governments in China-ASEAN cooperation are different from those considered at the central government level. Local governments give primary consideration to local economic interests and do not pay attention to broader macroareas such as international politics, foreign relations, geostrategy and security. Although the considerations and starting points of the central and local governments are not necessarily contradictory, in the practice of foreign exchanges, the interests of the central and local governments will also differ from time to time, and there will be conflicts between local and central policies.

The outstanding problem in relation to cooperation between local provinces and cities and ASEAN countries is that in the course of exchanges with the ASEAN countries, some localities are vague about their role as "limited participation actors", unilaterally promote local-led ASEAN cooperation strategy and often lack communication and coordination with the central government. This has led to confusion in ASEAN countries.

5.2 The Role of Chinese Provinces in China-ASEAN Relations

In China's relations with the ASEAN countries, the role played by China's local governments cannot be ignored. China's diverse topography, uniqueness and vast geographical area give local governments the advantage of participating in international cooperation. The economic development of local governments, especially in coastal provinces and municipalities such as Guangdong, Shanghai, Zhejiang and Jiangsu provinces that rely on foreign trade and foreign investment, cannot be separated from foreign economic and trade cooperation and the expansion of international ties.

Chinese President Xi Jinping delivered a speech at the "Symposium on China's Peripheral Diplomacy" held in October 2013: "Accelerate the opening up of border areas and deepen mutually beneficial cooperation between border provinces and regions and neighbouring countries". President Xi's statement has laid the foundation for local provinces and cities to strengthen ties with ASEAN countries and participate in multilateral cooperation in the subregion.

Extensive and in-depth local cooperation is a highlight of China-ASEAN relations and an integral part of bilateral cooperation. The breadth and depth of local provinces and municipalities participating in bilateral relations between China and ASEAN countries are not commonly replicated in China's cooperation with countries in other regions.

Local areas are among the players affecting China-ASEAN relations and have an important role in the development of bilateral relations. Chinese localities, especially provinces with land and water borders with Southeast Asian countries, are very active in engaging in cooperation and bilateral exchanges with ASEAN.

Local economic and trade cooperation with ASEAN countries is more conducive than central government activities to diluting ASEAN's sense of inequality in cooperation with China and eliminating ASEAN countries' suspicions and concerns about China's expansion of geopolitical influence through bilateral trade. For ASEAN countries, working with Chinese provinces and cities can help them to feel more equitable in cooperating with China, reducing resistance and eliminating anxiety and inequality. This, in turn, will help promote bilateral economic and trade exchanges between China and ASEAN.

Local areas' cooperation with ASEAN countries is conducive to their own economic development and opens up foreign trade markets for enterprises. For many provinces and cities in China, ASEAN is an important partner in carrying out foreign economic and trade cooperation. Regional economic integration and the establishment of the China-ASEAN Free Trade Area have led to the strengthening of bilateral relations between China and ASEAN countries. This also gives local provinces and regions more space to participate in bilateral cooperation and expand the field of bilateral exchanges. Local governments in China are actively seeking central support from the central government, hoping to incorporate local-ASEAN cooperation into the country-ASEAN cooperation framework in order to win central fiscal and other preferential policy support.

5.3 Overview of the China-Singapore Relations

Singapore is strategically located to guard the Strait of Malacca. It is also one of the most important financial centres in the Asia–Pacific region, a major commodity trading market and transshipment logistics centre in Southeast Asia, and an important financial and shipping centre.

Singapore has a comprehensive range of international leading professional intermediaries in finance, auditing, legal, consulting and intellectual property protection. In addition, it has world-class infrastructure, a first-class business environment, clean and efficient government, high social stability, a sound rule of law system, predictable policies and transparent governance, and an open economy with low tax rates.

These factors have, in combination, attracted the attention of Chinese companies. Singapore's unique strengths place it in a prime position to act as a bridge between East and West. The strengthening of bilateral relations between China and Singapore can act as a template for the development of relations between China and the ASEAN as a whole.

Singapore's relationship with China can be dated back to the forging of personal friendship between Singapore's late founding Prime Minister Lee Kuan Yew and Chinese paramount leader Deng Xiaoping. Lee Kuan Yew had always supported China's reform and opening up, believing that Singapore had to strengthen its engagement with China. Up to his death, he was always concerned with convincing China of Singapore's relevance as a reference for China's reform and development.

China's leadership is well aware that Singapore, despite being a small island economy, is uniquely positioned to be a trusted partner that can add value to China's reform and development. Bilateral cooperation between the two countries has been developing with the times and is today focused on infrastructure construction, financial services and the third-country market, and professional services cooperation, among other fields.

Since the formal establishment of diplomatic relations between China and Singapore in 1990, bilateral relations have developed rapidly. In 2015, Chinese President Xi Jinping visited Singapore, and China and Singapore established an all-round cooperative partnership that is keeping pace with the times. Based on mutual trust and the particularity of their bilateral relations, China and Singapore have launched four intergovernmental cooperation projects, including Suzhou Industrial Park (launched in 1994), Tianjin Eco-City (launched in 2007), China-Singapore (Chongqing) Strategic Connectivity Project (launched in 2015), and Guangzhou Knowledge City (launched in 2009 and upgraded to a state-level cooperation project in 2018). In addition, the two countries have collaborated on numerous other bilateral cooperation projects, such as the Jilin Food Processing Zone, the Sichuan-Singapore Innovation and Technology Park, and the Shenzhen Smart City.

Singapore has been deeply involved in China's opening up and regional economic development. Although Singapore is a small city-based economy, it has special advantages that have enabled it to become a reliable partner of China and add value to China's development. On 6 September 2020, Singapore's Minister of Trade and Industry, Chan Chun Sing, spoke in an interview with Singapore's Lianhe Zaobao about the reasons for the enhancement and consolidation of relations between China and Singapore over the past 30 years:

> Deep and updated understanding of China's different stages of development and regional needs, deep mutual trust, and a common pragmatic work culture. ... The relationship between the two countries is not static or one-dimensional, but multifaceted and evolving, and the two sides set the theme and approach of cooperation in line with China's priorities, which is quite different from Singapore's relationship with other countries (Han, 2020).

Economic and trade cooperation between the two countries has in recent decades played a leading and forward-looking role in China's foreign economic and trade policy. The bilateral trade in goods between the two countries reached US$89 billion in 2020. China has been Singapore's largest trading partner, largest export market and largest source of imports since 2013. With bilateral trade in services worth US$36.9 billion in 2020, Singapore is China's fourth-largest services trading partner. In 2021, bilateral trade in goods between China and Singapore reached US$94.05 billion.

Singapore has also been the largest source of foreign direct investment to China since 2013. According to the Ministry of Commerce of the People's Republic of China, the cumulative direct investment of Singaporean enterprises in China reached US$102.78 billion as of the end of December 2019 and was mainly focused on manufacturing, services and transportation. Singapore's investment in China accounts for more than 87% of all investment in China by BRI countries (see Table 5.1).

Table 5.1 Milestones in development of bilateral economic and trade ties between China and Singapore

1	Consecutively from 2013 to 2022, China was Singapore's largest trading partner
2	As of the end of 2019, there were more than 7500 Chinese-funded enterprises registered in Singapore
3	Singapore accounted for 87.7% of the total inflow of foreign direct investment into China from the Belt and Road countries
4	As of November 2018, 100 of the 750 companies listed on the Singapore Stock Exchange were from China. SGX-listed Chinese concept companies had a total market capitalization of nearly RMB130 billion

Source Compiled by the author

Singapore, as a tiny city-state economy, is highly dependent on foreign trade and investment, since it lacks a hinterland for the domestic market. Therefore, supporting Singapore's sustainable economic growth requires external raw material and consumer markets, as well as markets for outbound investment, to achieve capital investment appreciation. China and Singapore are geographically close and culturally connected, and China has become an important destination country for Singapore's national capital and private enterprises and provided an export market for its products.

Since the two countries formally established diplomatic relations in 1990, Singapore's direct investment in China has surged from just US$50 million in 1990 to US$10.3 billion in 2021 (see Fig. 5.1). In 2021 alone, Singapore set up nearly 1300 new enterprises and investment projects in China.

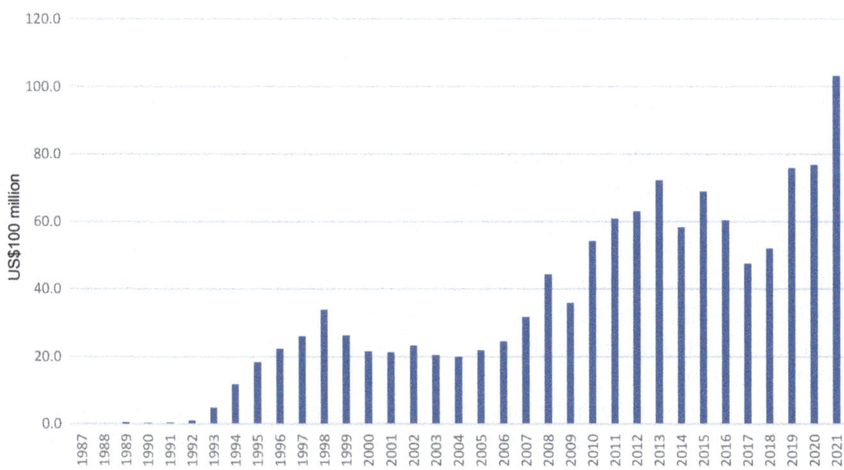

Fig. 5.1 Singapore's outbound investment to China. *Source* Ministry of Trade and Industry, Singapore; National Bureau of Statistics, Singapore

Temasek Holdings is a Singapore-based sovereign investment company with active investments worldwide. China has become Temasek's largest investment destination, based on investments spanning a wide range of sectors, including financial services, telecommunications and media, technology, real estate, transport and logistics, industrial manufacturing, life sciences and agri-food manufacturing. According to Temasek's Annual Investment Report, 27% of its global portfolio (S$381 billion) was invested in China as of March 2021, accounting for S$102.9 billion.

Temasek was established in 1974, in which the Singapore government has a 100% controlling stake. Temasek is also a state-owned enterprise registered in a private name. Temasek manages 23 multinational companies, commonly referred to as subsidiaries, on a holding basis, including 14 wholly owned companies, seven listed companies and two limited liability companies. These companies are also about 2000 large and small enterprises, with a total number of 140,000 employees and total assets of more than S$42 billion. These firms combined under Temasek account for about 8% of the country's GDP. Temasek controls Singapore's key sectors such as finance, transport, communications, real estate and energy and dominates Singapore's economic lifeline.

In the 46 years since Temasek's establishment and 16 years into China, China has become Temasek's largest single market for global investment, and the development of the Chinese market is an important factor in the enduring prosperity of Temasek. Today, Temasek's investment in China has already been pervasive, including China Construction Bank, Industrial and Commercial Bank of China, Ping an Insurance of China, Alibaba, JD.com, Didi Chuxing, Huiyuan Juice and other well-known enterprises.

Furthermore, Singapore is one of the three important overseas RMB offshore settlement centres, alongside Hong Kong and London. It has also become an important destination for Chinese outbound investment and has attracted the largest share of Chinese investment among all the Belt and Road countries. Between 2007 and 2018, Chinese direct investment in Singapore grew nearly ninefold, from US$398 million to US$3.55 billion. By the end of 2019, China's investment stock in Singapore reached US$33.45 billion, accounting for more than 20% of China's total investment in countries along the Belt and Road routes.

Building on the four bilateral country-level cooperation projects, Singapore can leverage its advantages as an international financial centre to enhance China's ability to open up to the outside world and accelerate the pace of internationalisation of Chinese enterprises through increasing China's investment in the region and throughout the world.

Singapore plays a special and important role in China's Belt and Road Initiative, having been one of the first countries to endorse and participate in the BRI. On 17 March 2023, Singapore's Prime Minister Lee Hsien Loong said in an exclusive interview with China Central Television (Prime Minister's Office Singapore 2023):

> The Belt and Road Initiative, in our view, is a way for China to contribute to regional development. The Belt and Road Initiative has been welcomed by the entire region as it helps China integrate into this regional network of cooperation and interdependence, which is mutually beneficial and win-win. Regional development requires infrastructure, and infrastructure

> needs financing. China has these capabilities to build infrastructure, provide financing, and develop economic and trade ties with countries in the region. With the Belt and Road Initiative, there is a framework within which these ideas can be realized. ... China is the largest economy in our region, and it is important to have an open, sustainable and mutually beneficial relationship with China. From this perspective, we believe that the Belt and Road Initiative is meaningful and we support it. From Singapore's perspective, what are we contributing to the Belt and Road? First of all, we are a financial center and many projects can be financed and evaluated in Singapore. This is an important infrastructure for the Belt and Road, that is, soft infrastructure. In fact, Singapore is one of the largest offshore RMB trading centers internationally. This is one aspect, on a legal level, Singapore is an arbitration and mediation hub with many international law firms. It is also important to us that countries participating in the Belt and Road Initiative can meet these needs if they need to find a seat of arbitration or provide legal advice.

The cooperative relationship between China and Singapore is also evolving with the times. At present, the investment of Chinese enterprises in Singapore covers e-commerce, financial services, shipping, third-party market cooperation, trade, energy, and infrastructure, logistics, professional services, tourism, real estate and education and training. In addition, Chinese and Singaporean enterprises have successfully joined forces to carry out third-party market cooperation based on their respective advantages (see Table 5.2 for details). Singaporean companies hope to participate with Chinese partners in cooperation with neighbouring countries in Southeast Asia.

In April 2018 and April 2019, China's National Development and Reform Commission and Singapore's Ministry of Trade and Industry signed the Memorandum of Understanding on Third-Party Market Cooperation and the Memorandum of Understanding on Strengthening the Implementation Framework for China-Singapore Third-Party Market Cooperation, which encourages enterprises of the two countries to use their respective advantages to carry out third-party market cooperation in the fields of logistics, e-commerce, infrastructure, finance and legal and other professional services to achieve mutual benefit and win–win results.

The Singapore government has set a goal of making Singapore a global technology and innovation hub. As a result, China and Singapore have gradually established and developed close cooperation in science and technology and innovation. To keep pace with future competition, countries must vigorously encourage and pursue innovation in science and technology to drive productivity growth and as an important engine of future development. China and Singapore share similar views on the important role of innovation in accelerating the country's economic transformation and sustainable development. At present, the two countries are engaging in close cooperation in high-tech fields such as artificial intelligence, big data, electric vehicles, new energy development and utilisation, biotechnology and aerospace, and there has been an increase in exchanges of scientific and technological personnel between the two countries.

Table 5.2 Selected third-party country cooperation projects between Chinese and Singapore enterprises

Project	Company name	Project detail
1	State grid and Singapore energy invest in Australian energy grid project	In 2014, state grid acquired a 60% stake in Australian Asset Company and a 19.9% stake in Australian open for US$2.8 billion
2	Shandong Weiqiao and Singapore's winning group form Guinea's "Win Alliance"	Hongqiao Group, a subsidiary of Shandong Weiqiao Group, forms a consortium "Win Alliance" with Yantai Port Group, Singapore Winning Group and Guinea UMS Company, which is responsible for Guinea bauxite mining, port transportation, land transportation and maritime transportation respectively. As of April 2019, the cumulative investment of the project had exceeded 500 million US dollars, and the annual export capacity is 50 million tonnes
3	China Machinery Engineering Corporation and CapitaLand are based in India	China Machinery Engineering Co., Ltd. and China automotive international are responsible for the promotion and investment attraction of Chennai Yihui Industrial Park in the Chinese market. The park is a joint venture between CapitaLand, IREO India, Nippon and Mizuho Bank
4	CMEC Group and CapitaLand Group are based in India	China Machinery Engineering Corporation Limited and CapitaLand Group have partnered to develop the Chenguang Industrial Logistics Park in Olagadam, Chennai
5	China State Construction Group cooperates with Singapore Dakuo Water Technology in Southeast Asian countries	Singaporean environmental protection company Dakuo Water Technology cooperated with China State Construction Group to supply regional pneumatic waste conveying systems to China and ASEAN countries, China State Construction was responsible for project construction, and Dakuo was responsible for providing relevant technology and ASEAN market information to achieve mutual benefit and win–win cooperation

(continued)

Table 5.2 (continued)

Project	Company name	Project detail
6	Sinopec Group cooperated with Singapore Tat Fung Holdings on a number of third-party market construction projects	Tat Fung Holdings is the largest crawler crane supplier in Asia, cooperating with Chinese enterprises in Southeast Asia and South Asia, providing machinery leasing, local machinery storage and other services, and providing assistance to Chinese enterprises in import and export procedures and business communication. Tat Fung Holdings and Sinopec Refining and Chemical Engineering Group and other project contractors jointly built the Bienjaran Petroleum Complex for Petronas
7	Fuchun Holdings cooperated with Ye Shuifu Group to establish a "Belt and Road" logistics assets private equity fund	Fuchun Holdings and Ye Shuifu Group set up the "Fuchun Ye Shuifu Belt and Road Logistics Asset Private Equity Fund" with an initial scale of US$150 million, focusing on the development and acquisition of logistics assets along the "Belt and Road" and assisting regional countries in the construction of infrastructure projects

Sources National Development and Reform Commission of China; Lianhe Zaobao; China Council for the Promotion of International Trade (2019)

5.4 Chongqing Connectivity Project and the Western Corridor

In March 2015, the Chinese government issued the "Vision and Actions for Jointly Building the Silk Road Economic Belt and the 21st Century Maritime Silk Road", which emphasises the following objectives:

> To promote the construction of the Belt and Road, China will give full play to the comparative advantages of various regions in China, implement a more proactive opening strategy, strengthen interaction and cooperation between the Eastern, Central and the Western regions, and comprehensively enhance the level of an open economy.

Since the Chinese government proposed the Belt and Road Initiative in 2013, central ministries and commissions have issued preferential policies to promote the Belt and Road Initiative. Moreover, all of China's provinces and regions (especially those along the ancient Silk Road) have put forward their own schemes for promoting the initiative, hoping to gain a strategic position in the nation's promotion of the BRI and win preferential policy support from central government, to promote economic development in their local areas.

The China-Singapore (Chongqing) Connectivity Project, which is a flagship project between the two countries under the BRI, is the third government-to-government cooperation project between the two countries and the only one to be established in the western region of China. In November 2015, during China's President Xi Jinping's state visit to Singapore, the two governments signed the Framework Agreement on the Construction of the China-Singapore (Chongqing) Strategic

Connectivity Demonstration Project and other relevant supplementary agreements in Singapore, which marked the official launch of the China-Singapore (Chongqing) Connectivity Project (the Chongqing Connectivity Project). In 2021, the governments of China and Singapore jointly completed the China-Singapore (Chongqing) Strategic Connectivity Demonstration Project Master Development Plan (2021–2025), and both countries intend this project to become a flagship project under the Belt and Road Initiative.

With Chongqing as the fulcrum, the China-Singapore Connectivity Project will help enhance the internationalisation of the entire western region. The western region needs to open up more in order to attract foreign investment. The China-Singapore Connectivity Project and the construction of new land-sea corridors will promote vitality of the provinces in the western region, accelerate their industrialization and create more local employment opportunities, as well as promote the overall economic and social development of the western region.

The implementation of the China-Singapore Chongqing Connectivity Project is a vote of confidence in the Singapore government's continued openness towards development of China. Modelled on Singapore's experience, the China-Singapore Connectivity Project will contribute to China's new round of opening up and the development of the vast western region.

This platform will also enable Singaporean enterprises to participate fully in the development of the BRI and the western region. In particular, it will encourage sharing of the opportunities brought by the development of the Chengdu-Chongqing Twin Cities Economic Circle. This project expands the hinterland of the overseas market of Singapore enterprises, since it encompasses one of the fastest-growing regions in China in recent years, with a total population of 52.18 million. The Chengdu-Chongqing Economic Circle accounted for about 4.2% of China's total economy and 12.4% of China's total foreign investment in 2020.

Chongqing was chosen for the China-Singapore Connectivity Project because of its preferential geographical location and administrative structure as a municipality directly under the central government. Chongqing is the only municipality directly under the central government in the western region and enjoys political resources and preferential policies that other cities in the western region cannot match.

Although it has been 20 years since China promoted the strategy of large-scale development of the western region, this region is still the soft underbelly of China's development. Economic development in the western region lags far behind not only that of the eastern coastal areas, but also the central region. While the western region accounts for 70% of China's land area and 27% of China's total population, it makes only a 20% contribution to the national economy.

However, under China's "dual-circulation" development strategy, the western region is not only the biggest driving force behind China's new round of opening up, but also has the greatest potential in terms of building a robust and dynamic domestic economy.

From the Chinese perspective, leveraged on Singapore's investment, urban management and knowhow on connectivity and industrial development, the strategic goal behind developing the Chongqing connectivity project and the western corridor is to build a convenient trade corridor and integrate the western region into the global economy.

Geographically speaking, Chongqing is located at the junction of the Silk Road Economic Belt and the Maritime Silk Road and therefore plays an important role in the initiative. It is also located in the upper reaches of the Yangtze River waterway, which connects to the domestic Yangtze River Economic Belt. Chongqing has developed into one of the main economic centres in western China and a major global assembly and production base for notebook computers.

The International Land-Sea Trade Corridor (or Western Corridor) is a key cooperation project under the Chongqing Connectivity Project, while the Qinzhou Port in Guangxi is at the intersection of water and land routes in the Western Corridor. The Western Corridor connects Chongqing and Western China with Singapore and Southeast Asia as a whole. The cargo transit route under the Western Corridor is based on the use of a variety of transport modes, including expressways, railways and inland waterways, and maritime shipping, to the southward route reaching Singapore and ASEAN major logistics nodes, and then radiating to the Middle East, Australia and other regions.

The New International Land-Sea Trade Corridor has been gaining political momentum in both countries over the past few years. In June 2022, the governments of China and Singapore jointly signed the Cooperation Plan for the China-Singapore (Chongqing) Strategic Connectivity Demonstration Project "New International Land-Sea Trade Corridor", proposing to build an efficient, convenient, open and competitive trade logistics channel by 2025. Singapore's Prime Minister Lee Hsien Loong recently commented on the significance of Chongqing Connectivity Project and the Western Corridor:

> The integrated transport corridor of the new international land-sea trade corridor from Chongqing to Guangxi to Beibu Gulf is part of the Belt and Road initiative, opening up new routes connecting Chinese mainland abroad. China has established access roads to foreign countries through the Yangtze River, but the distances are long and water transportation is very busy. Therefore, we believe that the establishment of another shorter and faster corridor with Southeast Asian countries and the rest of the world makes a significant contribution to the joint construction of the Belt and Road Initiative.

For Singapore, participating in the construction of a new land-sea corridor in China's western region, will help cement its position as a key maritime trade hub in the region. Singapore is no stranger to Chongqing, which has been the largest source of foreign investment for many years. Many Singaporean companies have settled in Chongqing and subsequently radiated across the entire western Chinese market. For example, CapitaLand, Mapletree, Raffles Medical Group and BreadTalk all have entered Chongqing. The three major banks in Singapore, including DBS Bank, United Overseas Bank (UOB) and OCBC Bank, have also established presences in Chongqing.

With Singapore and Chongqing as the hub, the China-Singapore Connectivity Project can facilitate the connection and further integration of China's western provinces with the ASEAN countries. Through the interconnection between

Chongqing and Singapore, Chongqing and other western provinces will be more widely interconnected with Singapore and Southeast Asia.

The Chongqing Connectivity Project has made substantial progress in the past five years, and the Western Corridor is attracting further participation by 13 provinces, municipalities, and autonomous regions, including Inner Mongolia, Guangxi, Chongqing, Sichuan, Guizhou, Yunnan, Shaanxi, Tibet, Gansu, Qinghai, Ningxia, Xinjiang and Hainan, as well as the Zhangjiang city of Guangdong, which have already signed the agreements and formally participated in the project.

The China-Singapore connectivity project focuses on the areas of transport and logistics, financial services, aviation and information and communications, through which bilateral cooperation is progressing. Enterprises from Singapore and China have cooperated to establish the China-Singapore (Chongqing) Huilian Pucheng Multimodal Intelligent Logistics Base to enhance the external connectivity of Chongqing's logistics industry.

In the financial services industry, western provinces, including Chongqing, have received more than US$10 billion in different forms of financing through Singapore, which is conducive to the economic development of the western region. In the aviation sector, Singapore's Changi Airport Group has worked with local partners to manage Chongqing Jiangbei Airport's catering, retail and advertising businesses to enhance the airport's international service standards. In the field of information and communication, Singapore Press Holdings Group cooperated with ZBJ.com in Chongqing to build a bilingual e-commerce platform, which has been launched in Singapore.

The Chongqing Connectivity Project uses Chongqing as its operation centre, but it is an open and shared development platform for the entire western region of China and the ASEAN. The project welcomes the participation of all 12 provinces in western China, as well as ASEAN partners. Openness is a feature of the Chongqing connectivity project that represents one of its biggest advantages.

The port of Qinzhou, located in Guangxi, is the meeting point of the sea and land routes of the Western Corridor. The Western Corridor connects Chongqing and Western China with Southeast Asian countries (via Singapore). Once the new international land-sea trade corridor, a southbound strategic channel with equal emphasis on railway, sea and land, is open and its operations start to mature, it will effectively reduce the costs and transit time of logistics in the western region. For western provinces such as Yunnan, Guizhou and Sichuan, the new international land-sea trade route is more advantageous than the existing land transport through China-Thailand and China-Myanmar, or the sea freight through ports such as Guangzhou, Shanghai or Shenzhen, which can greatly reduce the distance, transportation cost and transit time of goods (Table 5.3).

The Western Corridor provides convenient and direct access to the sea for the western provinces of China and is also the most convenient passage connecting western China with the world. On the one hand, more Singaporean enterprises will be attracted to invest in the western region, including Chongqing, through the Western Corridor. On the other hand, more western enterprises and products will enter Singapore, ASEAN countries and even the global market through the Corridor.

Table 5.3 Comparison of cargo shipping routes from Chongqing to Singapore

Transportation routes	Transport distance (km)	Transit time (days)	The degree of facilitation of land-sea combined transport	Efficiency of the customs clearance process
Chongqing—Guangxi Beibu Gulf Port—Singapore	3240	6–7	Low	Low
Chongqing—Shanghai Yangshan Port—Singapore	3700	9–10	High	High
Chongqing—Shenzhen Yantian Port—Singapore	5300	20	High	High

Source Compiled by the author based on relevant port information

Since the launch of the new corridor, the volume of goods transported through the corridor has grown rapidly, from 3382 TEUs in 2017 to 756,000 TEUs in 2022 (Fig. 5.2). Singapore is an important node of the BRI, based on its status as one of Asia's main trading hubs. This new trade corridor connecting China's western hinterland with Singapore will enable fresh agricultural products from China's vast western provinces to be quickly transshipped through Singapore to markets in such as Southeast Asia, South Asia, the Middle East, Europe, the South Pacific and Africa.

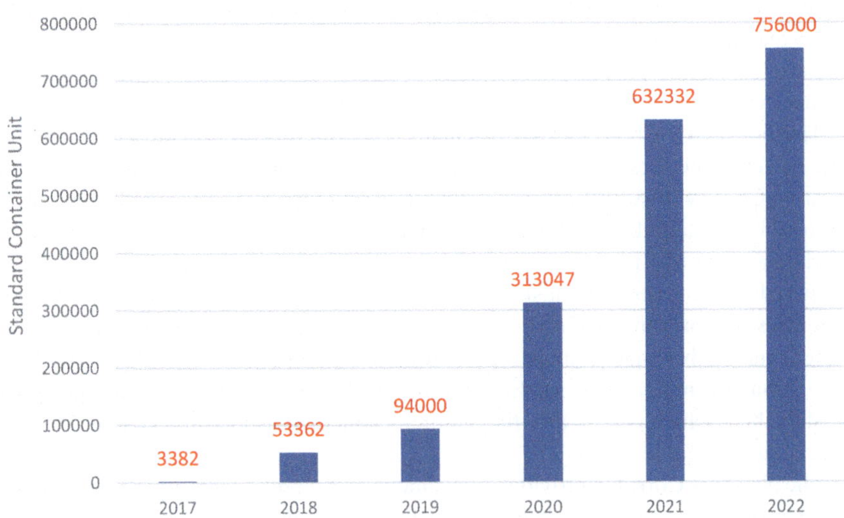

Fig. 5.2 Cargo transportation volume by Western Corridor. *Source* Ministry of Commerce of China; Ministry of Trade and Industry, Singapore

5.5 Building the Western Corridor Requires the Participation of More Partners

The new international land-sea trade corridor or Western Corridor is gaining strong political support and development momentum, based on endorsement by the Chinese and Singapore authorities. Nevertheless, its development sustainability and commercial viability not only depend on political support, but also the participation of the private sector and other multiple stakeholders, such as the Chinese western provinces and the ASEAN countries.

The Western Corridor is still in its infancy and the relatively high costs of operation and logistics are thorny issues facing the Western corridor. First, Li's study (2020) found that the Western corridor faces the problem of insufficient volumes of cargo goods for transport, especially for the return trip from Southeast Asia to China's western provinces. Although Chongqing is an important economic centre in the western region, its economic volume is small and it lacks regional economic radiation capacity. In 2019, Chongqing's GDP was RMB2.36 trillion (S$472 billion), accounting for only 2.3% of China's economy. In terms of foreign economic ties, Chongqing accounts for only 2.4% of the bilateral trade volume between China and ASEAN.

In economic development terms, Chongqing not only lags far behind coastal provinces such as Shanghai and Zhejiang, but its total economic output is smaller than that of other western cities, namely Sichuan and Shaanxi. The supply of goods from Chongqing alone is not enough to support the sustainable development of inflow of goods through the Western Corridor.

The western corridor faces the problems of insufficient sources of foreign trade goods. The Western Corridor needs to attract active participation of more enterprises from western provinces and ASEAN countries in order to achieve economies of scale and further reduce logistical costs. This will help to strengthen economic momentum and achieve sustainable development of the Western Corridor.

Moreover, the China-Singapore connectivity project needs to enhance the commercial attractiveness of the western corridor by reducing the cost of transporting goods, improving operational efficiency and facilitating customs clearance. For example, at present, there is considerable imbalance between southbound cargo transportation and northbound cargo transportation in the western corridor.

To achieve smooth operation of the corridor, it is essential to break down the institutional barriers in transportation, logistics, trade and other fields along the route, coordinate the customs systems and standards for market access and supervision, and establish mutual recognition of quality and qualifications between regions. It is necessary to deepen international collaboration on customs, focusing on the efficiency of multimodal customs declaration and convenient customs clearance policies.

While attracting more participation in western China is critical to the prospects of the China-Singapore connectivity project and the western corridor, in the case of the China-Singapore Chongqing Connectivity Project, there is as yet no institutionalised coordination mechanism covering all participating provinces and regions in the western region. The Chinese central government needs to further demonstrate leadership by coordinating the participation of western provinces and regions in the Chongqing connectivity project and the construction of the Western Corridor at the national level. Such a mechanism, led by the Chinese central government, would help to resolve the interprovincial disputes and to standardise cross-provincial customs clearance.

Local governments in China are oriented towards economic development and strive to pursue local interests by strengthening external connectivity and international cooperation. Therefore, local participation in the China-Singapore connectivity project will depend on whether the project can meet the local economic development needs.

The changing global geopolitical environment could also have a potential impact on regional logistics and transportation and industrial chain layout, thus bringing new variables and uncertainties to the Chongqing connectivity project and the development of the western corridor. Hence, the China-Singapore connectivity project needs to demonstrate flexibility and resilience in response to external changes.

References

Chen, Zhimin. 2014. A New Starting Point for Urban Diplomacy. *Shanghai Foreign Affairs* (6): 25–26.

Chen, Nan. 2018. City Diplomacy and Major Country Diplomacy with Chinese Characteristics. *International Outlook* (1): 70–85.

China Council for the Promotion of International Trade. 2019. *Business Environment Guide for Countries (Regions) for Outbound Investment 2019—Singapore.*

Han, Yonghong. 2020. Interview with Minister of Trade and Industry Chan Chun Sing on the Management of Singapore-China Relations: Encouraging Each Other and Not Forgetting to Remind Blind Spots. *Lianhe Zaobao*, 6 Sept 2020. https://www.zaobao.com.sg/special/report/supplement/singapore-china-30-years-diplomatic-relations/news/story20200906-1082655.

Hocking, Brian. 1993. *Localizing Foreign Policy: Non-Central Governments and Multilayered Diplomacy.* London: Palgrave Macmillan.

Li, Mingjiang. 2014. "Local Liberalism: China's Provincial Approaches to Relations with Southeast Asia," *Journal of Contemporary China, 23*(86), pp. 275–293.

Li, Nan. 2020. *Connecting Chongqing and Southeast Asia: Progress, Potential and Challenges.* ISEAS Perspective No. 99, 7 Sept 2020.

Prime Minister's Office Singapore. 2023. PM Lee Hsien Loong at the Interview with CCTV-13 for Leaders' Talk, 24 Mar 2023. https://www.pmo.gov.sg/Newsroom/PM-Lee-Hsien-Loong-at-the-Interview-with-CCTV-13-for-Leaders-Talk-Mar-2023.

Su, Changhe. 2010. China's Local Government and Sub-Regional Cooperation: Dynamics, Behavior and Mechanisms. *World Economy and Politics* (5): 4–24.

van der Pluijm, Rogier. 2007. *City Diplomacy: The Expanding Role of Cities in International Politics*, 1–42. Issue 10 of Clingendael Diplomacy Papers, Netherlands Institute of International Relations.

Yang, Xiangzhang. 2018. The Power, Process and Characteristics of China's Local Governments' Participation in China-ASEAN Cooperation. *Peace and Development* (4).

Chapter 6
Riding on the BRI Train: Issues Relating to China's Strengthening Ties with Cambodia

6.1 Bilateral Political Relations Between China and Cambodia

The effects of China's rising economic ascendency and geopolitical clout are being felt throughout the Southeast Asian countries but most prominently in Cambodia. Cambodia is one of the smallest and least developed nations in Southeast Asia. It has a strategic location between Thailand and Vietnam, two powerful rivals in the region, and borders Laos to the north and the Gulf of Thailand to the southwest.

China's ties with Cambodia have deep historical roots. Since establishing diplomatic relations in July 1958, Cambodia's late King Norodom Sihanouk had built friendly ties with China's late Premier Zhou Enlai and other Chinese leaders. Sihanouk sought Chinese support to avoid his country being sucked into the Sino-Vietnam tensions. With the assistance and support of the United States, the then Cambodian Prime Minister Lon Nol launched a military coup against Sihanouk in 1970, while he was travelling abroad, and he was sentenced to death. With the Chinese leaders' agreement, Sihanouk remained in exile in China from March 1970 until December 1975. The Chinese leadership still recognised and respected Sihanouk as the king and head of the state, treating him with extreme courtesy (Jeldres 2012).

Historically, Cambodia used China as a heavy counterweight against its two bigger and more powerful neighbours, namely Vietnam and Thailand. Cambodia's relations with Vietnam and Thailand are not without contention. Following the fall of the Khmer Empire in the fifteenth century, Cambodia felt constantly threatened by both Vietnam and Thailand (Heng 2022). In particular, although Cambodia has had a long history of engagement with Vietnam, there had been many wars between Cambodia and Vietnam in the past.

Most recently, Vietnam launched a full-scale invasion in Cambodia in 1979. The Vietnamese army overthrew the Khmer Rouge and occupied Cambodia. Cambodia has widespread anti-Vietnamese sentiment, largely due to the border disputes,

H. Yu, *Understanding China's Belt and Road Initiative*, Asia in Transition 26,
https://doi.org/10.1007/978-981-99-9633-9_6

Cambodians' perceptions on Vietnam's expansionist intentions and illegal immigrants from Vietnam. Unlike the Vietnamese, the Cambodians have never regarded the Chinese as invaders or aggressors. Indeed, China was deemed to be useful to preserve Cambodian sovereignty from its immediate bigger neighbours.

In 2013, the two countries signed a "Comprehensive Strategic Partnership agreement", the first for Cambodia with another country, demonstrating common interests on security and economy. The year 2023 marks the 65th anniversary of bilateral ties between China and Cambodia. Hun Sen's visit to China in February 2023 demonstrated the "ironclad relationship" between Cambodia and China, based on a long traditional friendship.

In November 2020, the Chinese government awarded the "Medal of Friendship" of the People's Republic of China to Cambodia's Queen Mother Norodom Monineath Sihanouk. The medal was also intended to honour the late King Sihanouk for his efforts to build close relations with the Chinese people. The past relations between the countries' late leaders have laid the foundation for the close ties between the two countries today (Yu 2023). Sihanouk's son is now the King of Cambodia.

The Chinese and Cambodian governments have established regular high-level exchanges between the two countries. China's President Xi Jinping visited Cambodia in October 2016 and Cambodia's Prime Minister Hun Sen visited China in February 2020. The latter was the first visit by a foreign leader to Beijing since the outbreak of the COVID-19 pandemic in the city of Wuhan. Hun Sen wanted to show political support for China and personally sent a message of solidarity from Cambodia to the Chinese people. Meanwhile, in his appreciation of Hun Sen's visit and affirmation of the friendship between the two countries, Xi Jinping commented that "a friend in need is a friend indeed".

Given its pro-China foreign policy stance, the Cambodian government has consistently supported China's approach of bilateral negotiation towards dealing with the South China Sea issues. In June 2016, Prime Minister Hun Sen clearly stated that the territorial disputes surrounding the South China Sea are matters between China and the claimant states in Southeast Asia, and not matters of dispute between China and ASEAN (Youtube June 2016).

On its part, China has made clear its preference for bilateral negotiation on the territorial and maritime disputes surrounding the South China Sea with specific claimant states involved rather than multilateral arraignments such as the China-ASEAN leader summits. By proceeding in this way, China can fully exploit its asymmetrical advantages of economic power and military might over the smaller Southeast Asian countries to gain the dominant position in negotiation.

Meanwhile, Cambodia has been criticised by some ASEAN countries, such as the Philippines, for "doing Beijing's bidding". They see Cambodia as taking a policy stance that favours China's interests. For example, at the conclusion of the 45th ASEAN Foreign Ministers Meeting held in Phnom Penh in 2012, although the Philippines and Vietnam urged Cambodia, as the Chair, to highlight the South China Sea issue in the joint communiqué, Cambodia refused to do so, which resulted, for the first time in ASEAN's history, in the grouping's failure to issue a joint communiqué (Charadine 2021). In July 2016, Cambodia also blocked an ASEAN statement that referred to the international tribunal's ruling on the South China Sea territorial disputes (Thul 2016). Cambodia, like China, insists that the South China Sea issue should be dealt with by China and the relevant ASEAN claimant states, and is not an issue for the ASEAN as a grouping. However, Cambodia is still perceived by some external critics as being in strong alignment with China's position. Given the asymmetrical relationship between Beijing and Phnom Penh, these critics largely view Cambodia as China's "vassal state" or "a pawn" of China. (Chong 2017).

Cambodia's strongman Prime Minister Hun Sen is one of the longest-serving Prime Ministers in Southeast Asia. His Cambodian People's Party (CPP) has dominated Cambodian domestic politics for a long time. Hun Sen's government has effectively shaped Cambodia's foreign policy to support China's interests. When speaking to Nikkei's Future of Asia Conference in May 2021, Hun Sen defended his close ties with Beijing, and he bluntly stated this, "If I don't rely on China, who will I rely on?" (Nikkei May 2021). After the CPP won an overwhelming victory in Cambodia's general election in July 2023, which was criticised by the West as not "a fair and free election", Hun Sen announced his will step down as Cambodia's Prime Minister and hand over power to his son Hun Manet (The Straits Times July 2023). At the time of writing, Hun Manet already became Cambodia's prime minister and led a new government in August 2023. Nevertheless, Mr Hun Sen will not disappear into retirement, and he is still head of the CPP and a member of the National Assembly. He is likely to remain an influential figure of Cambodia's government and to control politics.

Cambodia's pro-China policy is expected to continue under the Hun Manet's government. In his separate thank-you letters to China's President Xi Jinping, and China's Premier Li Qiang, which dated on 26 July 2023, Mr Hun Sen reassured to Chinese leader that the new Cambodian government under Prime Minister Hun Manet will maintain the current pro-China policy and to further strengthen comprehensive strategical cooperative partnership with China. (Khmer Times July 2023).

Hun Sen's pro-China stance has facilitated investment in Cambodia by Chinese firms. His pro-China stance has facilitated investment in Cambodia by Chinese firms. Chinese investors and construction firms had made an accumulated investment of US$12.02 billion to Cambodia from 2013 to 2022. The transport and energy sectors accounted for the lion share of the Chinese investments to Cambodia during the same period, with US$7.31 billion and US$4 billion, respectively (Table 6.1). These two sectors of energy and transport combined accounted for 94.1% of the stock of Chinese investments and constructions in Cambodia between 2013 and 2022.

Prime Minister Hun Sen made a three-day visit to China from 9 to 11 February 2023, during which the "Joint Statement on Building a China-Cambodia Community with a Shared Future in the New Era" was signed, which reflects the strong and robust bilateral ties on political, economic and defence cooperation. China and Cambodia also signed a series of bilateral cooperation agreements in several areas, notably infrastructure financing and construction, and agriculture.

The Cambodian authority has granted China access to its Ream Naval Base, a site of strategic significance. Chinese companies have started to build new infrastructure there, including new roads, port upgrading and ship repair facilities, which will

Table 6.1 Chinese BRI-affiliated investments and construction in Cambodia, 2013–2022

Year	Chinese investor/Builder	Sector	Amount (US$ million)
March 2013	Shanghai Construction	Transport	250
December 2013	Huaneng Power	Energy	410
May 2015	China Communications Construction	Transport	130
June 2015	Shanghai Construction	Transport	120
March 2016	China National Machinery Industry	Energy	100
April 2016	Guangdong Heng Fu	Agriculture	360
October 2016	China National Machinery Industry	Energy	120
April 2017	Sino Great Wall	Energy	560
December 2017	Hengtong Group	Energy	200
March 2018	Kunming Iron	Transport	500
April 2018	Sino Great Wall	Transport	300
May 2018	China Communications Construction	Transport	220
December 2018	China Communications Construction	Transport	2080
January 2019	Shanghai Construction	Transport	260
March 2019	China Communications Construction	Transport	1950
June 2019	State Construction Engineering	Tourism	200
June 2019	China International Trust and Investment	Agriculture	320
October 2019	China Energy Engineering; China National Machinery Industry	Energy	190
November 2019	China Railway Construction	Tourism	190
March 2020	China Communications Construction	Transport	190
June 2020	China Huadian Corporation	Energy	1190
August 2020	State Construction Engineering	Transport	600
November 2020	Minmetals	Transport	410
November 2020	Sinosteel	Energy	670
August 2021	China National Machinery Industry	Energy	170
January 2022	Hodo Group	Transport	300
July 2022	China National Machinery Industry	Energy	390

Note Chinese investments and construction cover energy, transport, agriculture and tourism sectors only

Source Extracted from "China Global Investment Tracker", American Enterprise Institute

enable the Ream to host large naval warships in future (Asia Maritime Transparency Initiative 2021). This has raised suspicions in regional countries and the West over China's military presence in Cambodia and future use of the base by the People's Liberation Navy vessels. If these plans come to fruition, Ream Naval Base will provide China with a secure military foothold in the Indo-Pacific region (Detsch 2022).

This will allow China to project its naval power further across the region amid the China-US rivalry. Ream thus has become an arena for competition between China and the United States for strategic influence in Southeast Asia. Nevertheless, despite China gaining military access to Ream Naval Base, it cannot match the United States' network of military bases around the region, or throughout the world.

6.2 China's Strengthening Economic Ties with Cambodia Under the BRI

Cambodia is a close friend and partner of China in the ASEAN (Association of Southeast Asian Nations). China has strong trade and economic ties with the Kingdom and is Cambodia's largest trading partner. According to statistics from the Ministry of Commerce of China, the bilateral trade volume between China and Cambodia had increased from US$3.77 billion in 2013 to US$13.67 billion in 2021. The trade balance is in China's favour, and China enjoyed a growing trade surplus with Cambodia from 2013 to 2021 (Fig. 6.1). Meanwhile, China is Cambodia's second-largest export market, accounting for 8.3% of its total export value in 2021, and Cambodia's largest source of imports, accounting for 33.9% of its total import value.

The China-Cambodia Free Trade Agreement (CCFTA), which came into effect on 1 January 2022, was the first bilateral free trade arrangement signed by Cambodia. The CCFTA has given Cambodia impetus to further strengthen its trade and economic ties with China and gain wider market access to the Chinese domestic market through applying the Kingdom's "Four Corners Development Strategy (2018–2023)".

Under the CCFTA implementation, Cambodia will reap economic benefits from exporting agricultural products to China. China has set zero tariffs for Cambodia on 97.53% of tariff lines for trade in goods, and Cambodia has set China zero tariffs on 90% of tariff lines. China's tariff reduction rate under the Cambodia-China Free Trade Agreement exceeds that under the CAFTA by 3.16%. China's zero tariffs cover almost all Cambodia's main exports to China, including polished rice, bananas, mangoes, cassava, fishery products and clothing.

The CCFTA also provides more scope for Cambodia to stabilise its foreign trade amid the severe economic sanctions imposed by both the United States and the European Union. In August 2020, due to concern over human rights violations and lack of democracy in Cambodia, the European Union cut 20% of the tariff concessions on Cambodia's exports (Everything but Arms). In addition, the United

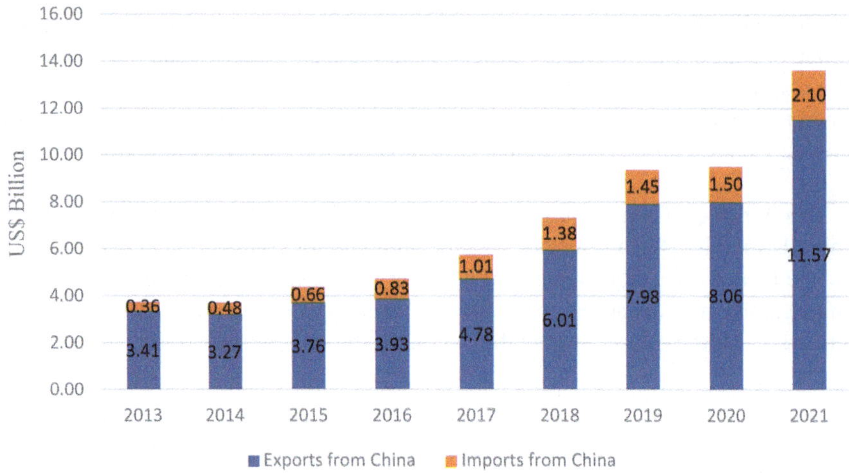

Fig. 6.1 Bilateral trade in goods between China and Cambodia. *Source* Ministry of Commerce of the People's Republic of China (2022, 2018)

States has suspended its GSP preferences and imposed several economic sanctions on Cambodia.

From a geopolitical perspective, Cambodia could use the CCFTA as a leveraging tool to mitigate the impacts of the Western economic sanctions by increasing its exports to China (Vannarith 2023). The CCFTA will also help the Chinese firms to export machinery, vehicles, electronic and telecommunication products to Cambodia.

Based on its trade and economic ties with China, ASEAN, Japan and Republic of Korea, Cambodia has been one of the fastest-growing economies among ASEAN countries for the past decade. According to ASEAN Secretariat's statistics (2022), Cambodia's average annual growth rate was 5.7% between 2012 and 2021, due to the boom in garment and textile industries, tourism and infrastructure construction funded by the increasing foreign direct investment. With its rapid economic growth, urbanisation and dynamic young population, Cambodia has become a hotspot for foreign investors, including Chinese companies.

Cambodia has been seen as one of the countries in Southeast Asia most supportive of the BRI, and it has been one of its major beneficiaries since 2013. Besides being the largest foreign investor in Cambodia, China is the Kingdom's biggest financier of transportation, hydropower plants and other infrastructure development. The Cambodian government views BRI implementation as important for boosting national economic and social development. It is therefore keen to ride on the BRI train to accelerate domestic infrastructure improvement and industrial take-off.

BRI implementation during the Xi Jinping era has led to Cambodia becoming the closest partner and ally of China in Southeast Asia on geopolitical and geoeconomic collaboration. Several large Chinese-funded infrastructure projects in Cambodia have been completed and are in operation, including a 190-km-long expressway connecting Cambodia's capital, Phnom Penh, with the port city of Sihanoukville.

Due to the underdevelopment of its roads and port and maritime infrastructure, Cambodia has in the past been unable to bring down its high logistics costs or tap the potential of the coastal areas. Road transport accounts for over 90% of Cambodia's passenger and freight movement. Meanwhile, the World Economic Forum's 2019 report on infrastructure competitiveness described road infrastructure in Cambodia as being of poor quality due to such as inadequate roads and expressways, insufficient road maintenance, poor traffic safety and underdeveloped urban and rural transport infrastructure.

Cambodia desperately needs foreign investment in its domestic infrastructure sector in order to realise its economic growth potential. According to the estimation by PWC in October 2022, to achieve sustained growth and improve social and economic standards among its population, Cambodia will need infrastructure investment of around US$28 billion in the period up to 2040. The poor quality of Cambodia's infrastructure is reflected in its ranking in the 2019 Global Competitiveness Report as 106th out of 141 economies.

The Royal Government of Cambodia has over the past several years earmarked infrastructure development and connectivity improvement as priorities for enhancing Cambodia's integration into the ASEAN and global economy. Specifically, transport connectivity improvement (building roads, bridges, seaports, expressways, railways and airways), the expansion of energy coverage (power supply) and digital connectivity (fibre-optic infrastructure and modernising the mobile telephone network) are three areas at the top of the government's infrastructure development agenda. Cambodia welcomes foreign investment in its domestic infrastructure construction and other industrial sectors, including investment from China, due to its need to address the weaknesses in its economy. Cambodia attracted US$4.35 billion of fixed asset investment in 2021, while China accounted for over 50% of the inflow of fixed asset investment to Cambodia.

Under China's push for BRI implementation, there has been a massive inflow of Chinese investment to Cambodia for the past several years. In the years from 2013 to 2021, accumulated Chinese investments in Cambodia totalled US$6.96 billion. In the year 2021 alone, Chinese investments to the Kingdom amounted to US$0.46 billion (Fig. 6.2), accounting for about 67% of total inflow of foreign investment to Cambodia. China's economic presence is visible everywhere in the Kingdom, from the capital city of Phnom Penh to the coastal province of Sihanoukville. The Chinese are investing in sectors ranging from mining, energy, transport, digital communication, agriculture and hotels to real estate and casinos. Chinese firms now have a 50% market share in Cambodia's domestic construction sector via the BRI platform. According to Vasim Sorya (2023), Under Secretary of State at Cambodia's Ministry of Public Works and Transportation, the total value of BRI-affiliated projects, either completed or under construction, which have been financed with concessioned loans and grants from Chinese banks, is around US$3.2 billion.

China's economic and strategic influence in Cambodia has grown steadily over the past decade and China has been Cambodia's largest source of foreign investment since 2013. According to statistics from Cambodia's Chamber of Commerce, Cambodia received US$18 billion from Greater China between mid-1994 and end-2021, far

Fig. 6.2 Inflow of Chinese investments to Cambodia. *Source* The ASEAN Secretariat database

exceeding the Republic of Korea's US$4.9 billion and Singapore's US$2.7 billion. Greater China accounted for 43.9% of total foreign direct investment inflows to Cambodia during this period (Phanet 2022). Apparently, the COVID-19 pandemic has not affected the inflow of Chinese investment to Cambodia. Furthermore, in June 2021, the Cambodian firm Cellcard chose ZTE, a Chinese telecommunication equipment provider, as its 5G partner.

Nevertheless, Cambodia has also developed close trade and economic ties with Japan and the Republic of Korea to mitigate the impacts of sanctions imposed by the United States and European Union. In particular, Japan's long-standing active diplomacy in Southeast Asia has helped to develop cordial relations with Cambodia under Hun Sen. Nevertheless, Japan lags far behind China regarding economic and trade ties with Cambodia. China's overall trade and economic influence in the Kingdom is unparalleled by any other major power, including the United States and Japan.

Compared to China, which is the top foreign investor in Cambodia and accounted for nearly half of the total inflow of FDI to the country in 2021, Japan only accounted for 5.9% of total inflow of foreign direct investment to Cambodia during the same year (National Bank of Cambodia 2022). In terms of bilateral trade, in 2020, China's trade volume with Cambodia (UA$8.12 billion) was almost five times larger than Japan's trade with Cambodia (US$ 1.69 billion). In addition, China was the top origin country for foreign tourist arrivals in Cambodia, accounting for 28.2% of total inbound tourist arrivals, compared to merely 0.9% of Cambodia's inbound tourists arriving from Japan (Ministry of Foreign Affairs and International Cooperation 2021).

6.3 Positive Effects of Chinese Investments in Cambodia

There are positive spillover effects of Chinese investments in terms of rapid cross-provincial infrastructure improvement and urban development in cities, and industrial development. As an example, the US$2 billion Phnom Penh-Sihanoukville Expressway, which was financed and built by China, has been operational since late 2022. This 190 km-long expressway is the first expressway to be built in Cambodia. Since 2022, it has enhanced transport links between the capital of Cambodia and the coastal city of Sihanoukville by cutting in half the transportation time and logistics costs.

The Chinese investment has led to an urban infrastructure boom in Cambodia's major cities such as Sihanoukville. This port city, which is located 226 km from Phnom Penh and has a population of around 200,000, once was a sleepy coastal town, but it is now being transformed into a modern metropolis with many high-rise buildings.

Moreover, these Chinese investments enable the Cambodian governments to extract more tax revenue which can be used to improve the living standards of ordinary Cambodians through creating jobs and constructing transport facilities, schools and hospitals, in particular for the remote rural areas.

The Sihanoukville Special Economic Zone (SSEZ) is a high-profile bilateral cooperation project between China and Cambodia under the BRI. The SSEZ, which is focused on the garment and textile industries, houses 174 firms, over 85% of which are Chinese-run enterprises. Moreover, since the SSEZ became operational in March 2020, nearly 30,000 jobs for locals have been created. Besides contributing to Cambodia's industrial and social development, the SSEZ is also becoming the nation's largest export base.

Tourism is one of the pillar industries of Cambodia's economy. In 2019, Cambodi's tourism revenue was US$4.92 billion, contributing 17.8% to Cambodia's gross domestic product (GDP) and directly creating 630,000 jobs for locals. Cambodia is a country with ancient civilisations; in particular, the "Khmer" civilisation is an attraction for tourists the world over.

China was the biggest source of inbound foreign tourists for Cambodia during the pre-pandemic era. In 2019, Chinese tourists visiting Cambodia numbered 2.36 million, accounting for 35.7% of the total number of foreign tourists visiting Cambodia, and almost equivalent to the total number of tourists from the second to eighth-largest source countries. However, the COVID-19 pandemic from 2020 to 2021 hit the Cambodian economy hard and the government has had to implement various measures to mitigate its negative impact on businesses and people's incomes and to support economic recovery. Cambodian Prime Minister Hun Sen's visit to China in 2020 was intended to lay the foundation for attracting Chinese tourists after the epidemic and rejuvenating Cambodia's struggling tourism industry. Following China's recent reopening, it is likely that over one million Chinese tourists will visit the country in 2023, compared to merely 110,000 in 2022 (Xie 2023).

6.4 Issues and Challenges Under BRI Implementation

Through becoming the largest investor and financier for Cambodia, China's influence in Cambodia has rapidly increased. Nevertheless, the massive inflow of Chinese investments and the influx of many Chinese to Cambodia have come at a price for the local community, since rental and property prices in the Kingdom have shot up over the past decade.

In the case of Sihanoukville, Chinese investments are highly concentrated in the sectors of gambling, real estate, and resorts. Chinese-run casinos have mushroomed in the city in the past several years. The exact number of casinos is hard to know, but the estimation is between 30 and 80 (Fifield 2018; Faulder and Kawase 2018; Po and Heng 2019). According to the local authorities in Sihanoukville province, a rise in crimes such as kidnapping and gun violence has reportedly been associated with the increasing number of casinos in Sihanoukville city.

China's economic presence in Cambodia in general, and Sihanoukville in particular, has led to serious concerns among locals, who have voiced their anger on the Internet via social media and other platforms. Many feel strongly that the sense of "Cambodian-ness" has been lost in Sihanoukville. The locals even joke that Sihanoukville city should be renamed as "giant China Town" or "mini-Macau".

In February 2018, as reported by the local Cambodian media, the then-Chinese Ambassador to Cambodia, Xiong Bo, stated that China would stand in solidarity with the Cambodian law and enforcement authorities to catch Chinese nationals who committed crimes in Cambodia. He further commented that "The Chinese government appeals to all Chinese people who live abroad to abide by the Cambodian laws, respect the country's customs and co-live peacefully with locals" (Suy 2018). This unusual diplomatic gesture reflects the seriousness of a situation which required the Chinese government's top official representative to apologise for the crimes committed by Chinese nationals and attempt to pacify the anger expressed by local residents.

A more worrying trend is that Chinese "black societies" might have infiltrated into the local Cambodian economy and society. Chinese criminal scam gangs are actively operating in Cambodia and are trafficking many poor or debt-saddled youngsters from the regional countries to trap them in scam call centres in Cambodia.

The locals regard many Chinese as ignoring or disrespecting the Khmer language, culture and customs when doing business in Cambodia. The Chinese-invested industrial zones, restaurants and hotels often misspell Khmer words on their business signs and advertising boards.

The Cambodian authorities always assert that the Chinese investment and Chinese-funded infrastructure projects are conducted in a transparent manner, and are beneficial to Cambodia's development. By bringing in tax revenue and creating job opportunities, the Chinese investments and infrastructure projects are seen as shoring up the legitimacy of the Cambodian government and the ruling Cambodian People's Party under Hun Sen. Although the Cambodian authorities are embracing Chinese investment, the effects are not always positive for the Cambodian general public. Specifically, Chinese investors' business practices in Cambodia remain an issue (Phea 2020), with many local Cambodians believing that Chinese investments solely benefit the few ruling elites at the expense of financial, environmental and social impact on the local people in Cambodia.

Evidently, Chinese tourists and merchants tend to buy from Chinese businesses and spend money in Chinese hotels and restaurants. Any trickle-down economic effect to local community is therefore limited. As shown in the case of Sihanoukville, the casinos, resorts and restaurants are often built by the Chinese and run by the Chinese. Most of their customers are Chinese. Essentially, Sihanoukville is becoming a playground for rich Chinese and a place for them to let their hair down.

Lack of assessment of the environmental and social impacts of the Chinese-funded projects in Cambodia is an outstanding unresolved issue. For example, the Chinese-built beach resorts in Sihanoukville, such as the Golden Silver Golf resort, located at the Ream National Park and about 28 km from downtown Sihanoukville, were accused of having hazardous effects on forests containing valuable Siamese rosewood trees, and thus threatening local biodiversity (Po and Heng 2019).

According to Vannarith (2021) from the Asian Vision Institute, an independent think tank based in Cambodia, none of the major Chinese state-owned enterprises that have invested and operated in Cambodia (namely the China Road and Bridge Group, China Huaneng Group, Yunnan Construction Investment Group and Bank of China) have formulated any environmental, social and governance (ESG) policies at the corporate governance level for implementation in their operations. As is common practice among Chinese firms and business persons under BRI implementation in Southeast Asia, they tend to solely pursue their financial interests and profit maximisation from their investments in Cambodia, at the expense of local environmental and social considerations.

"The love-hate" or "rewards-risk" relationship with Chinese investment is most evident in the coastal city of Sihanoukville. While the massive Chinese investment in real estate and other service industries has brought about a construction boom in Sihanoukville, fast-rising housing prices, corruption and the surge in crime associated with the Chinese-invested casinos are generating bad press and anger among the local community in Cambodia, which, if left unchecked, could damage China's ties with Cambodia and Cambodians' perception and image of China.

The adverse social and environmental impacts on the local people that have accompanied the massive inflow of Chinese investment, business persons and migrants have led to rising anti-Chinese sentiment among many Cambodians. They are concerned that their country is being taken over by the Chinese. In interviews conducted with Cambodian officials and business elites, they urged their government to diversify the sources of foreign direct investment and to reduce Cambodia's over dependence on Chinese investments. More importantly, they view Cambodia's one-sided pro-China stance as risky and potentially harmful to its national interests, and, in the long term, would prefer Cambodia to take a "balance of power" diplomatic stance by strengthening its engagement with other powers, such as the United States, Japan and the European Union.[1]

To the older generation of Cambodians, Mao's support of the Khmer Rouge regime, which shared a similar ideological stance to the Chinese Communist Party in that era, still leaves lingering suspicions. The Khmer Rouge, led by the dictator Pol Pot, was a brutal regime that ruled Cambodia between 1975 and 1979, following the Cambodian civil war. It was estimated that about 2 million Cambodian people were killed at the hands of the Khmer Rouge in its campaign of mass violence and genocide, representing a quarter of Cambodia's population (Dunst 2020).

According to the latest *State of Southeast Asia 2023 Survey Report (ISEAS-Yusof Ishak Institute,* 2023*)*, only 2.2% of the respondents from Cambodia had utmost confidence that China would seek to maintain the rules-based order and uphold international law, down from 65.4% in the 2022 Survey Report. When asked which they would choose if ASEAN were forced to align itself with one of the two strategic rivals, 73.1% of respondents from Cambodia chose the United States, and only 26.9% picked China in the 2023 Survey Report. However, when asked the same question in the 2022 survey, 81.5% of the Cambodian respondents had voted for China. Beijing would do well to take note of this significant shift in attitude towards China among the Cambodian elites.

Indeed, Cambodia's overall foreign debt has been exacerbated due to the sharp increase attributed to BRI projects such as the expressway and seaport upgrading. Over 41% of Cambodia's accumulated external debt is estimated to be held by China (an approximate US$4.05 billion or 15% of Cambodia's GDP). China is Cambodia's largest creditor, accounting for 41.7% of its total foreign debt (estimated at US$9.47 billion), according to the statistics released by Cambodia's General Department of International Cooperation and Debt Management (2022). Cambodia, a small and underdeveloped economy with a population of around 16.59 million, will find it a challenging task to repay this massive foreign debt.

Nevertheless, given its small economic and population size, foreign trade and investment will be always important for boosting Cambodia's economy. Chinese investment will therefore continue to be an important source of local economic growth. Meanwhile, since Cambodia is China's close ally and large-scale infrastructure construction plays a flagship role in mainland Southeast Asia under the BRI, it is not in China's interest to bankrupt Cambodia over its infrastructure projects. This would generate a negative image of China's BRI that would hamper its future implementation, regionally as well as globally.

Both countries will have to promote the BRI in a more transparent, accountable, and inclusive manner to ensure the projects are truly beneficial to the local communities, economically, socially and environmentally. This will entail conducting due environmental and social impact assessments and strictly abiding by their findings during the construction and operation of future projects.

---

[1] Interviews with senior officials, scholars and businessmen in both Phnom Penh and Sihanoukville, Cambodia, were conducted on 15–16 June 2023.

Moreover, Chinese merchants, tourists and migrants need to understand the Khmer history, language, culture and customs. This is important not only for helping the Chinese to integrate into the local community in Cambodia but also for improving China's image and easing the local dissatisfaction about Chinese investments and the influx of Chinese people. Addressing these issues would help to convince Cambodians of the equal benefits and win–win potential of BRI participation.

References

Asia Maritime Transparency Initiative. 2021. "*Update: China Continues to Transform Ream Naval Base*. Available at https://amti.csis.org/changes-underway-at-cambodias-ream-naval-base/. Accessed 17 Feb 2023.

Cambodia's General Department of International Cooperation and Debt Management. 2022. *Cambodia Public Debt Statistical Bulletin*, vol. 16. Available at https://gdicdm.mef.gov.kh/en/2022/11/23/10987.html. Accessed 9 Feb 2023.

Charadine, Pich. 2021. *Cambodia's Chairmanship of ASEAN in 2022: What to Expect?* 69–72 In the Outcome Report titled "Facilitating Multilateralism: EU-Cambodia ASEAN Dialogue", Cambodian Institute for Cooperation and Peace.

Chong, Terence. 2017. *The Politics Behind Cambodia's Embrace of China*. Perspective No. 59, ISEAS-Yusof Ishak Institute, 2 August 2017. Available at https://www.iseas.edu.sg/images/pdf/ISEAS_Perspective_2017_59.pdf. Accessed 17 Feb 2023.

Detsch, Jack. 2022. U.S. Looks to Check Chinese Advances at Cambodian Naval Base. *Foreign Policy*. Available at https://foreignpolicy.com/2022/12/05/us-china-cambodia-ream-naval-base/. Accessed 18 Feb 2023.

Dunst, Charles. 2020. Xi's Fake History Lesson for Hun Sen. *Foreign Policy*. Available at https://foreignpolicy.com/2020/03/10/xi-jinping-fake-history-lesson-hun-sen-china-cambodia-khmer-rouge/.

Faulder, Dominic, and Kenji Kawase. 2018. Cambodians Wary as Chinese Investment Transforms Their Country. *Nikkei Asia*. Available at https://asia.nikkei.com/Spotlight/The-Big-Story/Cambodians-wary-as-Chinese-investment-transforms-their-country. Accessed 25 June 2023.

Fifield, Anna. 2018. This Cambodian City is Turning Into a Chinese Enclave, and not Everyone is Happy. *The Washington Post*. Available at This Cambodian City is Turning Into a Chinese Enclave, and not Everyone is Happy—The Washington Post. Accessed 24 June 2023.

Heng, Kimkong. 2022. *Cambodia-Vietnam Relations: Key Issues and the Way Forward*. ISEAS Perspective No, 36.

ISEAS-Yusof Ishak Institute. 2023. *The State of Southeast Asia 2023 Survey Report*. Available at https://www.iseas.edu.sg/wp-content/uploads/2025/07/The-State-of-SEA-2023-Final-Digital-V4-09-Feb-2023.pdf. Accessed 9 Feb 2023.

Jeldres, Julio A. 2012. A Personal Reflection on Norodom Sihanouk and Zhou Enlai: an Extraordinary Friendship on the Fringes of the Cold War. *Cross Currents, East Asian History and Culture Review*.

Khmer Times. 2023. Cambodia's Policy Toward China Remains Unchanged, Says PM. Available at https://www.khmertimeskh.com/501332389/cambodias-policy-toward-china-remains-unchanged-says-pm/. Accessed 28 July 2023.

Ministry of Commerce of the People's Republic of China. 2018. *Country (Region) Guidelines for Foreign Investment and Cooperation in 2018: Cambodia*.

Ministry of Commerce of the People's Republic of China. 2022. *Country (Region) Guidelines for Foreign Investment and Cooperation in 2022: Cambodia*.

Ministry of Foreign Affairs and International Cooperation of Cambodia. 2021. *Dashboard*, 1–40. Available at https://data.opendevelopmentcambodia.net/en/library_record/dashboard-series-about-cambodia/resource/ac3ffd22-e65c-4e5b-b474-dfc840016318. Accessed 21 Aug 2023.

National Bank of Cambodia. 2022. *Financial Stability Review 2021*. Available at https://www.nbc.gov.kh/download_files/publication/fsr_eng/Financial_Stability_Review_2021.pdf. Accessed 21 Aug 2023.

Nikkei. 2021. Cambodia's Hun Sen: 'If I Don't Reply on China, Who Will I Rely On? *Nikkei's The Future of Asia 2021*. Available at https://asia.nikkei.com/Spotlight/The-Future-of-Asia/The-Future-of-Asia-2021/Cambodia-s-Hun-Sen-If-I-don-t-rely-on-China-who-will-I-rely-on. Accessed 22 July 2023.

Phanet, Hom. 2022. Cambodia's FDI surges 11.2% to $41B in 2021", *The Phnom Penh Post*. Available at https://www.phnompenhpost.com/business/cambodias-fdi-surges-112-41b-2021. Accessed 18 Feb 2023.

Phea, Kin. 2020. Cambodia-China Relations in the New Decade. In *New Decade, Old Challenges?* 21–26. Diplomatic Briefing, Konrad Adenauer Stiftung.

Po, Sovinda, and Kimkong Heng. 2019. Assessing the Impacts of Chinese Investments in Cambodia: The Case of Preah Sihanoukville Province. In *Pacific Forum, Working Paper* vol. 19.

Prime Minister Hun Sen's Speech at the 65th Founding Anniversary of the Cambodian People's Party, 28 June 2016. Available at 28 JUNE 2016 the 65th Founding Anniversary of the Cambodian People's Party—YouTube. Accessed 25 June 2023.

PWC. 2022. *Cambodia's Infrastructure Market Update and Outlook*, 1–34.

Suy, Pav. 2018. Chinese Embassy Addresses Crime. *Khmer Times*. Available at Chinese Embassy Addresses Crime—Khmer Times (khmertimeskh.com). Accessed 26 June 2023.

The ASEAN Secretariat. 2022. *ASEAN Statistical Yearbook 2022*, 40.

The Straits Times. 2023. Cambodian Prime Minister Hun Sen to Step Down, Hand Over Power to son Hun Manet. Available at https://www.straitstimes.com/asia/se-asia/cambodian-prime-minister-hun-sen-announces-resignation. Accessed 26 July 2023.

Thul, Prak Chan. 2016. Chinese President Xi Jinping Visits Loyal Friend Cambodia. *Reuters*. Available at https://www.reuters.com/article/us-china-cambodia-idUSKCN12D0NV. Accessed 25 June 2023.

Vannarith, Chheang. 2021. *The ESG Practices of Chinese State-owned Enterprises in Cambodia*. Perspective No. 140, ISEAS-Yusof Ishak Institute. Available at https://www.iseas.edu.sg/wp-content/uploads/2021/10/ISEAS_Perspective_2021_140.pdf. Accessed 10 Feb 2023.

Vannarith, Chheang. 2023. *Cambodia-China Free Trade Agreement: A Cambodian Perspective*. ISEAS-Yusof Ishak Institute Perspective No. 46, 12 June 2023. Available at https://www.iseas.edu.sg/wp-content/uploads/2023/04/ISEAS_Perspective_2023_46.pdf.

Vasim Sorya. 2023. The BRI in Cambodia. Speech Given During the 2023 NEAT Working Group Meeting "Belt and Road Initiative: Partnership for Enhancing Regional Connectivity", 13 June 2023.

Xie, Kawala. 2023. Cambodia's Hun Sen to Head to China in Search of High-Speed Rail Support. *South China Morning Post*. Available at https://www.scmp.com/news/china/diplomacy/article/3206903/cambodias-hun-sen-head-china-search-high-speed-rail-support. Accessed 11 Feb 2023.

Yu, Hong. 2023. PM Hun Sen's Visit Reflects Strong Relations Between Cambodia and China. *CGTN Commentary*, 9 February 2023. Available at PM Hun Sen's Visit Reflects Strong Relations Between Cambodia, China—CGTN. Accessed 21 May 2023.

Chapter 7
China's Efforts to Deepen Its Ties with the Middle Eastern Countries: The Case of Saudi Arabia and Iran

7.1 Xi's Visit to Saudi Arabia

The trip to Saudi Arabia by President Xi Jinping in December 2022 came shortly after he won a third term as China's paramount leader at the 20th National Congress of the Chinese Communist Party in late October 2022. It also represents one of the Chinese leader's first overseas trips for high-profile diplomacy after an almost three-year hiatus due to the global COVID-19 pandemic.

Xi was feted with a lavish reception by his Saudi counterpart, the Saudi Crown Prince and de facto ruler, Mohammed Bin Salman. When Xi's aeroplane entered the Saudi airspace, four fighter jets from the Air Force of Saudi Arabia escorted the plane. These were also joined by six other planes that formed red and yellow contrails in a show of respect for the Chinese flag. Later, President Xi's car was greeted with a horseback parade at the Al Yamamah Royal Palace in Riyadh. All these gestures were symbolic, demonstrating the rise of Sino-Saudi relations.

It was President Xi's second visit to the Kingdom of Saudi Arabia since 2016. President Xi's visit to Riyadh is part of China's strategy to deepen its relations with the developing world, amid the United States' realignment with its allies and other like-minded partners under the Biden administration. The hero's welcome received by Xi stood in sharp contrast to an earlier bilateral meeting between American President Biden and Saudi Crown Prince Mohammed bin Salmon, where the former sought to avoid a handshake with a fist bump that looked weird and awkward. And the Saudi leader will surely not forget that President Biden once vowed to make Saudi Arabia a "pariah state" after the murder of Saudi journalist Jamal Khashoggi.

As part of their strategy to develop a global Saudi Arabia (see Map 7.1 for geographical location) and expand its ties with other countries in addition to the United States, the Saudi leaders are pursuing a visible strategic relationship with China, the world's second-largest economy. Bilateral trade between China and Saudi Arabia reached appropriately US$87.31 billion in 2021. China has already become

H. Yu, *Understanding China's Belt and Road Initiative*, Asia in Transition 26,
https://doi.org/10.1007/978-981-99-9633-9_7

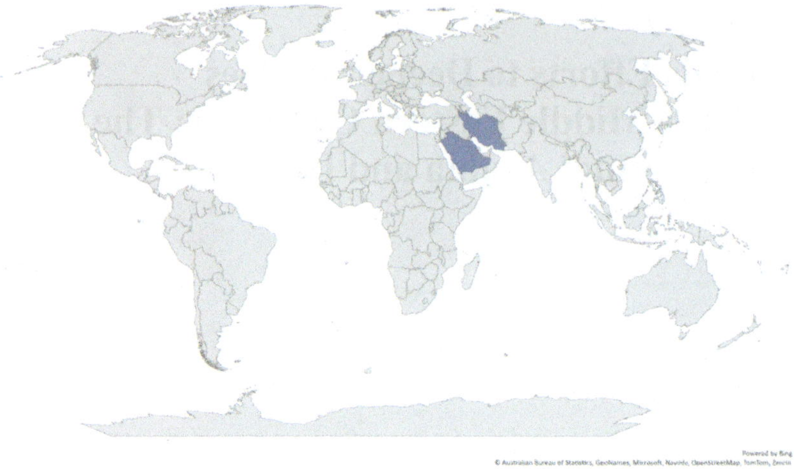

Map 7.1 Location of Saudi Arabia and Iran

Saudi Arabia's largest trading partner and the largest consumer of Saudi oil and petrochemical products.

Meanwhile, China sees the Kingdom of Saudi Arabia as both an influential country in the Middle East and a rising power itself, with strategic significance in the emerging multipolar world. To China, Saudi Arabia is an influential Muslim country. The Kingdom's endorsement is crucial for Beijing to gain international support from other Muslim countries in maintaining the stability of Xinjiang, one of the most troubled and politically sensitive regions in China, which is home to the ethnic Uyghur minority.

Both Beijing and Riyadh anticipate pursuing continuous domestic economic development by diversifying and globalizing their economies. During President Xi's three-day visit to Riyadh, both countries signed "The Comprehensive Strategic Partnership Agreement between the People's Republic of China and the Kingdom of Saudi Arabia", "Joint Statement Between the People's Republic of China and the Kingdom of Saudi Arabia" (Ministry of Foreign Affairs of the People's Republic of China 2022). In addition, a series of bilateral commercial agreements worth up to US$30 billion were signed, although these agreements are not binding. These agreements will no doubt strengthen the economic ties between Beijing and Riyadh and bring the Kingdom closer to China's Belt and Road Initiative circle. One of these agreements is between the Saudi-based Sumou and China-based ENOVATE Motors to build an electric vehicle plant in the Kingdom with a capacity of up to 100,000 cars per year.

In the Joint Statement Between the People's Republic of China and the Kingdom of Saudi Arabia, which was signed by Saudi King of Salman bin Abdulaziz Al Saud and President Xi in December 2022, both countries reaffirmed that they will continue to firmly support each other's core national interests, support each other in safeguarding national sovereignty and territorial integrity, including Taiwan. To coordinate their development, China and Saudi Arabia agreed that their respective leaders will hold biannual meetings.

President Xi's trip to Saudi Arabia has largely been viewed through the lens of U.S.-Saudi relations by the international media coverage. The Kingdom sees China as a reliable alternative to the United States in the emerging multipolar world. To further strengthen its ties with China, the Saudi leader wants to develop oil-rich Saudi Arabia into a self-reliant power, with a thriving economy, a stable society and a capable national defence. To play a more influential role in the regional and global affairs, Saudi Arabia wants to obtain full membership of both the Shanghai Cooperation Organization (SCO) and the BRICS (Brazil, Russia, India, China and South Africa) grouping. China has also become a key player in many regional cooperation institutions, such as BRICS and SCO. Thus, obtaining Beijing's endorsement is crucial for Saudi Arabia's bid for membership of both organizations.

As part of its overall strategy to deal with the rise of China, the United States is shifting its focus from the Middle East to the Indo-Pacific region. U.S.-Saudi relations have become strained in the aftermath of the Saudi assassination of the journalist, Jamal Khashoggi, and the Saudi-led OPEC's decision to cut oil production by around two million barrels a day. President Biden warned the Saudi leadership that the United States would reassess its ties with Saudi Arabia (Al-Atrush and White 2022). In contrast, China's silence on the murder of the Saudi journalist in Saudi Arabia's Istanbul consulate has reinforced the Saudi leader's belief that its view on the region and the world is more closely aligned with Beijing's than those of Western capitals.

During his three-day visit to Riyadh, the Chinese President also attended the China-Arab States Summit and the China-GCC (Gulf Cooperation Council) Summit. The China-Arab States Summit, the first of its kind ever to be held, was attended by nearly 20 Arab leaders from the region. It was hailed by the Chinese officials as a milestone in Sino-Arab relations. Besides the co-hosts, Xi Jinping and the Saudi Crown Prince Mohammed Bin Salman, President Abdel Fattah El-Sissi of Egypt, Qatar's Emir Tamim bin Hamad Al Thani, King Hamad bin Isa Al Khalifah of Bahrain and the Crown Prince of Kuwait, Sheikh Mishal Al-Ahmad Al-Jaber Al-Sabah, were among the high-profile leaders who attended the summit. This was China's largest and highest-level diplomatic interaction with the Arab world since the founding of the People's Republic of China in 1949. Xi's visit signals that there will be no slowing down in China's economic engagement with the world in the post-COVID-19 era.

Bilateral trade between China and the Arab countries reached over US$300 billion in 2021. China has become one of the largest trading partners for the Arab countries. While the shifting of global power dynamics has increased the appeal of China within the Middle East region, the much-anticipated China-GCC Free Trade Agreement is yet to be finalized, mainly due to disagreements over oil tariffs.

Amidst the shift of U.S. strategic priorities away from the Middle East and the strained relations between the U.S. and Saudi Arabia, the Saudi leadership is seeking to diversify its foreign relations by forging partnerships with other emerging powers, including China, India, the Republic of Korea, and Indonesia. Concurrently, Beijing is grabbing a golden opportunity to capitalize on the strained relations between Saudi

Arabia and the United States by securing a foothold in the resource-rich Middle East. China pursues a carefully crafted "balanced" foreign policy in the Middle East. Beijing has made efforts to strengthen its strategic ties with the Arab world. In the meanwhile, China has established good diplomatic, economic, cultural and military ties with Israel and Iran too.

In view of the complex situation and diplomatic relations in the Middle East, China has adopted a strategic approach of balanced diplomacy in the Middle East and not wanted to be involved in regional disputes and bilateral conflicts. President Xi's interactions with his counterparts in the region are a testament to this approach. Xi Jinping made a state visit to Saudi Arabia in December 2022, while he warmly greeted Iranian President Ebrahim Raisi in Beijing by rolling out the red carpet and with a 21-gun salute during his visit to Beijing in February 2023. With the support from China, Iran became a full member of the Shanghai Cooperation Organization in 2021.

Unlike the American approach of supporting one side against the other and creating division in the Middle East, China is playing a delicate diplomatic balancing role by trying to bring together the rival parties in the region. Balancing is a diplomatic strategy used by China to maintain stable power relations between itself and other Persian Gulf states or groups of states in the region, which involves using the tools of hard and soft power. China is willing to promote economic and trade ties and develop cooperation without political strings attached. China wants to project an image of a trusted but neutral power in the region by forging friendships with all countries in the region, big and small, democratic, or authoritarian.

7.2 Energy as the Core of the Bilateral Ties Between China and Saudi Arabia

Against the backdrop of Chinese economic growth and the boom in its export-oriented manufacturing industries over the last two decades, China's demands for oil, gas and other commodities have rapidly increased accordingly. According to China Customs data, China's total crude oil imports had increased to 542.39 million tonnes in 2020 from 335.5 million tonnes in 2015, although they dopped slightly in 2021 due to the COVID-19 pandemic, local lockdowns and factory shutdowns in certain localities in China (Fig. 7.1). China imports annually a very substantial amount of oil to meet its domestic economic demand, sourced from a variety of countries. In 2021, China's total spending on crude oil imports sat at US$257.3 billion, compared to the corresponding figure of US$134.5 billion in 2015 (Fig. 7.2). To power domestic manufacturing and economic growth, China has to spend heavily on energy imports due to its own inadequate domestic supply. In fact, after semiconductors (chips), energy was its second-largest import in terms of value.

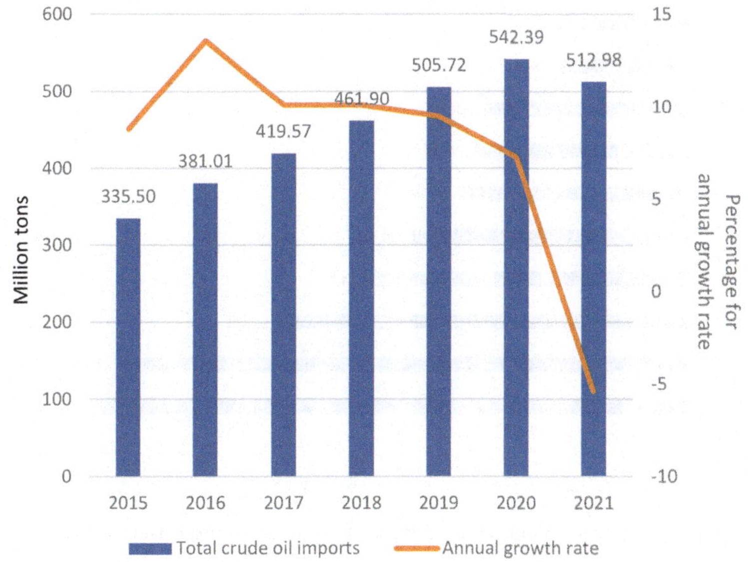

Fig. 7.1 China's total crude oil imports, 2015–2021. *Source* Qianzhan Industry Research Institute, 2022

Fig. 7.2 China's total spending on crude oil imports, 2015–2021. *Source* Qianzhan Industry Research Institute, 2022

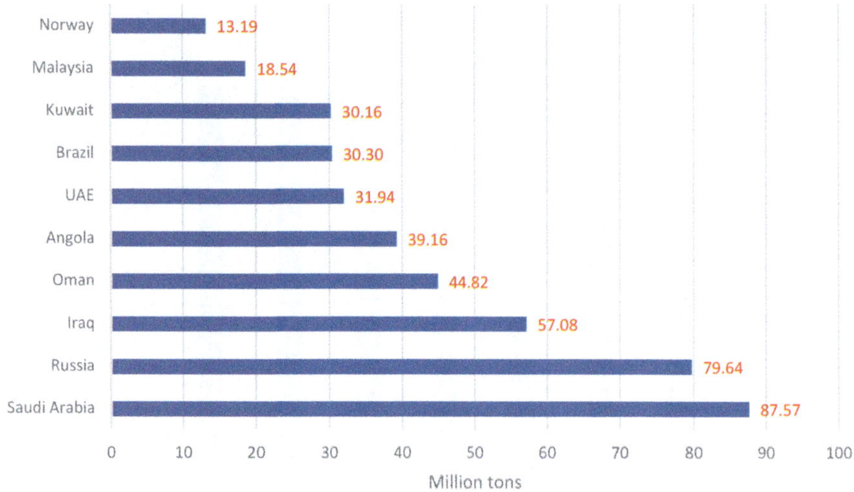

Fig. 7.3 Top 10 suppliers of crude oil to China in 2021. *Source* China Customs, 2022

Since the Chinese leadership started to shift its "Zero COVID-19" pandemic containment policy to a "live with COVID-19" strategy in late 2022, China has gradually been reopening its economy, and industrial production will certainly gradually recover to pre-pandemic levels. China's demand for energy and commodities will concomitantly bounce back.

According to Fig. 7.3, in 2021, five Arab countries including, Saudi Arabia, Iraq, Oman, United Arab Emirates and Kuwait, were among China's top 10 sources of imported oil. The Arab states combined supplied 212.57 million tonnes oil to China in 2021, accounting for appropriately half of China's total imports of crude (estimated at 512.98 million tonnes). The Arab states play a pivotal role in supplying energy to power China's domestic industrial and economic development. China is reliant on the energy-rich Arab nations for its energy security.

Saudi Arabia is the world's top oil exporter, while China is the largest buyer of Saudi oil and the world's biggest energy consumer. In 2021, it bought around 16.5% of total oil production by Saudi Arabia. Figure 7.3, which lists the ten top suppliers of crude oil to China in 2021, shows that Saudi Arabia was the top-ranking supplier of oil to China in that year. China imported 87.57 million tonnes of crude oil from the Kingdom, accounting for 17% of China's total imported oil. Energy collaboration was the core of all discussions between Xi and his Saudi counterpart. Energy serves as the bedrock of the partnership between Beijing and Riyadh. Both countries reaffirmed their cooperation on achieving stability of global energy markets. As stated in the Joint Statement:

> In terms of energy, the two sides emphasized that strengthening energy cooperation is a manifestation of the important strategic partnership between the two countries. Saudi Arabia is rich in oil resources, and China has a vast market. The two sides mentioned the scale of oil trade between the two countries and a good foundation for cooperation. It is in the common

> interests of China and Saudi Arabia to promote and consolidate bilateral cooperation in the oil field. The two sides emphasized the importance of stability in the global oil market. China welcomes Saudi Arabia's role in supporting the balance and stability of the global oil market, and welcomes Saudi Arabia as a major and reliable source of crude oil for China.

The Sino-Saudi economic cooperation is mainly centred on energy and infrastructure construction, including buying oil from Saudi Arabia and investing considerably in each other's critical oil and petrochemical refinery infrastructure. On the one hand, in early 2022, Aramco, the Saudi state oil conglomerate, made a decision to invest in a refinery and petrochemical complex in Liaoning Province, China's heavy industry heartland. The project was worth US$10 billion, and it is expected to be operational in 2024, combining a 300,000-bpd refinery and 1.5 million tonnes per year ethylene plant, with Aramco set to supply up to 210,000 bpd of crude oil. This project marks the Kingdom's single largest investment in China. Aramco's other investments in China include a 25% stake in the Refinery and Petrochemical Company Ltd in Fujian province, which is controlled by Sinopec. The project began in 2008 to operate a 280,000-bpd refinery and a 1.1 million tonne per year ethylene plant. On the other, China's state oil giant, Sinopec (China Petroleum & Chemical Corporation) owns a 37.5% stake in the Yanbu Aramco Sinopec Refinery Co, which is located on the coast of the Red Sea. The Yanbu project is a joint venture between Sinopec and Aramco that operates a 400,000-bpd refinery.

7.3 China's Ties with the Middle Eastern Countries Under the BRI

China sees the GCC states and the entire Middle East as a promising emerging market for Chinese companies. Importantly, the region was situated along the historical Silk Road and is now involved in its modern version, the Belt and Road Initiative (BRI). China is pushing hard for the implementation of the BRI by expanding its trade and increasing investment in the region. In 2021, China's total trade volume with the Middle Eastern countries reached US$259 billion.

The BRI is the hallmark of China's emergence. Through this platform, China is rapidly extending its economic influence in Asia and other parts of the world. The rise of China and its growing clout in the world have enhanced its leaders' confidence and the ambition to continue to promote and implement the BRI internationally (Yu 2022a). The BRI serves as the new cooperation platform to advance China's relations with the Arab world. The BRI is helping to expand member countries' cooperation in various areas covering infrastructure financing and construction, energy, finance, industrial parks, manufacturing, telecommunication technology, high-tech industry, tourism, education and cultural exchanges. Beijing aims to expand its trade, investment and economic ties with the region, as well as expand its influence amid the BRI push, slowly but steadily.

Saudi Arabia and Iran both served as important regional transportation and trade hubs along the ancient Silk Road, where silk was traded as a commodity between the Arab, Persian and Chinese merchants. Through Arabia and Persia, China established a trade and transportation route to Europe. Hence, China's new strategic partnership with both countries could facilitate deepening of BRI implementation in the region. China hopes to counter the confrontation and containment of the United States and allied allies by strengthening its relations with both Iran and Saudi Arabia, further advancing the BRI in the Middle East and expanding its circle of partners and friends of China's strategy. China's warming relations with both Saudi Arabia and Iran will help strengthen China's strategic influence in the region.

With its rise in the region and beyond, China has interests that go far beyond the Asia–Pacific region. Xi's visit to Riyadh amounted to far more than boosting energy cooperation between the two countries. China plans to train 1500 police and cybersecurity officials to deepen the security cooperation between China and the Arab countries. It also seeks to play a more important role in resolving many long-standing conflicts and crises afflicting the region, ranging from the rivalry between Iran and other Arab states to the Israeli-Palestinian conflict. The recent development of rapprochement between Saudi Arabia and Iran, which was facilitated by China, is such a case in point.

Under the BRI framework, China's increasing influence has greatly unsettled the existing global landscape and geopolitics. The BRI has attracted increasing attention from the international community. According to official data from China, 150 nations (including all Arab and GCC States) had signed various BRI cooperation agreements with China by the end of 2022. Since launching the BRI in 2013, China has spent billions on overseas investments and construction contracts for BRI projects in more than 100 nations. The BRI is currently the world's largest geoeconomic initiative, involving 150 countries. The other major Western-oriented infrastructure initiatives, namely the European Union's Global Gateway, the United States' Bule Dot Network, Japan's Quality Infrastructure Investment and the G7's Partnership for Global Infrastructure and Investment have not yet produced enough geoeconomic momentum globally to seriously rival the BRI (Yu September 2022b).

Chinese investment in the infrastructure construction industries is welcomed by the Middle Eastern countries, particularly those countries affected by conflicts, as a source for boosting economic growth and industrial take-off. Calabrese (2022) argues that China's push for the BRI in the region is expanding from its primary focus on infrastructure construction to the health, science and technology and digital domains.

China has cemented its ties with Saudi Arabia and the other Gulf states over the past decade, Qatar being a case in point. Qatar recently hosted the 2022 FIFA World Cup, marking the first time the World Cup has been held in an Arab country. Despite not qualifying for the World Cup finals, China's influence was to be seen everywhere at the Qatar World Cup 2022, ranging from the construction of stadiums, including the Lusail Stadium, the main stadium for the 2022 World Cup and worth US$764 million, the development of the Al Kharsash Solar Power Plant, which served as one of the main power sources for the tournament, to provision of electrical vehicles operating within the sport venues and souvenirs made by Chinese factories (Rakhmat and Purnama 2022). According to GlobalData, a London-based information services firm, Chinese companies were among the main sponsors for the tournament, with their sponsorship revenue sitting at US$1.4 billion, in contrast to US$1.1 billion from U.S. firms.

7.4 The Saudi Arabia-Iran Deal Mediated by China: A Major Geopolitical Shift in the Middle East

Saudi Arabia and Iran are leaders of the two largest sects of Islam, with Riyadh considering itself the guardian of Sunnis and Iran assuming a similar guardian role for Shiites. The Sunni majority in Saudi Arabia and the Shia majority in Iran have long seen each other as a threatening power with its eyes on regional dominance. Their relations have been highly complicated and contentious, which has affected regional peace and security in the Middle East.

The rapprochement between Saudi Arabia and Iran, which was facilitated by China, took the region and the world by surprise. Following four days of secret talks in Beijing in March 2023 between Musaad bin Mohammed al-Aiban, Saudi Arabia's Minister of State, and Ali Shamkhani, National Security Advisor and Secretary of Iran's Supreme National Security Council, Saudi Arabia and Iran agreed to restore their diplomatic ties, to reopen embassies within two months, and to prepare for exchange of ambassadors, according to the tripartite joint statement signed by Saudi Arabia, Iran and China on 10 March 2023. Both countries have further agreed to put aside their respective concerns and differences and to open a new page in their bilateral relations. In addition, Saudi Arabia and Iran have agreed to abide by the principle of sovereignty, non-interference in each other's internal affairs, and jointly work to maintain long-term peace and stability in the region. Both countries also agreed to activate a bilateral security cooperation agreement signed in 2001, and a general agreement on economy, trade, investment, scientific research and technology, which was signed in 1998, according to the tripartite joint statement (Ministry of Foreign Affairs of the People's Republic of China 2023a).

Saudi Arabia cut its diplomatic ties with Iran in January 2016 after angry Iranian protestors stormed its embassy in Tehran following Riyadh's execution of a prominent Shia Muslim cleric. The signing of the agreement signifies both countries could be ending seven years of estrangement and hostility. The development marks a major geopolitical shift in the Middle East. The China-brokered agreement reached by Saudi Arabia and Iran has sent multifaceted messages across the region and beyond.

First, the Saudi-Iran agreement is expected to reestablish development and security in the region. The Saudi Arabia-Iran agreement is both historical and symbolic, and it could help to de-escalate the tensions between the two countries and ensure badly needed long-term peace and stability in the region. The deal could generate wide-reaching implications for the Middle East. It is expected to boost regional cooperation among the Persian Gulf countries and other Islamic countries.

China has stunned the Middle East and the world by achieving an unexpected diplomatic breakthrough. Wang Yi, China's top diplomat and director of the Chinese Communist Party Central Foreign Affairs Office, claimed, while chairing the closing ceremony of the Beijing dialogue among Saudi Arabia, Iran and China, that the deal is a victory for peace and diplomacy. This Saudi-Iran reproachment has become a successful practice of China's Global Security Initiative (Ministry of Foreign Affairs of the People's Republic of China 2023b).

Second, Saudi Arabia and Iran are the two most powerful countries in the Middle East, and both are influential powers in the Muslim world. The Iran-Saudi Arabia deal could cause a "ripple effect" in the security arrangements and geostrategic landscape for the region. It could also pave the way to finally ending the conflicts and security crises in Yemen, Lebanon and Syria. António Guterres, the United Nations' Secretary General, remarked that the deal is a very positive development, and he thanked China for brokering the deal and helping to ensure durable peace and security in the region (Reuters March 2023).

Third, the Saudi Arabia-Iran deal shows Beijing's influence in the region is sharply increasing. Saudi Arabia and Iran both thanked China for hosting the peace talks and its leadership role in them (Turak 2023). President Xi Jinping was personally involved in brokering the Saudi-Iranian agreement, having expressed to Saudi Crown Prince Mohammed bin Salman during his visit to Riyadh in December 2022 that Beijing could play a "bridge" role between Saudi Arabia and Iran. Before that, China rarely became involved in solving regional conflicts as either a meditator or external player which could change the balance of power in the Middle East. Beijing is clearly becoming far more proactive and forthcoming in its foreign policy towards the region. Both countries now view China as not only an important trade and economic partner, but also as a security partner in the region.

Both Saudi Arabia and Iran are rich in oil resources. Their economies are highly dependent on oil exports. China is the world's largest oil consumer and the largest oil importer. In this sense, China is not just a general buyer for Saudi and Iranian energy products, but their primary strategic customer. China's influence on both countries' economies has been rising in recent years, and China is their most important export market and largest trading partner.

Just as the United States is seeking a strategic pivot to the Indo-Pacific region based on reducing its involvement in the Middle East, China is seizing the opportunity to step into the region. The Americans' rushed withdrawal from Afghanistan in 2021 reinforced the impression formed by many Middle Eastern countries that the United States is withdrawing from the region (Parsi and Aljabri 2023). More important, as it is the largest trading partner and the top energy buyer for both Saudi Arabia and Iran, China has the economic leverage to influence both countries. It can capitalize this leverage to take on the significant role of power broker in the Middle East which was traditionally held by the United States.

By brokering the Riyadh-Tehran deal, China has established itself as a reliable and trusted meditator for both countries. China has played a pivotal role in mediating the agreement on normalizing diplomatic relations between Riyadh and Tehran and bringing reconciliation between the two long-term arch-rivals. In addition to the trade and economic arenas, China's greater involvement in regional security and conflict mediation is welcomed by the regional countries. As stated in the following extract from the tripartite joint statement:

> In response to the positive initiative of President Xi Jinping of the People's Republic of China on China's support for the Kingdom of Saudi Arabia and the Islamic Republic of Iran to develop good-neighborly and friendly relations, according to the agreement reached by President Xi Jinping and the leaders of Saudi Arabia and Iran on China's hosting and supporting the talks between Saudi Arabia and Iran Consensus, in order to resolve their differences through dialogue and diplomacy within the framework of fraternal relations, to abide by the purposes and principles of the Charter of the United Nations, the Charter of the Organization of Islamic Cooperation, as well as international regulations and practices, the Saudi Minister of State, cabinet members, National Security Adviser Musaid bin Mohammad Alban and Iran's Supreme National Security Council Secretary Ali Shamkhani respectively led Saudi and Iranian delegations to hold talks in Beijing from March 6 to 10, 2023.

China has long advocated that conflicts and differences in the world should be resolved peacefully and politically through dialogue and negotiations, as reflected in the Global Security Initiative (GSI), which was first proposed by President Xi Jinping in April 2022. The official concept paper of the GSI calls on countries to adapt to the profoundly changing international landscape in a spirit of solidarity, and address the complex and intertwined security challenges with a win–win mindset. The GSI aims to eliminate the root causes of international conflicts, improve global security governance, encourage joint international efforts to bring more stability and certainty to a volatile and changing era and promote durable peace and development in the world. The core concepts and principles of the GSI refer to the following six points: stay committed to the vision of common, comprehensive, cooperative and sustainable security; stay committed to respecting the sovereignty and territorial integrity of all countries; stay committed to abiding by the purposes and principles of the United Nation Charter; stay committed to taking the legitimate security concerns of all countries seriously; stay committed to peacefully resolving differences and disputes between countries through dialogue and consultation; and stay committed to maintaining security in both traditional and non-traditional domains (Ministry of Foreign Affairs of the People's Republic of China 2023c).

Fourth, Beijing has a long-term geostrategic plan to insert China not only into economic areas but also the overall security arrangements of the region. By stepping up its efforts in the region, China is competing with the United States for influence in the Middle East. The agreement reached in Beijing demonstrates that China has ability to project its power and diplomatic influence beyond the Asia–Pacific region. China is becoming an indispensable power, politically and economically, in a region where it has long been geostrategically dominated by the United States.

Its successful brokering of the agreement between Saudi Arabia and Iran is telling the world that Beijing can do big things, while Washington is simply incapable of making such a deal between these two long-term arch-rivals. Iran has long been considered by the United States as a foe and a security threat. The United States has long accused Iran of backing terrorist groups or armed militias in the region. Meanwhile, Saudi Arabia is a long-term security ally of the United States in the Middle East. Nevertheless, both Iran and Saudi Arabia seem to be determined to implement foreign policies which are independent from those of the West in general and the United States in particular.

The China-mediated agreement is not only a big victory for China's diplomacy, but also it strikes a major blow against American's foreign policy towards the Middle East. It could signal the waning of American influence in the region. The China-mediated Saudi Arabia-Iran agreement presents an alternative to a Washington-led order in the region. As a New York Times report commented (Baker 2023):

> The Americans, who have been the central actors in the Middle East for the past three-quarters of a century, almost always the ones in the room where it happened, now find themselves on the sidelines during a moment of significant change. The Chinese, who for years played only a secondary role in the region, have suddenly transformed themselves into the new power player.

The objective of China's foreign policy towards the Middle East is to seek strategic balance, but not regional control and domination. Without taking sides or getting entangled in their disputes, Beijing could avoid being perceived as a party in the conflicts and has won praises from countries in the region. Beijing's approach has enabled it to rise as a credible power that can mediate conflicts and resolve disputes.

By strengthening its ties with Saudi Arabia, China has been developing close relations with Iran for the past decade. Both China and Iran are facing the pressures of US sanctions and geopolitical competition from the West. In March 2021, Wang Yi's visit to six Middle Eastern countries, in particular, Iran, attracted much attention from the international community. During Wang Yi's visit to Iraq, he and then Iranian Foreign Minister Zarif formally signed on behalf of the two governments the Agreement on "Comprehensive Cooperation between the People's Republic of China and the Islamic Republic of Iran" for the next 25 years (China-Iran Comprehensive Cooperation Plan). This plan injects substance into China's strategic partnership with Iran. According to publicly available information, the China-Iran Comprehensive Cooperation Plan lays out a roadmap for future comprehensive cooperation between the two countries and is a strategic framework guiding the development of bilateral relations. The agreement covers politics, economy, energy, finance, infrastructure construction, defence security and a wide range of other fields such as medical and health care and people-to-people exchanges. Despite domestic opposition to the partnership, the Iranian leadership has given due consideration to ending Iran's isolation and countering the US sanctions. Ayatollah Ali Hosseini Khamenei has explicitly supported the deepening of Iran's cooperation with China and the agreement, clearing the path for its signing.

Iran, with a population of more than 83 million, is a young country that has great consumption potential. China hopes that its signing and implementing of the China-Iran Comprehensive Cooperation Plan will help Chinese enterprises further expand into the Iranian market through their exports of goods and services. Iran has an especially urgent need to improve its infrastructure facilities, including domestic roads, airports, ports and power stations, and improve the efficiency of transportation, logistics and transportation. According to the World Economic Forum's Global Competitiveness Report 2019, Iran ranks very low internationally in areas such as road quality, port operational efficiency, air transport, power supply and telecommunications infrastructure. Iran's need to improve infrastructure and operational efficiency provides opportunities for Chinese companies to enter relevant markets.

Trade with China accounted for more than a quarter of Iran's total foreign trade in 2019. Many Chinese enterprises have long been involved in Iran's domestic economic development, industry and infrastructure construction. Despite the US sanctions, China has not stopped importing oil and energy products from Iran. To avoid and reduce transaction risks due to the sanctions, China has continued to import Iranian oil through third parties and unofficial channels. According to data from Refinitiv Oil Research, China imported 17.8 million tonnes of Iranian crude oil, averaging about 300,000 barrels per day, during the 14-month period from January 2020 to February 2021. On the one hand, in the face of US sanctions and blockade, Iran urgently needs foreign investment, technology and expansion of trade space, and the implementation of the China-Iran Comprehensive Cooperation Plan will allow Iran to cope with economic difficulties and provide urgently needed foreign investment in domestic infrastructure. On the other hand, the agreement will also allow China to obtain a stable supply of oil from Iran at a more favourable price, which will help to further strengthen China's energy import diversification strategy and ensure its domestic energy security (Yu 2021).

The China-mediated agreement between Riyadh and Tehran indicates that its policy towards the region is quite effective and forceful. China is emerging as the new power broker in the Middle East, a region burdened by crises and conflicts. After successfully brokering the reestablishment of diplomatic ties between Saudi Arabia and Iran, Beijing could turn its attention to other hotspot issues, such as the long-standing Israeli-Palestinian conflict.

7.5 Limitations of the Sino-Saudi Economic Ties

Although bilateral trade between Beijing and Riyadh is increasing, it remains narrowly based. The bulk of imports from the Kingdom to China has consisted of crude oil and petrochemical products. China's trade deficit with Saudi Arabia has increased thanks to the former's huge demand for oil imports. In 2021, according to the Chinese official statistics (Ministry of Commerce of the People's Republic of China January 2022), China spent US$39.73 billion on buying Saudi oil, while crude oil accounted for around 70% of the value of China's imports from Saudi Arabia (US$ 56.99 billion).

As shown in Table 7.1, the total value of Saudi exports of mineral fuels, oils and products thereof to China reached US$44.87 billion in 2021. Meanwhile, China mainly exports electrical machinery and electrical equipment, vehicles and auto parts, furniture and home appliances to Saudi Arabia. According to the ITC Trade Map (Table 7.2), in 2021, China exported electrical machinery and equipment with a total value of US$12.58 billion to Saudi Arabia, accounting for appropriately 41% of total value of China's exports to the Kingdom (estimated at US$30.32 billion).

Beijing and Riyadh are seeking to develop a partnership that goes beyond the traditional supplier–buyer relationship in terms of Saudi oil. Both countries seek to expand this cooperation to other areas, such as telecommunication, cloud computing, nuclear technology, aerospace, finance, logistics and medical industries. Both Saudi Arabia and China share the convergence of interests in seeking sustainable economy by going global, and greater autonomy and diplomatic space in the international system.

Oil and petrochemical products accounted for over 90% of the value of Saudi exports and appropriately 87% of total revenue received by the Kingdom. Oil and

Table 7.1 Top 5 products exported from Saudi Arabia to China in 2021

Rank	Product category	Amount (US$ billion)
1	Mineral fuels, mineral oils and products of their distillations, bituminous substances and mineral wax	44.87
2	Organic chemicals	5.67
3	Plastics and articles thereof	4.89
4	Ores, slag and ash	0.56
5	Salt, sulphur, earths and stone, plastering materials, lime and cement	0.28

Source ITC Trade Map

Table 7.2 Top 5 products exported from China to Saudi Arabia in 2021

Rank	Product category	Amount (US$ billion)
1	Electrical machinery and equipment and parts thereof; sound recorders and reproducers, television image and sound recorders and reproducers, and parts and accessories of such articles	7.79
2	Machinery, mechanical appliances, nuclear reactors, boilers, parts thereof	4.79
3	Vehicles other than railway or tramway rolling stock, and parts and accessories thereof	2.31
4	Ships, boats and floating structures	1.96
5	Furniture, bedding, mattresses, mattress supports, cushions and similar stuffed furnishings, lamps and lighting fittings, not elsewhere specified or included; illuminated signs, illuminated nameplates and the like, prefabricated buildings	1.46

Source ITC Trade Map

other related industries accounted for over 40% of Saudi's GDP. To diversify its industrial development and reduce the dependence on the oil sector, the Kingdom needs China. Given that China is the world's largest manufacturing country, and the top producer of renewable energy equipment for such as solar and wind power, it has strong production capacity in a variety of industries.

During Xi's visit, both countries resolved to accelerate the synergy between China's Belt and Road Initiative and Saudi Arabia's 2030 Vision (China Briefing 2022). Both countries committed to jointly construct the BRI and "2030 Vision" in order to forge collaboration on non-oil sectors and boost non-oil trade. Saudi's 2030 Vision is referred to as a strategic framework aimed at reducing Saudi Arabia's reliance on oil, diversifying its economy and expanding public service areas such as health, education, infrastructure, recreation and tourism. One of the Vision's main objectives is to promote a softer and more secular image of the Kingdom, in addition to bolstering economic and investment activity.

7.6 Xi's Call for RMB Settlements for Energy Trading and China's RMB Internationalization Strategy

During President Xi's meeting with the Saudi leader and other fellow leaders from the GCC states, he promoted the use of Renminbi (Chinese currency or *yuan*) for trading in oil and gas with the GCC countries (Ng 2022). During the China-GCC summit, President Xi's call for RMB settlement for oil, gas and other energy products with the GCC countries, based on the platform of the Shanghai Petroleum and National Gas Exchange, could be seen as a sign of China's push for an RMB internationalization strategy. If the move is materialized, it could weaken the US dollar's hold on global trade and also help to boost the internalization of the Chinese currency. It is widely perceived as part of China's plan to challenge the U.S. dollar (USD)'s dominance in the global energy markets, the so-called Petrodollar system, which has helped to preserve the dollar's status as the top international reserve currency and payment medium for oil, gas and other commodities. Due to its status as the world's second-largest economy and one of the largest trading nations, China is still one of the biggest holders of U.S. dollars.

Beijing's unhappiness with the global reserve system being de facto based on the USD dates back to the 2008/2009 period, soon after the outbreak of the global financial crisis. The Western financial and economic sanctions which have been imposed on Russia due to its war on Ukraine, have heightened China's will to expedite the Renminbi internationalization strategy in order to safeguard China's national economic interests. Amid the fast-changing global geostrategic environment, and the intensified power rivalry between the United States in general and the technological decoupling in particular, China's dependence on the USD for both inward and outward foreign investment, international trade payment, as well as for trading on imports of energy and other critical commodities to power domestic industrial growth, has exposed vulnerability in its national economic security.

From Beijing's perspective, since the policymakers in Washington are increasingly taking a hostile attitude towards China, which is widely perceived as the U.S.'s top long-term enemy, it makes no sense for China to continue to rely on its rival's currency, the USD, as the main payment medium for its external trade and international economic engagement. President Xi and the Chinese leadership team are undoubtedly taking note of the devastating effects of economic and financial sanctions on the Russian economy. If China were to engage in a war against Taiwan, it would almost certainly trigger the United States and its other Western allies to impose severe sanctions on China, which could have large impacts or even cripple the Chinese economy. Beijing thus has stepped up its preparation efforts to insulate its economy and vital trade linkage from over reliance on the USD.

China's plan to accelerate the internationalization of the RMB is an effort to wean itself off the current international monetary system and Society for Worldwide Interbank Financial Telecommunication (SWIFT) system, both of which are led by the United States. Under its RMB internationalization strategy, China has for the past decade been focusing on the vast developing countries in Southeast Asia, Central Asia, South Asia, the Middle East, Africa and Latin America in its global push for the RMB. The RMB is becoming more widely used around the world, and it could become a more serious international payment currency.

Moreover, Beijing has been making efforts to increase deployment of its digital currency (e-RMB) during the same period. Chan (2023) argues that although its Central Bank Digital Currency (CBDC) initiative is still in the early experimental phase, China has emerged as a forerunner in the light of its influence over the standardization of digital payment infrastructure. China is building a scalable e-RMB model by partnering with UnionPay (the largest card firm in the world, with 8.4 billion cards issued and accepted in 179 countries) and China Mobile (with over 975 million customers worldwide), as well as with Alipay (with 1.3 billion users) and WeChat Pay (with 900 million users), which are two leading mobile payment platforms.

China is one of the major trading partners for these vast developing countries, which regard maintaining good relations with Beijing as key to their economic development. These countries are therefore more receptive to gradually accepting the Chinese currency for cross-border transactions. China's international settlements in RMB with the BRI countries reached RMB5.42 trillion (estimated at US$763.4 billion) in 2021 (Chan and Yang 2022). Given that the amount of international settlement in RMB was negligible just five years ago, this development is surely astonishing.

The US dollar still maintains its status as the world's predominant reserve currency, its influence is gradually diminishing. According to the IMF data, 58% of global reserves were held in the US dollar in the last quarter of 2022, compared to the US dollar accounted for 73% of reserves in the world in 2001. George Yeo, Singapore's former foreign minister, recently remarked during the annual ISEAS-Yusof Ishak Institute's regional outlook forum 2023, that "US weaponization of the US financial system is causing the establishment of an alternative system. At some point, the growth of an alternative system will threaten the primacy of the US dollar" (Yeo 2023).

The increasing usage of the Chinese currency stems from China's status as the second-largest economy in the world and its dominant position in the global merchandise trade. China is the largest trading partner for over 100 countries, many of these countries have signed up for the BRI and are in Southeast Asia and Central Asia. The internationalization of the RMB is expected to accelerate.

Nevertheless, while Xi's call for trading of oil and gas in RMB is part of China's efforts to push for the RMB internationalization strategy, it is still too early for Saudi Arabia and other GCC countries to ditch the USD in pricing their oil and gas sales. In addition, cross-border settlement of Saudi oil payments with Chinese currency has encountered various geopolitical and practical difficulties. As the RMB is not a fully convertible currency like the USD or EURO, holding the Chinese currency is not of much benefit to the Saudis. Very few Saudi-made products are being exported to China to date, except for oil and the other petrochemical products. The days of USD supremacy as the world's dominant reserve currency are therefore far from numbered.

7.7 Sino-Saudi Defence Ties

Sino-Saudi Arabia defence ties remain limited in scope despite the rise in bilateral trade and close political engagement. According to MERICS's estimation, in contrast to the value of Saudi-U.S. arms trade, sitting at US$17.85 billion, the value of Sino-Saudi arms trade was a very modest US$245 million between 2013 and 2021 (Al-Tamimi 2022). The value of U.S. arms sales to the Kingdom was over 72 times higher than that of Chinese arms sales. Saudi Arabia is the world's largest defence spender, and in the past, the Kingdom has imported weapons mostly from the United States. According to the Stockholm International Peace Research Institute, the United States supplied up to 82% of Saudi arms imports between 2017 and 2021. Other Western countries, such as France and the United Kingdom, were also among the main suppliers of weapons to Saudi Arabia (Fig. 7.4).

The Kingdom is now keen to diversify its imports of weapons and has thus sourced weapons from a range of countries, including France, Germany, Italy, and the Republic of Korea. China has yet to become a top alternative for supplying weapons and other defence equipment to Saudi Arabia. The arms trade between China and Saudi Arabia dates back to the late 1980s, when the Kingdom started to purchase middle-range missiles, drones and self-propelled artillery from China (Xie 2022). Nevertheless, security cooperation between Beijing and Riyadh remains limited. Despite the deepening bilateral political and economic relations between Beijing and Riyadh, the United States remains the Kingdom's most significant ally in general and on defence cooperation in particular. America's President Biden has vowed that the United States will not walk away from the region and leave a vacuum to be filled by China, Russia or Iran.

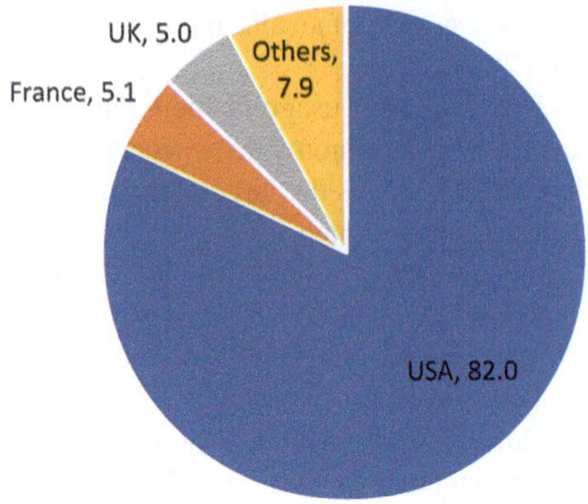

Fig. 7.4 Main suppliers of Saudi Arabia's arms imports, 2017–2021 (Unit: Percentage). *Source* Stockholm International Peace Research Institute (March 2022)

From Washington's perspective, it can't afford to break the ties with Saudi Arabia, as the Kingdom serves as a critical ally for helping the United States to stabilize the crisis-ridden Middle East and keep the Iranian influence under control. The United States' influence in Saudi Arabia and the region as a whole will not decline significantly in the foreseeable future. Saudi Arabia and the other Arab states want to maintain good relations with both China and the United States. As Saudi Arabia's foreign minister commented recently, "We do not believe in polarization or in choosing between sides. … cooperating with the world's number two economy is necessary, however, this does not mean not cooperating with the world's number one economy". The Saudi leadership is aware that maintaining good relations with Uncle Sam remains, of necessity, a key foreign policy objective for the Kingdom.

7.8 Conclusion

The debate among Chinese experts over the necessity and wisdom of China getting more involved in the Middle East in order to protect Chinese economic interests and safeguard its national energy security has now drawn to a conclusion. It is increasingly argued that China should increase its presence in the region and thereby ditch its image of being a free rider.

China is making efforts to deepen its ties with the Middle Eastern countries, economically, politically as well as strategically. China's President Xi Jinping's visit to Saudi Arabia in December 2022 is a case in point. It came on the tail of his winning a third term as China's paramount leader at the 20th National Congress of the Chinese Communist Party in late October 2022. To the Chinese leader, Saudi Arabia is both an influential country in the Middle East and a rising power with strategic significance in a multipolar world. Saudi leaders' pursuit of a visible strategic relationship with China, the world's second-largest economy, is part of their strategy to develop a global Saudi Arabia and expand its ties with countries apart from the United States.

China is Saudi Arabia's largest trading partner and the largest consumer of Saudi oil and petrochemical products. Energy serves as the bedrock of the partnership between Beijing and Riyadh. Beijing and Riyadh's bilateral trade volume is increasing, the structure of this bilateral trade remains narrowly based. Saudi Arabia exports mostly crude oil and petrochemical products to China. Sino-Saudi Arabian defence ties remain limited in scope even with the rise in bilateral trade and the close political engagement.

The two countries are seeking to develop a partnership that goes beyond the traditional supplier–buyer relationship in terms of Saudi oil. The BRI has a role to play in expanding China's cooperation with the regional nations in areas that go beyond the energy industry. Other areas of cooperation include telecommunication, cloud computing, nuclear technology, aerospace, finance, logistics and medical industries. A series of non-binding bilateral commercial agreements worth up to US$30 billion have also been signed. These agreements will doubtlessly strengthen the economic ties between Beijing and Riyadh.

During his three-day visit to Riyadh, the capital of Saudi Arabia, the Chinese president also attended the China-Arab States Summit and China-Gulf Cooperation Council Summit. The China-Arab States Summit, the first of its kind ever to be held, was attended by nearly 20 Arab leaders from the region. This was China's largest and highest-level diplomatic interaction with the Arab world since the founding of the People's Republic of China in 1949. Xi's visit signals that there will be no slowing down in China's economic engagement with the world in the post-COVID-19 era. The Middle Eastern states supply critical energy to power China's domestic industrial and economic development.

China has developed good relations with both Saudi Arabia and Iran over the years, and they see China as an honest broker. This allows Beijing to play a mediator role to bring the two rival parties closer to reconciliation in the interests of peace and stability in their countries and the Middle East. The China-mediated agreement between Riyadh and Tehran is historic, indicating a major geopolitical shift and realignment in the region. China has intensified its diplomatic, economic and political engagement in the region, and it will continue to do so.

China has great interest in the Middle East becoming a stable and prosperous region, rather than one of conflict and confrontation. On the one hand, from the geostrategic perspective, China has stepped up its efforts to be involved in the Middle East, in a strategic position between the East and the West. On the other, from the geoeconomic point of view, the oil-rich Middle East is crucial to ensuring its national energy security. The emerging Middle East with its young population and increasing middle class, is an important market for Chinese firms engaged in sectors ranging from infrastructure construction, agricultural, food, automobiles, home appliances to smartphones and the 5G telecommunication network.

Nevertheless, it must be emphasized that both Saudi Arabia and Iran have pursued an independent foreign policy of "Neither East nor West" and will not fully lean towards China. Based on ancient and magnificent civilizations, the modern Saudi Arabia and Iran both retain too strong a sense of national pride to allow that to happen.

References

Al-Atrush, Samer, and Edward White. 2022. Xi Jinping Hails 'new era' in China-Saudi Arabia Relations. *Financial Times*. https://www.ft.com/content/a3ad8e0c-d8e5-4fb3-b3af-39320ecf6b0d. Accessed 30 Dec 2022.

Al-Tamimi, Naser. 2022. *Saudi Arabia's Once Marginal Relationship with China has Grown Into a Comprehensive Strategic Partnership*. MERICS. https://merics.org/en/saudi-arabias-once-marginal-relationship-china-has-grown-comprehensive-strategic-partnership. Accessed Dec 30.

Baker, Peter. 2023. Chinese-Brokered Deal Upends Mideast Diplomacy and Challenges U.S. *The New York Times*. Available at https://cn.nytimes.com/world/20230313/saudi-arabia-iran-china-biden/dual/. Accessed 14 Mar 2023.

Calabrese, John. 2022. *China's Health Silk Road and the BRI Agenda in the Middle East*. Middle East Institute. https://www.mei.edu/publications/chinas-health-silk-road-and-bri-agenda-middle-east.

Chan, Elgin. 2023. *Renminbi Internationalization: China's Central Bank Digital Currency*. RSIS Commentary No. 037. https://www.rsis.edu.sg/rsis-publication/rsis/renminbi-internationalisation-chinas-central-bank-digital-currency/#.ZBE1DnZBzb1.

Chan, Elgin, and Zi Yang. 2022. *China's Renminbi Internationalization*. Singapore: Nanyang Technological University RSIS Commentary No. 135.

China Briefing. 2022. Saudi Arabia—China Ties: Several Investment Agreements, MoUs Signed During President Xi's Visit. https://www.china-briefing.com/news/saudi-arabia-china-relations-xi-jinping-visit/. Accessed 30 Dec 2022.

China Customs. 2022. Online Customs Statistics. http://stats.customs.gov.cn/indexEn. Accessed 8 Feb 2023.

Ministry of Commerce of the People's Republic of China. January 2022. *Country (Region) Guidelines for Foreign Investment and Cooperation: Saudi Arabia*.

Ministry of Foreign Affairs of the People's Republic of China. 2022. Joint Statement Between the People's Republic of China and the Kingdom of Saudi Arabia. https://www.fmprc.gov.cn/zyxw/202212/t20221209_10988250.shtml.

Ministry of Foreign Affairs of the People's Republic of China. 2023a. *Tripartite Joint Statement of the People's Republic of China, the Kingdom of Saudi Arabia, and the Islamic Republic of Iran*. Available at https://www.fmprc.gov.cn/zyxw/202303/t20230310_11039137.shtml. Accessed 11 Mar 2023.

Ministry of Foreign Affairs of the People's Republic of China. 2023b. *Wang Yi: The Saudi Arabia-Iran Dialogue in Beijing is a Victory for Peace*. Available at https://www.fmprc.gov.cn/zyxw/202303/t20230310_11039102.shtml. Accessed 14 Mar 2023.

Ministry of Foreign Affairs of the People's Republic of China. 2023c. *The Global Security Initiative Concept Paper*. Available at https://www.fmprc.gov.cn/mfa_eng/wjbxw/202302/t20230221_11028348.html. Accessed 13 Mar 2023.

Ng, Teddy. 2022. China Pushes to Boost the Role of the Yuan in Global Energy Markets as Xi Jinping Wraps Up Saudi Arabia Visit. *South China Morning Post*. https://www.scmp.com/news/china/diplomacy/article/3202831/china-pushes-boost-role-yuan-global-energy-markets-xi-jinping-wraps-saudi-arabia-visit. Accessed 28 Dec 2022.

Parsi, Trita, and Khalid Aljabri. 2023. How China Became a Peacemaker in the Middle East: Washington's Missteps Paved the Way for Beijing's Saudi-Iranian Deal. *Foreign Affairs*. https://www.foreignaffairs.com/china-became-peacemaker-middle-east.

Qianzhan Industry Research Institute, 2022. *From January to December 2021, The Production Scale of China's Crude Oil Industry and the Panorama of the Import Market: The Annual Crude Oil Import Volume Exceeded 500 million tons*. https://d.qianzhan.com/xnews/detail/541/220321-7a62c3a3.html. Accessed 16 Feb 2023.

Rakhmat, Muhammad Zulfikar, and Yeta Purnama. 2022. China's Prominent Role in the 2022 Qatar World Cup. *The Diplomat*. https://thediplomat.com/2022/12/chinas-prominent-role-in-the-2022-qatar-world-cup/. Accessed 28 Dec 2022.

Reuters. 2023. *Reaction to Iran and Saudi Arabia Resuming Ties*. Available at https://www.reuters.com/world/middle-east/reaction-iran-saudi-arabia-resuming-ties-2023-03-10/. Accessed 14 Mar 2023.

Stockholm International Peace Research Institute. March 2022. Trends in International Arms Transfers. https://www.sipri.org/sites/default/files/2022-03/fs_2203_at_2021.pdf. Accessed 29 Dec 2022.

Turak, Natasha. 2023. Arch-rivals Iran and Saudi Arabia Agree to Revive Ties, Reopen Embassies in China-Brokered Seal. *CNBC*. Available at https://www.cnbc.com/2023/03/10/arch-rivals-iran-and-saudi-arabia-agree-to-revive-ties-reopen-embassies.html. Accessed 12 Mar 2023.

Xie, Kawala. 2022. Why is Saudi Arabia Looking to China to Buy Weapons After Years of Arms Deals with the US? *South China Morning Post*. https://www.scmp.com/news/china/diplomacy/article/3202245/why-saudi-arabia-looking-china-buy-weapons-after-years-arms-deals-us?module=hard_link&pgtype=article. Accessed 28 Dec 2022.

Yeo, George. 2023. ASEAN's Advantage in an Emerging Multipolar World. Keynote Address of the ISEAS-Yusof Ishak Institute's Regional Outlook Forum 2023. *ThinkChina*. https://www.thinkchina.sg/george-yeo-aseans-advantage-emerging-multipolar-world?utm_source=newsletter&utm_medium=email&utm_campaign=weekly_newsletter. Accessed 12 Jan 2023.

Yu, Hong. 2021. China-Iran Deal Complements the BRI, But Faces Iranian Domestic Opposition and US Sanctions. *ThinkChina*. Available at https://www.thinkchina.sg/china-iran-deal-complements-bri-faces-iranian-domestic-opposition-and-us-sanctions. Accessed 14 Mar 2023.

Yu, Hong. 2022a. Is the Belt and Road Initiative 2.0 in the Making? The Case of Central Asia. *Journal of Contemporary Asia*. https://doi.org/10.1080/00472336.2022.2122858.

Yu, Hong. September 2022b. *G7's Global Infrastructure and Investment Plan: An Alternative to China's Belt and Road Initiative?* Singapore: National University of Singapore, East Asian Institute Background Brief No. 1665.

Chapter 8
G7's Plan for Partnership for Global Infrastructure and Investment: An Alternative to the BRI?

8.1 Sino-US Strategic Competition and the U.S.'s "Indo-Pacific Strategy"

Sino-U.S. strategic competition presents a major obstacle to China's BRI implementation. US-China rivalry is intensifying and the world appears to be on a path to great power confrontation. The two countries hold increasingly divergent views on their respective strategic roles in the region and worldwide, with each country suspicious of the other's geopolitical intentions. The U.S. fears that the rise of China, as reflected by the launch of the Belt and Road Initiative, poses the most consequential long-term threat to U.S. interests and national security.

Despite their many differences on domestic issues, ironically, the Democratic Party and the Republican Party share the same view that China has both the geopolitical intention and economic resources to reshape the US-dominated global order. While from China's perspective, it is concerned that the U.S. is forging an alliance network through such as the AUKUS and the QUAD, to contain and suppress the rise of China.

Since the era of former U.S. President Donald Trump, the United States has begun to take various measures to try comprehensively to contain China's rising influence at the regional and global levels. As part of his strategy to counter China, in December 2017, Trump published his first U.S. National Security Strategy Report since taking office, calling China "a revisionist power that engages in economic aggression against the United States and endangers regional security and their sovereignty". The report describes China as "a peer competitor against U.S. values and interests" designed to challenge U.S. influence and wealth (U.S. Department of Defense 2018).

The U.S. elite view a rising China as having the power to shape a new international order, rules and global governance system, exert increasing influence in international affairs and suspect it of intending to replace the Western-dominated international order and rules system (Mazarr et al. 2022). Since President Biden took office in January 2021, the current US administration has basically continued the Trump-era

H. Yu, *Understanding China's Belt and Road Initiative*, Asia in Transition 26,
https://doi.org/10.1007/978-981-99-9633-9_8

policy of containing and countervailing China, characterizing China as "the only compound competitor" and "the only competitor potentially capable of combining its economic, diplomatic, military and technological power to mount a sustained challenge to a stable and open international system".

President Biden emphasized that the United States will increase investment in domestic infrastructure, as well as in key areas such as artificial intelligence, quantum computing and biotechnology, to ensure that the United States wins in the competition with China.

U.S. national strategy and foreign policy have been reshaped, with increasing focus on the competition with major powers, especially China. When Xi Jinping came to power in 2012, he repeatedly called for an equal relationship with the United States, under the framework of a "new type of major power relationship". Nevertheless, the U.S. has largely ignored such calls, as it is intent on retaining its status as the world's sole superpower. In order to boost its position in the competition with China, the Biden administration has tried to build a global alliance network, focusing on strengthening cooperation between the United States and allies such as Japan, Australia, Canada and the United Kingdom.

Intense competition is emerging in Asia and beyond between the United States as the established superpower and China as the rising global power. In another attempt to counterbalance the rise of China and its increasing prominence in the region, since the Trump era, the United States has been implementing "Indo-Pacific Strategy" to strengthen cooperation between the United States and its allies and other like-minded partners, to which the Biden administration attaches much more importance than his predecessor President Trump. The QUAD, AUKUS, and the IPEF are all United States-led multilateral cooperation mechanisms, which are long-term strategies designed to exclude, contain and constrain China and its rising influence. Specifically, the QUAD and IPEF seek to exclude China from the global economy and global supply chain, while the AUKUS seeks to contain China's military might in the region.

The United States joined up with Japan, Australia and India to reactivate the Quadrilateral Mechanism (QUAD) after a ten-year hiatus. Meanwhile, the United States joined up with the United Kingdom and Australia to form the "U.S.-UK-AU" Trilateral Military Partnership (AUKUS), which is perceived as the military and security component of the "Indo-Pacific Strategy". Through the QUAD and AUKUS mechanisms, the United States intends to reshape China's surrounding geopolitical environment, to counter China's BRI and thereby curb China's rising influence in the Indo-Pacific region.

On the military and security side, the U.S.'s moves to increase military cooperation with Australia, Japan, South Korea and the Philippines have caused concern for China. In the eyes of many Chinese scholars and policymakers, the U.S. "Indo-Pacific" strategy is essentially a tool to enable the United States to reinforce regional security alliances and its dominance in the region, primarily by counteracting the influence of China.

As the economic component of the "Indo-Pacific Strategy", on 23 May 2022, President Biden officially launched the "Indo-Pacific Economic Framework" (or the

IPEF in short) during his visit to Japan. This framework is an attempt to suppress China's rising economic influence and BRI implementation in the region. At present, the Indo-Pacific Economic Framework includes 14 member countries, accounting for 40% of the world's total economy and involving a total population of about 2.5 billion people. The IPEF is not a single agreement, but a series of loose institutional arrangements covering four pillars: digital trade, strengthening supply chain resilience, clean energy, infrastructure and taxation and anti-bribery. These arrangements constitute a platform for the Biden administration to strengthen trade and economic ties with regional countries. It is particularly worth emphasizing that the United States hopes to use this framework to exclude China from economic rule-making, and to undermine the China-centred regional supply chains by forming supply chain alliances, thereby reducing dependence on China in key industries and services and maintaining its advantage over China in high-tech fields such as semiconductors.

The Biden administration views reducing dependence on China-centric supply chains as an important part of strategic competition with China as a great power. It intends to work with regional allies to build "resilient and reliable supply chains", based on joint development of technical standards and specifications in key industrial sectors, such as the semiconductor industry, and joint inventory mechanisms for critical raw materials. In addition, participation in these supply chains will be extended through "friendly shore outsourcing" (the transfer of supply chains to allied countries) and "nearshoring" (the transfer of supply chains to geographically close neighbours).

The Biden government hopes to collaborate closely with both Japan and South Korea to create an IPEF as a model for reshaping supply chains, especially in key industries such as the digital economy and manufacturing of semiconductors and electric vehicle batteries. The United States wants to expand imports of chips made in South Korea and chip equipment and key raw materials made in Japan, thereby reducing dependence on the Chinese mainland and Taiwan in the semiconductor industry.

Semiconductors are among the few products for which China is still highly dependent on foreign imports, and represent the soft underbelly of China's scientific and technological development. China spends a lot of money every year on importing large quantities of semiconductor integrated circuit products. China is aware that the semiconductor industry is a "stuck neck" technology and has been seeking breakthroughs, with little success. The U.S.'s "Chips and Science Act of 2022" is expected to have a negative impact on the development of China's semiconductor industry. The bill will enable the United States to use administrative intervention and industrial policy to reshape the global semiconductor industry supply chain and will restrict and slow down the development of China's semiconductor industry, but without completely stifling it.

Despite its rising international status, China is not yet ready to challenge the U.S.-led Western primacy and needs to acknowledge the limitations of its power. Neither should it exaggerate the U.S.'s decline in strength or underestimate its resilience, since the U.S. economy is still much larger than that of China. Furthermore, the United States still leads the world in terms of technological capability, innovation, science and military might, due in no small part to its ability to attract a plentiful supply of skilled talent to its shores from every corner of the world.

According to the International Monetary Fund, although China is the world's second-largest economy after the United States, the per capita gross domestic product (GDP) of the United States reached US$63,051 in 2020, while the average Chinese GDP was only around one-sixth of that total, at US$10,582. As the world's only superpower, the United States still has absolute superiority in the fields of military, education and scientific and technological research and development. Meanwhile, infrastructure construction has become an important area of the fierce competition between the United States and China.

8.2 The U.S. To Compete with China on Infrastructure Financing and Construction

In terms of infrastructure development, China has the world's best ports, the fastest railways, the largest airports and the best telecommunications infrastructure. China has become a global leader in infrastructure construction, with great strength in infrastructure hardware construction and software operation management (Cheong 2022). In contrast, many transportation facilities in the United States, such as roads, bridges and airports, are in a state of disrepair. The U.S. and its allies are concerned that China is using its infrastructure-based BRI to establish a Sino-centric regional order.

In March 2021, Hillman and Sacks of the Council on Foreign Relations published a report entitled "How the United States Should Compete with China's Belt and Road Initiative", which pointed out that the BRI poses comprehensive challenges to U.S. politics, economy, national security, and climate change interests. To ensure that U.S. interests are not compromised, the United States needs to formulate a new strategy that can effectively respond to the BRI, based on high-quality and environmentally sustainable infrastructure development. (Hillman and David, 2021)

On 25 March 2021, at the first presidential press conference since his inauguration, President Biden said that during his term of office, China would never be allowed to surpass the United States as the most powerful country in the world. The Biden administration has realized that China's massive Belt and Road Initiative poses challenges to the United States in areas ranging from politics and economy to national security and overseas interests.

The BRI is the hallmark of China's emergence as an economic power. Through this platform, China is rapidly extending its economic influence in Asia and other parts of the world. Yu (2022) pointed out that the growing clout of China throughout the world has enhanced its leaders' confidence and their ambition to continue to promote and implement the BRI internationally. The BRI has greatly unsettled the existing global geopolitical landscape, since it is largely welcomed by developing and middle-income countries across Asia, the Pacific Island states, Africa and Latin America.

China's global influence is rapidly growing through the BRI implementation, and new geopolitical and geoeconomic realities in Asia and beyond are unfolding. China's push for the BRI has created considerable pressure and impetus in the United States to rebuild and strengthen its relations with like-minded partners in the Indo-Pacific region, such as Australia, Japan, Republic of Korea and the Philippines, to counter the rising Chinese influence.

In Biden's view, infrastructure development will be an important arena for the US to compete with China. President Biden intends for the PGII "to be one of the hallmarks of the Biden administration foreign policy over the remainder of his tenure" (Jenny and Jennifer 2022). Biden cop an initiative similar to the BRI by bringing together its allies in democratic nations to help developing nations upgrade their infrastructure. In June 2021, at the G7 summit held in the United Kingdom, Biden unveiled the Build Back Better World initiative (known as the B3W), focusing on addressing climate change, digital infrastructure, gender equality and healthcare system issues. The B3W was perceived as the G7's alternative to China's BRI. Nevertheless, the Biden administration offered few details about what exactly B3W would involve. Around one year after the B3W initiative was announced, the Biden administration had made a commitment to the cause of global infrastructure renewal of only up to US$6 million (Charles and Scott 2022).

This paltry amount is a far cry from the billions in infrastructure investment promised by Biden's original announcement. It compares poorly with the billions of dollars provided by Chinese companies and banks under the BRI umbrella. In the period since its announcement, the B3W attracted little regional or international attention in terms of its capability to finance infrastructure development.

In June 2022, the U.S. and other fellow G7 countries officially launched the rebranding of the B3W as the Partnership for Global Infrastructure and Investment (PGII), an initiative that aims to mobilize up to US$600 billion over the next five years, with US$200 billion, US$317.5 billion and US$65 billion coming from the U.S., European Union (EU) and Japan, respectively.

China and the United States are now competing fiercely for influence over the developing countries across the world. In June 2022, Xi Jinping, China's President, hosted a special high-level dialogue on global development for representatives of developing countries across all continents (Ministry of Foreign Affairs of the People's Republic of China 2022),[1] which included infrastructure financing and construction as its key components.

The PGII could potentially offer developing countries the option to seek external loans to finance infrastructure development in addition to funding from Beijing's Belt and Road Initiative. Meanwhile, several countries in the region and beyond are

[1] The leaders from China, Algeria, Argentina, Egypt, Indonesia, Iran, Kazakhstan, Russia, Senegal, South Africa, Uzbekistan, Brazil, Cambodia, Ethiopia, Fiji, India, Malaysia and Thailand attended the High-Level Dialogue on Global Development in June 2022.

pushing back against the BRI on the grounds that its China-invested infrastructure projects are costly and impractical, with internal transactions tainted by corruption issues.

8.3 What is the PGII All About?

The PGII is a private enterprise-led initiative, intended to bring together democratic nations to help developing nations to upgrade their infrastructure, whereas the BRI is a state-driven initiative. Consequently, China's state-owned banks and firms have played a dominant role in infrastructure financing and construction overseas, while the United States and other Western countries have committed very little money to the PGII, since most of the funds are expected to come from private companies.

The idea for financing the PGII is that it will comprise a combination of government grants and funding from G7 countries. The funding will be mobilized primarily from multilateral development banks (MDBs), as well as leveraged on sovereign wealth funds and complementary private capital from pension funds, private equity funds and insurance funds, among others. Using this strategy, the G7 countries seek to develop the influence of the PGII through achieving multiple positive impacts on global infrastructure development and national economies. Nevertheless, details of the working mechanisms for financing and implementing PGII projects are not available yet; for example, it is not known how the MDB source will be tapped.

The existing MDBs have over the years leveraged on their experience and expertise to provide loans and technical services to developing countries for infrastructure development. MDB loans can help tackle environmental sustainability and social safeguard issues and promote transparency and better governance in the developing countries. For example, the Asian Development Bank's (ADB) loans had increased from US$14 billion in 2014 to over US$20 billion in 2020, with 70% of these ADB loans going towards infrastructure development (Asian Development Bank 2022). In 2021, the World Bank approved around US$17 billion in loans to the developing countries for infrastructure, in sectors ranging from transport, energy and water to information and communication technologies (The World Bank 2021). Partnership between PGII and the MDBs is crucial to the execution of PGII projects. The G7 can provide a credible alternative to China's BRI by using the existing MDBs as implementing agencies for building and maintaining infrastructure projects in the developing countries while reducing reliance on public funds and grants (e.g. taxpayers' money).

In March 2022, US Secretary of the Treasury Janet Yellen, an important member of the PGII project, held a meeting to discuss global infrastructure investment with the presidents of many major MDBs, including the World Bank, African Development Bank, ADB, European Bank for Reconstruction and Development and the Inter-American Development Bank (US Department of the Treasury 2022). The Biden administration intends to build on its relationships with the MDBs in its drive for future PGII implementation.

As part of a whole-of-government approach, Biden appointed Ambassador Amos Hochstein as Special Presidential Coordinator for PGII implementation and coordination works. The PGII aims to deliver game-changing projects that will fill the infrastructure gaps in developing countries. Details of the U.S.-led G7 Countries' Partnership for Global Infrastructure and Investment (PGII) remain vague. Some infrastructure investment projects under the PGII, worth US$3 billion in total investment, are under implementation, including those in the following countries and sectors (White House 2022a):

- US$2 billion investment for a solar power project located in Angola.
- US$600 million US investment to build a subsea high-speed telecommunications cable, which will connect Singapore to France via Egypt and the Horn of Africa.
- US$50 million from the United States for the World Bank's Childcare Incentive Fund.
- US$14 million investment to Senegal for developing a multivaccine manufacturing facility, provided by the United States, partnered with the World Bank and the G7 partners.
- US$14 million investment from the United States for deployment of a small modular reactor plant in Romania.
- US$16 million of investment from the United States for renovating or constructing over 100 hospitals and clinics across Côte d'Ivoire.

Shortly before the G7 countries' announcement of the PGII, Jake Sullivan, the United States National Security Advisor, stated that the US-led initiative will provide "an alternative to what the Chinese are offering". Then, at the launch of the PGII, President Biden made the following comment on the initiative (White House 2022b):

> What we're doing is fundamentally different because it's grounded on our shared values of all those representing the countries and organizations behind me. It's built using the global best practices: transparency, partnership, protections for labor and the environment. We're offering better options for countries and for people around the world to invest in critical infrastructure that improves the lives …

There is a huge demand for financing infrastructure projects in the developing countries. As estimated by the Asian Development Bank, Asia and the Pacific countries will require over US$22.5 trillion for climate-adjusted infrastructure development up to 2030. No plan proposed by a single country or grouping could come close to meeting the developing nations' infrastructure investment needs. To accelerate infrastructure investment and development in the developing countries, the G7 PGII and China's BRI could collaborate to promote "third-party market" cooperation. Nevertheless, the Biden administration has promoted the PGII as a "democratic" alternative to the "autocratic" BRI. The latter has been criticized by the Biden administration for lack of transparency and low standards on environment and social issues. This positioning is likely to limit the scope for cooperation between the two.

8.4 The Infrastructure Investment Push Amidst the China-U.S. Rivalry

The PGII is a rebrand of the B3W and represents a bid for a head-to-head matchup with China. As evidenced by the announcements of the B3W and the PGII, the U.S.-led G7 seems to be playing a catch-up game with China on global infrastructure development.

Since its announcement by President Xi Jinping in 2013, the Belt and Road Initiative has formed the central pillar of China's drive to become a global power. China has financed and built thousands of infrastructure projects abroad, ranging from railways, seaports, airports, power plants and bridges to industrial parks and telecommunication networks around the world. China's total investment in infrastructure in the Belt and Road countries was estimated at between US$156.2 billion and US$332.6 billion from 2013 to 2021.

The G7 countries must convince the global community that they can provide a credible alternative to China's BRI that has the capability to undertake the urgent upgrading of infrastructure needed in a vast number of developing nations. It is noteworthy, however, that U.S. investments in many developing nations have declined and have been unable to meet their development needs in recent years.

On the domestic front, China has the best container port, the fastest rail, the largest airport and the most complete telecommunications infrastructure in the world. It has become the global leader in infrastructure, with solid capabilities in facility construction and operations management (Yu 2021). In contrast, many transportation facilities in the U.S., such as roads, bridges and airports, are in disrepair. In the stiff competition with China, the U.S. is playing to its weaknesses rather than its strengths. For example, in the field of technological capacity and infrastructure construction, according to the ENR ranking of construction revenue generated outside of each company's home country in 2020, fourteen Chinese construction firms are listed among the 20 largest infrastructure contractors in the world, whereas none are from the United States.

Building connectivity based on infrastructure development is the key to China's BRI and also the key selling point in encouraging the regional countries' participation. According to official data from China, 150 nations had already signed up for the BRI by the end of 2022. Since launching the BRI in 2013, China has spent billions in overseas investments and construction contracts for BRI projects in more than 100 nations. The U.S. and the wider world cannot ignore the potential impacts of the rise of China and the BRI implementation.

While the Belt and Road Initiative is Xi Jinping's pet project and has been a central pillar of China's foreign policy initiative since 2013, it is not China's only outreach strategy. To advance its national economic interests and its geostrategic ambition, China has also become a key player in many regional cooperation institutions, such as a grouping comprising five emerging economies: Brazil, Russia, India, China and South Africa (BRICS), Shanghai Cooperation Organization (SCO) and Regional Comprehensive Economic Partnership agreement (RCEP). China's endeavour to play a more influential role in both the regional and global affairs is multipronged and extends beyond the BRI.

8.5 Unfolding of Competing Regional and Global Connectivity Initiatives

Recent years have seen the unfolding of a successive wave of competing regional and global initiatives, all of which aim to accelerate interregional connectivity through infrastructure investment and construction. Examples include the ASEAN Master Plan for Connectivity, the Belt and Road Initiative, Japan's Partnership for Quality Infrastructure, ASEAN-Korea Infrastructure Fund, Russia's Eurasian Economic Union (EAEU), the European Union's "Connecting Europe and Asia", and the PGII as the newest initiative of this kind. However, many of these competing connectivity initiatives are still at the vision stage, without concrete achievements. None of these initiatives so far have been able to compete with the BRI from the perspective of scale, geographical coverage and geostrategic influence.

The Belt and Road Initiative is currently the world's largest geoeconomic initiative. Neither the other Western-oriented infrastructure initiatives, namely, the EU's Global Gateway, the United States' Blue Dot Network, Japan's Quality Infrastructure Investment, nor the G7's B3W have yet produced enough geoeconomic momentum globally to seriously rival the BRI.

Vast capital is required for infrastructure upgrading in developing nations, and the risks are high. Private enterprises do not have the required capital or the ability to undertake the associated risks. China is continuing to implement and expand the BRI, whereas the U.S. is currently unable to put forward a more effective alternative. Through the BRI implementation, China hopes to establish a new model for global infrastructure financing and development. Its state-led model is China's unique advantage in the BRI, a model not found in the U.S. and the West. Moreover, this infrastructure development model is implemented through China's state-owned enterprises and banks. China's leaders deem private enterprises to be ill-disciplined, have the tendency to expand indiscriminately, and be incapable of fulfilling China's strategic objectives.

Meanwhile, China is globally competitive in industries such as infrastructure construction, equipment manufacturing, metallurgical building material and communications equipment. The BRI could be used by China to transform its economic and financial power into geostrategic leverage and influence, by continuing to promote infrastructure connectivity as an important national strategy in its attempts to gain control over markets and industrial supply chains. (Khanna 2016)

However, China's self-imposed Zero-COVID strategy (or the Dynamic Clearing policy) and the ongoing Ukraine war created obstacles for Beijing's push for BRI implementation worldwide. The strict lockdown and control measures made it extremely difficult for Chinese officials, business executives and engineers to travel abroad to conduct in-person promotion and management of the BRI projects. The pandemic also pushed up the construction and labour costs of the BRI infrastructure projects due to supply chain disruption, soaring energy prices and manpower shortages of supplies of critical raw materials and equipment for infrastructure construction projects.

Russia's war in Ukraine could potentially cause collateral damage to the BRI, as China's land-based connectivity with the European Union via the China–Europe Express may be jeopardized. The China–Europe Express is crucial for overland-based connectivity between China, Eurasian countries and the European Union. Almost half of the routes and lines (78 lines reaching 180 cities in 23 European countries by 2021) pass through Russia; however, due to the massive sanctions imposed on Russia and the ongoing war, European firms may choose not to ship goods via Russia.

More significantly, China views Russia as an indispensable ally and strategic partner. From the long-term perspective, China's refusal to condemn Russia's aggression in the Ukraine war and its alignment with Russia have deepened the strategic distrust between China and the West, which could make Beijing's BRI push in the Western countries more challenging.

The BRI is still, by and large, a China-centric solo or bilateral initiative. China has thus far been unable to project the BRI as a credible multilateral endeavour. President Biden hopes to take advantage of the dissatisfaction of these nations along the BRI routes and engage with them and US allies to form an alliance against the BRI.

In the face of these increasing challenges, China must modify its original BRI model in order to respond effectively to the new geopolitics of the post-COVID-19 era.

References

Asian Development Bank. 2022. https://www.adb.org/what-we-do/knowledge#:~:text=ADB%20is%20scaling%20up%20its,this%20amount%20going%20toward%20infrastructure. Accessed 27 Aug 2022.

Charles, Kenny, and Scott, Morris. 2022. *America Shouldn't Copy China's Belt and Road Initiative*. Foreign Affairs, 22 June 2022.

Cheong, Danson. 2022. China's Belt and Road Initiative is Shifting Gears. *The Straits Times*, A15.

Hillman, Jennifer, and David, Sacks. 2021. *China's Belt and Road: Implications for the United States*. Independent Task Force Report No. 79, Council on Foreign Relations. Available at https://www.cfr.org/report/chinas-belt-and-road-implications-for-the-united-states/download/pdf/2021-04/TFR%20%2379_China%27s%20Belt%20and%20Road_Implications%20for%20the%20United%20States_FINAL.pdf. Accessed 12 Nov 2022.

Jenny, Leonard, and Jennifer, Jacobs. 2022. *Biden Plans to Launch a G7 Global Infrastructure Push to Counter China*. Bloomberg, 16 June 2022. Available at https://www.bloomberg.com/news/articles/2022-06-16/biden-to-launch-g7-global-infrastructure-push-to-counter-china. Accessed 27 June 2022.

Khanna, Parag. 2016. *Connectography: Mapping the Future of Global Civilization*. New York: Penguin Random House.

Kissinger, Henry. 2012. *On China*. New York: Penguin Books.

Kissinger, Henry. 2015. *World Order*. New York: Penguin Books.

Mazarr, Michael, Bryan Frederick, and Yvonne Crane. 2022. *Understanding A New Era of Strategic Competition*, 1–53. RAND Corporation.

Ministry of Foreign Affairs of the People's Republic of China. 2022. *President Xi Jinping Chairs and Delivers Important Remarks at the High-level Dialogue on Global Development*. Available at https://www.fmprc.gov.cn/eng/zxxx_662805/202206/t20220625_10709866.html. Accessed 27 June 2022.

The World Bank. 2021. *Annual Report 2021*. Available at https://www.worldbank.org/en/about/annual-report#anchor-annual. Accessed 27 Aug 2022.

U.S. Department of Defense. 2017. *Summary of the 2018 National Defense Strategy of the United States of American*. https://www.defense.gov/Portals/1/Documents/pubs/2018-National-Defense-Strategy-Summary.pdf.

US Department of the Treasury. 2022. *Statement by Secretary Yellen on President Biden's Announcement of the Partnership for Global Infrastructure and Investment*. Available at https://home.treasury.gov/news/press-releases/jy0835. Accessed 27 June 2022.

White House. 2022a. Fact Sheet: President Biden and G7 Leaders Formally Launch the Partnership for Global Infrastructure and Investment. Available at https://www.whitehouse.gov/briefing-room/statements-releases/2022/06/26/fact-sheet-president-biden-and-g7-leaders-formally-launch-the-partnership-for-global-infrastructure-and-investment/. Accessed 27 June 2022.

White House. 2022b. Remarks by President Biden at Launch of the Partnership for Global Infrastructure and Investment. Available at https://www.whitehouse.gov/briefing-room/speeches-remarks/2022/06/26/remarks-by-president-biden-at-launch-of-the-partnership-for-global-infrastructure-and-investment/. Accessed 27 June 2022.

Yu, Hong. 2021. Can Biden's New Infrastructure Plan rival China's BRI?. *ThinkChina*. Available at https://www.thinkchina.sg/can-bidens-new-infrastructure-plan-rival-chinas-bri. Accessed 23 June 2022.

Yu, Hong. 2022. *Is the Belt and Road Initiative 2.0 in The Making?* EAI Background Brief No. 1635, National University of Singapore.

Chapter 9
Asian Infrastructure Investment Bank's Role in Regional Infrastructure Financing

9.1 Establishment of the China-led Asian Infrastructure Investment Bank

The Asian Infrastructure Investment Bank (AIIB), proposed by China in 2013 and founded in 2014, is one of the world's newest multilateral development banks (MDBs). However, it has already become the second-largest multilateral institution in the world by membership after the World Bank. Its membership had expanded from 57 founding members in 2015 to 106 approved countries by January 2023, with the African country of Mauritania the latest country to join the bank. The bank's approved member countries account for over 80% of the world's population and 65% of the global gross domestic product (GDP). This is a testimonial to AIIB's evolution from a regional MDB to a global development institution.

The AIIB has been taking an open and inclusive approach towards applications for bank membership since its inception in 2016. The AIIB's success in attracting both developed and developing countries from Asia and beyond is in turn reinforcing the credibility of the bank regionally as well as globally (Bustillo and Andoni 2018). Nevertheless, the United States and Japan have yet to apply for prospective membership of the bank. These two countries view the creation of the AIIB as a challenge from China to the influence of established MDBs such as the World Bank (WB) and the Asian Development Bank (ADB). They have also expressed their concern that the AIIB may not comply with international norms and practices in terms of financing transparency and viability, and environmental, social and labour safeguards.

According to the bank's constitution, the mission of the AIIB is to provide infrastructure financing and technical assistance to developing countries in Asia and to promote greater interconnectivity across the region. The AIIB is not only the world's first MDB dedicated to infrastructure development, but also the first MDB established by China.

H. Yu, *Understanding China's Belt and Road Initiative*, Asia in Transition 26,
https://doi.org/10.1007/978-981-99-9633-9_9

Many developing countries in Asia lack both technological know-how and the financial capacity to raise the tremendous amounts of capital to fund their desperately needed infrastructure projects. Studies by the WB, International Monetary Fund (IMF) and ADB have shown that the low- and middle-income countries still need immense infrastructure financing to unleash their development potential and sustain their growth. For example, an updated estimation report, which was published by the ADB in 2017, pointed out that Asia alone will need over US$26 trillion for infrastructure development from 2016 to 2030 to realize its economic growth potential and improve human welfare (see Table 9.1). The established MDBs simply lack sufficient capital to accommodate the huge infrastructure investment need in Asia, giving China the opportunity to seize the initiative through the AIIB.

China's efforts to establish the AIIB were driven by its dissatisfaction with the lack of reform of the West-led international finance institutions over the past decade. With its growing economic clout and global geostrategic influence, China is now a rising global power. Nevertheless, in China's view, its financial power and economic weight in the world have not been proportionally reflected in the major established MDBs, particularly in terms of decision-making and voting power. China has lacked the discourse power to influence global development financing and international economic governance (Yu 2023). From the Chinese viewpoint, the World Bank, International Monetary Fund and Asian Development Banks are all dominated by the West and aligned too closely with the interests of the United States.

China is hence discontented with the perceived "second-class" treatment and its underrepresentation in the existing MDBs has pushed it to take a two-leg strategy towards the reform of global finance and economic governance. On the one hand, it continually seeks to take a greater role in the established MDBs. Yu's papers (2017a, b) pointed out that China asserts that it is not attempting to overturn the existing

Table 9.1 Estimated infrastructure needs by region, 2016–2030 (US$ billion in 2015 Prices)

Region	Projected annual GDP growth	2030 UN population projection (US billion)	2030 projected GDP per capita (2015 US$)	Climate-adjusted estimates		
				Investment needs	Annual average	Investment needs as % of GDP
Central Asia	3.1	0.096	6202	565	38	7.8
East Asia	5.1	1.503	18,602	16,062	1071	5.2
South Asia	6.5	2.059	3446	6347	423	8.8
Southeast Asia	5.1	0.723	7040	3147	210	5.7
The Pacific	3.1	0.014	2889	46	3.1	9.1
Asia and the Pacific	5.3	4.396	9277	26,166	1744	5.9

Source Asian Development Bank (2017)

international financing governance, but rather to reform it. On the other, China is ceaselessly striving to create its own multilateral development institutions, such as the AIIB and New Development Bank, over which it can exercise greater control and which will better reflect the changing realities of the global balance of power.

China is the founder and largest shareholder of the AIIB, contributing US$29.78 billion and owning 26.58% of the vote. This signals that China has the de facto veto power over key decisions made by the bank, which require a special majority of 75% of the vote, including the amendment of the bank's constitution (Articles of Agreement),[1] membership approval and suspension, drawing up the bank's long-term strategic plans, appointment of the president, increasing capital stock and changing the composition of the bank's board of directors (AIIB 2021). Other major shareholders of the AIIB include India (7.59% of the vote), Russia (5.97%), Germany (4.15%), South Korea (3.49%), Australia (3.45%), France (3.17%), Indonesia (3.16%), United Kingdom (2.89%) and Turkey (2.49%) (see Fig. 9.1).

9.2 The AIIB's "Asian First" Characteristic

The AIIB was created with a strong "Asian first" characteristic (Yu 2023). According to Article 1 of the bank's Articles of Agreement, the mission of the bank is "to improve infrastructure connectivity in Asia by investing in infrastructure and other productive sectors". The design of the AIIB membership structure is distinguished by its balance between regional and non-regional members. Regional members hold 72.8% of the total voting power in the AIIB and non-regional members hold 27.2%.

Meanwhile, the Asian Development Bank (ADB) (with 68 members, 49 from Asia and the Pacific, and 19 from other continents outside Asia), which was founded in 1966, has traditionally been the dominant player in development financing in Asia since its inception. Nevertheless, its regional members hold 65.04% of the ADB's total voting power, while non-regional members hold 34.96%. Therefore, Asian members of the AIIB tend to have more influence than their counterparts in the ADB. In addition, members from Asian countries account for seven of the top 10 shareholders in the AIIB, holding 53.2% of the bank's total votes.

The AIIB's unique governance structure and operational mechanism is reflected in its overwhelming dominance by Asian countries and thus the limited influence of non-regional countries. Compared with other international organizations, the AIIB gives Asian countries a greater say than in the past. Western countries, with their economic power, have usually had majority voting rights on MDBs' boards and councils and dominated their decisions. As argued in Yu's study (2023), the "Asian focus" and "Asian first" characteristic that has been institutionalized within the design of the AIIB will facilitate Asian countries' participation in the decision-making process of the bank and ensure that they have the dominant role in the bank's management and

[1] Articles of Agreement set the legal framework of the AIIB.

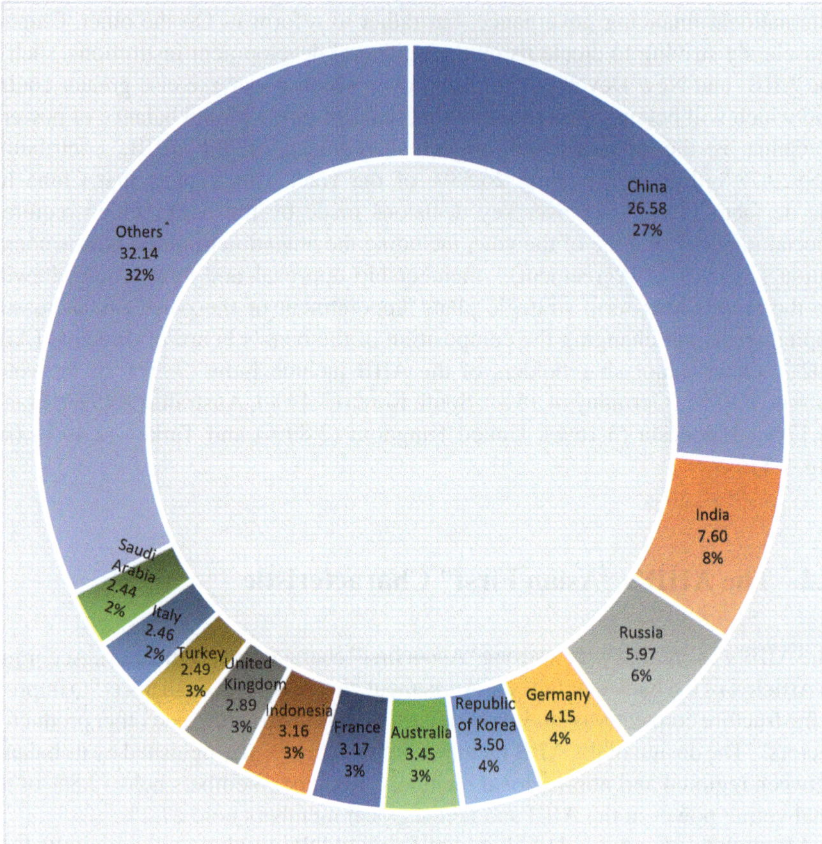

Fig. 9.1 Distribution of voting power among AIIB's members. *Source* AIIB (2022). "Members and Prospective Members of the Bank" available at https://www.aiib.org/en/about-aiib/governance/members-of-bank/index.html, updated on 26 October 2022

operation. This is reinforced by the fact that India, Indonesia and Turkey are the main Asian recipient countries in terms of project quantity and value.

Compared to other MDBs, the governance structure and voting rights arrangements of the AIIB are clearly tilted towards Asian countries. Among the bank's senior management team, its president is a Chinese national, while two among the five vice presidents are also from Asia (see Table 9.2). In addition, among the 11-member AIIB Board of Directors, the bank's highest decision-making body, seven are from Asian countries, namely Saudi Arabia, China, Pakistan, Bangladesh, Vietnam, Indonesia and South Korea. The creation of the AIIB has given Asian countries in general and the developing countries in particular a greater voice and role in regional development financing and infrastructure development.

Table 9.2 List of AIIB's senior management team

Name	Position in the bank	Previous senior position/s Held	Nationality
Jin Liqun	President and Chair of the Board of Directors	Vice President of ADB Vice Minister of the Chinese Ministry of Finance	China
Danny Alexander	Vice President, Policy and Strategy	Chief Secretary to the Treasury of the United Kingdom	United Kingdom
Konstantin Limitovskiy	Vice President, Investment Operations (Region 2)	Deputy Chairman of the Eurasian Development Bank	Russia
Urjit Patel	Vice President, Investment Operations (Region 1)	Governor of the Reserve Bank of India	India
Ludger Schuknecht	Vice President and Corporate Secretary	Deputy Secretary-General at the Organisation for Economic Co-operation and Development, and Chief Economist and Director General of Germany's Federal Finance Ministry	Germany
Luky Eko Wuryanto	Vice President and Chief Administration Officer	Deputy Coordinating Minister for Infrastructure Acceleration and Regional Development	Indonesia
Alberto Ninio	General Counsel	Deputy General Counsel for Operations, World Bank	Brazil
Antoine Castel	Chief Risk Officer	Country Head of Société Générale (SG) in India, and Deputy-CEO of SG in China	France
Andrew Cross	Chief Financial Officer	Deputy Treasurer at the International Finance Corporation	New Zealand
Erik Berglof	Chief Economist	Director of the Institute of Global Affairs, London School of Economics, and Chief Economist of the European Bank for Reconstruction and Development	Sweden

Source AIIB Governance

The bank's charter gives the AIIB's President and management a relatively greater degree of decision-making power, which enables the AIIB to act quickly and efficiently to make real-time decisions on project reserve and project design through to final operation, although its Board of Directors retains the veto power for project approval. The AIIB's governance structure is divided into three tiers: Board of Governors, Board of Directors, and Management. The Board of Directors is the highest authority of the Bank and may delegate certain powers to the Board of Directors and Management in accordance with the AIIB's Articles of Agreement

(Lichtenstein 2018). In contrast to the established MDBs, the AIIB has an unpaid non-resident Board of Directors. MDBs generally have permanent Boards of Directors to manage day-to-day working operations, but these are associated with high costs, low efficiency and bureaucracy.

The day-to-day operations of the AIIB are entrusted to the President and management. Its non-resident Board of Directors meets regularly once a year to deliberate on major issues, such as the AIIB's development strategy, lending policies and standards, but other meetings can be arranged as required. This streamlined approach helps to reduce operational expenditure, enhance operational efficiency and eliminate red tape, thereby freeing up more funds for project investments.

9.3 China's Role in the AIIB

China has played a critical and prominent role in the creation of the AIIB. Xi Jinping, China's President, announced the plan to create the bank during his official trip to Indonesia in October 2013, marking the first such initiative by a non-Western state (Ransdell 2019). Moreover, while the WB and IMF both have their headquarters in Washington DC, the AIIB's headquarters are located in Beijing, China's capital.

By leveraging on the AIIB, China seeks to take a lead in the new wave of Asian regionalism. Its injection of Chinese thinking/ideas and proposals into the establishment of the AIIB has enabled China to contribute to regional economic governance and regionalism in Asia while serving its own national interests.

China has been successful in attracting both developed and developing countries as the "followership" of the bank. The popularity of the AIIB's founding membership proposals and its current membership representing 106 countries worldwide reflect China's important role in a new form of regionalism in Asia.

Despite China leading the establishment of the AIIB and being the largest shareholder, with a de facto veto power, the AIIB does not belong to China. This was clearly acknowledged by the Ministry of Foreign Affairs (2023) in outlining China's official stance on its relationship with the bank:

> China actively plays its role as a shareholder, donor, and host country of the AIIB, follows multilateral rules and procedures, participates in decision-making through multilateral governance mechanisms such as the council and the board of directors, and strengthens communication and coordination with members and management.

In the years since the AIIB's inception, China has seemed intent on downplaying the influence of its voting power in the bank's decision-making mechanism and adhering to its commitment to make decisions on major issues in a multilateral, open and transparent manner on the basis of communication and consultation with relevant parties. Although it is the largest shareholder in the bank, the AIIB lends much less to China than many other member countries, such as India and Indonesia. As of January 2023, the AIIB had approved 15 projects in China, with a total loan commitment of US$3.445 billion.

In June 2023, Bob Pickard, the former Director General for Communications at the AIIB, publicly accused China of political interference in the AIIB's operation and management, and claimed that the bank was controlled by Chinese Communist Party members, who "operate like internal secret police" (Leahy et al. 2023). Following Pickard's accusation, the Canadian government announced that Canada would be halting all government-led activity with the bank and conducting a review. Ms. Chrystia Freeland, Canada's Finance Minister and Deputy Prime Minister, threatened that Canada might even withdraw its membership of the AIIB eventually. In a statement reacting to Pickard's accusation, the bank states that his allegation on the AIIB was baseless, and the AIIB welcomed the review announced by the Canadian government and would be cooperating fully (AIIB 2023a).

However, Bob Pickard has to date not offered any concrete evidence to substantiate this accusation. If the bank were controlled by the Chinese Communist Party and solely serving Chinese interests, the 105 member countries and territories would not have joined the AIIB. The AIIB's website has a comprehensive database listing all currently approved and proposed projects. Since every step of the AIIB project process has to comply with the abovementioned rules, regulations and norms, the bank has to undertake thorough evaluation of the merits, goals, costs and social and environmental impacts of all its projects. In its operations, the AIIB has thus far upheld its commitment to institutional transparency, accountability and openness.

In 2017, the AIIB further enhanced its worldwide credibility by securing short- and long-term triple-A issuers ratings from the three most important international credit rating agencies. Moreover, maintenance of the high standards and best practices required by the WB and IMF could facilitate low-cost borrowing by AIIB from the international capital market, which in turn would help the AIIB to lend at more favourable interest rates (Gu 2017).

Although the AIIB and the BRI were both initiated by China's President Xi Jinping, the AIIB was not created to serve such Chinese interests. Certainly, both the BRI and the AIIB are focused on investment in sectors such as energy, transportation, and telecommunications and promotion of interregional connectivity through regional infrastructure improvement. However, the BRI is China's own initiative, while the AIIB has to abide by internationally recognized standards that require a multilateral approach whereby lending is based on consultation and communication with all member countries. Some BRI-affiliated projects are indeed strategically guided and lack economic viability, but the projects financed by the AIIB have to be financially sustainable, environmentally friendly and welcomed by the local community in the recipient countries. In an interview, the director of the AIIB's Investment Operations Bureau commented as follows (Zhou 2018):

> The AIIB will never invest in 'white elephant' projects, or participate in some projects that consume huge cost resources but have low practicality. On the premise of profit, it serves a practical use for the local society, while not harming the local environment.

There have, however, been claims that the BRI's unilateral implementation approach has resulted in environmental damage, local community opposition, lack of project financing transparency and fair bidding, insufficient consultation with multiple local stakeholders in the BRI countries. A report published by the Asia Society Policy Institute in June 2019 claimed that "... China's laissez-faire approach to infrastructure development makes it easier for Chinese actors to secure project deals and allows developers to benefit by cutting corners and evading responsibility for legal, social, labour, environmental, and other issues". (Asia Society Policy Institute, 2019)

The AIIB Code of Conduct for Bank Personnel clearly states that bank personnel should remain independent from the influence of any governments, organizations and other entities. Meanwhile, China, although precluded from using the AIIB directly as a tool to fulfil its ambitious BRI agenda, is using the bank as leverage in pushing forward the BRI. It is hence not an exaggeration to claim that the AIIB is intended to project China's influence in Asia and beyond, and thereby to facilitate the BRI's implementation. In May 2017, the AIIB, and six other multilateral development banks, including the World Bank, signed the Memorandum of Understanding with China on Strengthening Cooperation in Related Areas under the BRI, aiming to build a stable, diversified and sustainable financing mechanism for the Belt and Road Initiative.

Behind China's efforts to create the AIIB lies an aim to influence developing Asian countries to follow its infrastructure and economic development model. China is Asia's largest economy and has the potential to challenge Japan's position as the traditional leader of economic development in Asia over the past decades.

China's de facto veto power and decisive influence in the AIIB could potentially undermine AIIB's legitimacy as a multilateral development organization if China were to choose to exercise its considerable powers in the bank's operation and management. Nevertheless, it is not in China's interest to undermine AIIB's operations and credibility by intervening in or controlling the bank's operations. China thus far has not made any attempts to do so and it is likely that China will in future continue to exercise restraint in this regard.

Before the creation of the multilateral AIIB, China predominantly provided bilateral financial support for infrastructure development, primarily through the domestic banks. The establishment of the AIIB not only signals China's shift towards a multilateral model for infrastructure investment but also reflects a broad change in its conduct of economic diplomacy.

9.4 The AIIB's Lending Operation in Practice

Since its commencement in January 2016, the AIIB has adhered to the same high international standards, norms and practices as the other established MDBs in its operations and management. Specifically, the AIIB's Board of Directors has successively approved and implemented the "Code of Conduct for Bank Personnel", "Environmental and Social Framework", "Policy on Prohibited Practices", "AIIB Project-affected People's Mechanism", "Procurement Policy" and "AIIB Debarment List",[2] among others, which are all publicly available for reference on the bank's website.

The AIIB had approved a total of 202 projects from 2016 to 2022, amounting to total financing of more than US$38.8 billion, involving sustainable infrastructure construction and green recovery of member economies in the fields of energy, transportation, water, telecommunications, education and public health, with projects located in 33 countries. Despite various challenges to its operations, including the shifting geostrategic environment, the COVID-19 pandemic and China's strict Zero-COVID policy, the bank is rapidly increasing its lending in regional countries.

The AIIB has approved infrastructure development projects ranging from transportation, telecommunications, energy to economic resilience programmes for countries suffering from the effects of the COVID-19 pandemic. The number of projects approved annually by the AIIB rose to 36 in 2022 from 8 in 2016 (Fig. 9.2). In total, the bank had approved 191 projects in 33 member countries, worth over US$36.44 billion, by October 2022, as an indication of China's new approach to international financing and infrastructure development abroad.

The bank is also opening up new positions and conducting new recruitment exercises to attract more infrastructure investment specialists in transportation, energy, water management, telecommunications, and urban development. Currently, there are around 400 full-time staff from over 65 countries working in its headquarters in Beijing. The AIIB aims to double its staff headcount to around 800–900 by 2030.[3]

The working language in the AIIB is English. The vice presidents and senior management team of the bank are very diverse in terms of nationality, background and expertise. According to an AIIB vice president, Chinese nationals account for barely 25% of total bank staff.[4] Although the United States and Japan are non-member states, the AIIB has hired both American and Japanese staff.

The AIIB has implemented several major measures to expand its lending, enhance its lending practices, and mitigate the impacts to its operations brought about by the three-year-long COVID-19 pandemic. Since commencing operations in 2016, the AIIB has been engaging in co-financing of AIIB-approved infrastructure projects

[2] The AIIB Debarment List aims to sanction firms and individuals that have engaged in fraud and corruption in AIIB-financed projects, contracts and activities in violation of the Policy on Prohibited Practices. Firms or individuals in this List would not be eligible to participate in or be awarded a contract in AIIB-financed projects and activities until the expiration of their respective debarment periods.

[3] Interview data with Senior Management member of the AIIB, conducted in July 2019.

[4] Interview data.

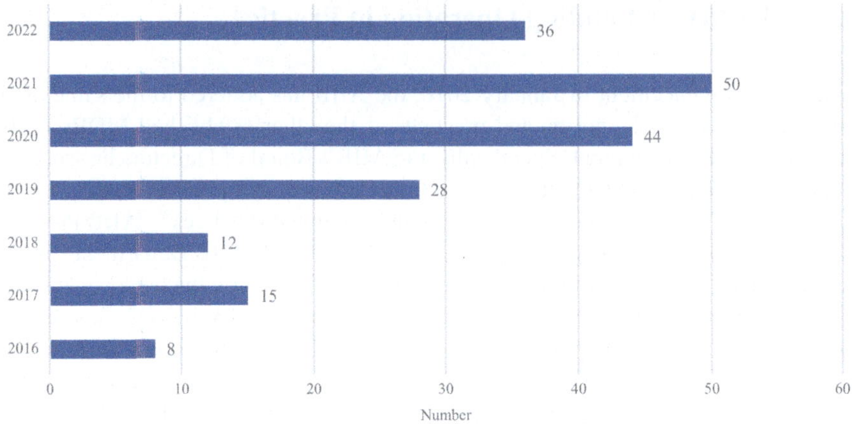

Fig. 9.2 Annual approved projects by the AIIB. *Source* AIIB, 2023b. "Project Summary", status as on 23 June, 2023

by partnering with existing MDBs which already have regional offices in project recipient countries. The AIIB has formed complementary working relationships with many other global and regional MDBs, such as the IMF, the World Bank and ADB, to jointly promote development financing in the region and beyond. On the one hand, cooperation with the established MDBs, governments and enterprises of the recipient countries has enabled the AIIB to diversify its lending risks by sharing the financial burden. Through such co-financing initiatives with other MDBs, the AIIB can draw on and learn from the partnering banks' rich experience in infrastructure financing and potentially avoid their mistakes.

Over 80% of AIIB's project lending practices (19 out of 23 AIIB-approved projects) in the first two operating years involved learning by doing through co-financing with the established MDBs. These initiatives helped the bank to quickly internalize the standards, norms and practices of international development financing which are respected and adhered to by the established MDBs.

On the other hand, engaging in such a co-financing model would allow the AIIB to involve the regional office staff of its partner MDBs in project selection, on-site project monitoring and supervision. The AIIB could use feedback from partnering MDBs within its own assessment of the vitality of its investment projects.

In July 2022, the AIIB's Board of Directors approved the establishment of a regional office in Abu Dhabi, United Arab Emirates (UAE), as the bank's first overseas office. The UAE is one of the fast-growing emerging economies and this new office will help the AIIB expand its investment business and lending operations in the Middle East, Africa and Latin America. Furthermore, having regional offices closer to its clients and front lines of its business could enhance the bank's supervision of its growing investment portfolio and strengthen its project monitoring and local implementation of services.

Another measure adopted by the AIIB to expand its lending was the establishment of the AIIB Project Preparation Special Fund. This offers financial support for borrowers from developing countries with less technical experience in terms of infrastructure project preparation. China, the United Kingdom and South Korea have contributed to the AIIB Project Preparation Fund, which had total assets of US$104.8 million as of 31 March 2019 (AIIB 2019a). This fund has disbursed US$0.3 million and US$0.02 million to Nepal and Pakistan for an urban infrastructure improvement project in the former and water and wastewater management projects in the latter.

The image of the AIIB among the international community has so far been largely positive. Its core values of "Lean, Clean and Green" are reflected in the AIIB's ethical Code of Conduct for Bank Personnel which was adopted in January 2016 and applied to all bank personnel, including the president, vice presidents and the whole senior management team. The AIIB's multilateral approach to infrastructure financing in the region involves commitment to an open tendering process, international competitive bidding and international procurement guidelines.

The AIIB has clearly shown that "flexibility" will not be allowed to creep in and compromise its standards and practices of loan selection and approval procedures. As Jin Liqun (AIIB, 2019b), the AIIB's president, stated during his opening address to the Meeting of the AIIB Board of Governors 2019:

> And – in adherence to our values of being lean, clean and green – we set the bar on a par with the governance structure of other MDBs, …. Quality means selecting projects with high economic returns, designing them well and financing them sustainably. Quality means ensuring that projects benefit the local population, do no harm to people or the environment and leave no chance for corruption. This is what it means to be lean, clean and green.

The increase in the bank's approved projects from 8 in 2016 to 50 in 2021, before slightly decreasing to 36 in 2022 due to the impacts of the global COVID-19 pandemic (Fig. 9.2), demonstrates that the bank is quickly building up its lending capacity. India is by far the largest borrower country by value, accounting for around a quarter of the bank's total loan portfolio, while China, Turkey, Indonesia and Bangladesh are the bank's other major borrowers. Its audited financial report indicates that although it is still in the start-up stage, the AIIB is making decent profit for its shareholders.

The AIIB has since 2018 been shifting towards a model of less reliance on co-financing. This shift implies that the AIIB is becoming more confident in its own lending practices and expanding the geographical footprint of its lending operations. In July 2019, AIIB President Jin Liqun stated that the bank intends to expand the reach of its loan programmes beyond Asia. In January 2022, the bank approved its first project in Brazil to fund Banco de Desenvolvimento de Minas Gerais SA (BDMG) (a Brazilian Development Bank) for the BDMG Renewables and Asia Connectivity Facility. This move indicates that the AIIB is on the right track to become a formidable competitor for the existing West-dominated MDBs in terms of infrastructure financing.

9.5 Moving Forward

In the past, many AIIB project loans were initially proposed and financed by the WB, ADB or the European Bank for Reconstruction and Development and supervised under WB and ADB rules and regulations. The AIIB has contributed additional funding to the existing financing mechanism for regional infrastructure development, but its involvement in such project financing has been merely as a minority or junior partner.

The AIIB still has much ground to make up in terms of its capacity to take a lead in financing regional development. While the AIIB has started to affect the established architecture of infrastructure financing in Asia, it has yet to become a dominant or influential player. For now, the Western countries and their four dominant MDBs (namely the WB, the IMF, the ADB, and the European Bank for Reconstruction and Development) still have relatively firm control of the international financial market.

The New Development Bank (NDB) is a multilateral development bank that was established by Brazil, Russia, India, China and South Africa (BRICS) in 2015, around the same time as the AIIB. The establishment of these two new MDBs resulted from shared geostrategic and geoeconomic dissatisfaction on the parts of China and other BRICS countries regarding the slow reform of an international financial governance system dominated by the West (Hofman and Srinivas 2022). In the eyes of the BRICS leaders, their countries' economic power is rising rapidly, but this is not reflected in the existing international financial and economic architecture, where their interests are underrepresented. Although BRICS countries combined accounted for over 30% of global GDP, they have little say in the way in which established MDBs, such as the WB, IMF and ADB, are run. This dissatisfaction was clearly stated in the III BRICS Sanya Declaration (2011):

> We call for a quick achievement of the targets for the reform of the International Monetary Fund agreed to at previous G20 Summits and reiterate that the governing structure of the international financial institutions should reflect the changes in the world economy, increasing the voice and representation of emerging economies and developing countries.

In 2021, the NDB admitted four new member countries, namely Bangladesh, Uruguay, the United Arab Emirates and Egypt. In comparison to the China-led AIIB, all five founding BRICS countries have equal voting shares in the NDB. The bank has an authorized capital of US$100 billion, which is divided into one million shares that have a par value of $100,000 each. Founding members each had a 20% share of the NDB's capital and were allocated equal shares (see Table 9.3).

Despite China's economy being far larger than those of the other four BRICS countries combined, the NDB shareholding structure provides equal voice to all BRICS countries. As stated in the Agreement on the NDB, the presidency of the bank is rotated among the founding BRICS countries. China's influence in the NDB is expected to be lower than in the AIIB as it has no veto power over the bank's critical decisions. (NDB 2014)

The NDB had approved 74 projects worth US$29.14 billion by December 2021. All of its lending has been to the five BRICS countries, whereas the AIIB had

Table 9.3 Shareholding of the NDB

Member country	Shares (number)	Subscribed capital
Brazil	Shares subscribed: 100,000 Exercisable votes: 100,000	Amount (million USD): 10,000.0 Per cent of total: 19.42%
Russi	Shares subscribed: 100,000 Exercisable votes: 100,000	Amount (million USD): 10,000.0 Per cent of total: 19.42%
India	Shares subscribed: 100,000 Exercisable votes: 100,000	Amount (million USD): 10,000.0 Per cent of total: 19.42%
China	Shares subscribed: 100,000 Exercisable votes: 100,000	Amount (million USD): 10,000.0 Per cent of total: 19.42%
South Africa	Shares subscribed: 100,000 Exercisable votes: 100,000	Amount (million USD): 10,000.0 Per cent of total: 19.42%
Bangladesh	Shares subscribed: 9420 Exercisable votes: 9420	Amount (million USD): 942.0 Per cent of total: 1.83%
United Arab Emirates	Shares subscribed: 5560 Exercisable votes: 5560	Amount (million USD): 556.0 Per cent of total: 1.08%
Total	Shares subscribed: 514,980 Exercisable votes: 514,980	Amount (million USD): 51,498.0 Per cent of total: 100.00%

Notes (1) Exercisable votes reflect status of paid-in capital received as of 24 May 2022; (2) The total per cent of subscribed capital may not add up to 100% due to rounding
Source NDB (2023)

approved a total of 191 projects in 33 member countries, with investments of over US$36.44 billion up to October 2022. The AIIB and NDB's partnerships with other established MDBs complement their efforts to finance regional infrastructure development in the region and beyond.

The AIIB is an ambitious project that demonstrates China's commitment to regional infrastructure financing. As stated by Xi Jinping in 2014, the AIIB's primary task is to finance infrastructure development in Asia, which echoes well the stated mission of the BRI (Yu 2017). Indeed, many projects currently financed by the AIIB are in countries along the Belt and Road routes, which have established friendly and trusted relations with China over the years (Yu 2022).

The AIIB is, however, facing global geostrategic challenges arising from the power rivalry between China and the United States, Russia's war against Ukraine and the deteriorating domestic economic and financing situations in many member countries largely due to the COVID-19 pandemic. Against the backdrop of intensifying power competition between China and the United States, funding of infrastructure by the AIIB is likely in the near future to play an increasingly important role in China's efforts to win over the support of developing countries in Asia and beyond.

The AIIB is a reflection of China's ambitions regarding development financing in Asia. However, in the face of international rules, standards and practices shaped by the West-dominated MDBs, at present it is performing a complementary role in international development financing by partnering with other MDBs and making additional financing contributions (Yu 2023). Compared to its existing MDB peers in general and the WB and ADB in particular, the AIIB's overall approved lending portfolio still has only a relatively small number of investment projects. China consequently still has some way to go before it can credibly claim the leadership role in Asian infrastructure financing.

References

AIIB. 2019a. AIIB Project Preparation Special Fund: Condensed Financial Statements for the Three Months ended March 31, 2019.

AIIB. 2019b. *Opening Address for Meeting of the AIIB Board of Governors 2019.* AIIB President Jin Liqun, 15 July 2019. Available at https://www.aiib.org/en/news-events/news/2019/20190713_002.html. Accessed 18 July 2019.

AIIB. 2022. *Members and Prospective Members of the Bank.* Available at https://www.aiib.org/en/about-aiib/governance/members-of-bank/index.html. Updated on 26 Oct 2022.

AIIB. 2023a. *AIIB Welcomes Canadian Review and Initiatives Internal Review to Ensure Transparency.* Available at https://www.aiib.org/en/news-events/news/2023/AIIB-Welcomes-Canadian-Review-and-Initiates-Internal-Review-to-Ensure-Transparency.html.

AIIB. 2023b. Project Summary, status as at 23 June 2023. Available at https://www.aiib.org/en/projects/summary/index.html.

AIIB, 2021. *Articles of Agreement.* Available at https://www.aiib.org/en/about-aiib/basic-documents/_download/articles-of-agreement/basic_document_english-bank_articles_of_agreement.pdf. Accessed 12 June 2021.

Asia Policy Society Institute. 2019. *Navigating the Belt and Road Initiative*, 1–44. Available at https://asiasociety.org/sites/default/files/2019-06/Navigating%20the%20Belt%20and%20Road%20Initiative_2.pdf. Accessed 18 July 2019.

Asian Development Bank. 2017. *Meeting Asia's Infrastructure Needs*, 1–106. The Philippines. Available at https://www.adb.org/sites/default/files/publication/227496/special-report-infrastructure.pdf. Accessed 17 Jan 2019.

Bustillo, Ricardo, and Maiza Andoni. 2018. China, the EU and Multilateralism: The Asian Infrastructure Investment Bank. *Revista Brasileira de Política International* 61 (1): 1–19.

Gu, Bin. 2017. Chinese Multilateralism in the AIIB. *Journal of International Economic Law* 20: 137–158.

Hofman, Bert, and P.S. Srinivas. 2022. New Development Bank's Role in the International Financial Architecture. *EAI Background Brief*, No. 1660, National University of Singapore, 8 July 2022.

III BRICS Sanya Declaration. BRICS Leaders Meeting, Sanya, China, 14 April 2011. Available at http://brics2022.mfa.gov.cn/eng/hywj/ODS/202203/t20220308_10649517.html. Accessed 7 Nov 2022.

Leahy, Joe, Arjun Alim, and James Politi. 2023. Canada Freezes aAtivity at 'China's World Bank' After Infiltration Claims. *Financial Times.* Available at https://www.ft.com/content/f582dc60-482b-4c9e-821a-958807f80a5c.

Lichtenstein, Natalie. 2018. *A Comparative Guide to The Asian Infrastructure Investment Bank.* Oxford: Oxford University Press.

Ministry of Foreign Affairs of the People's Republic of China. 2023. *China's Relationship with the Asian Infrastructure Investment Bank.* Available at https://www.fmprc.gov.cn/web/gjhdq_676201/gjhdqzz_681964/yzjcsstzyh_700178/gx_700182/.

New Development Bank, 2014. *Agreement on the New Development Bank*, signed on 15th of July 2014. Available at https://www.ndb.int/wp-content/uploads/2022/11/Agreement-on-the-New-Development-Bank.pdf. Accessed 8 February 2024.

New Development Bank, 2023. *Capital Structure and Subscription.* Available at https://www.ndb.int/aboutndb/shareholding/. Accessed 1 September 2023.

Ransdell, James. 2019. Institutional Innovation by the Asian Infrastructure Investment Bank. *Asian Journal of International Law* 9: 125–152.

Yu, Hong. 2017a. *Belt and Road Initiative, the Rise of China and International Cooperation* (in Chinese). Beijing: World Affairs Press.

Yu, Hong. 2017b. Motivation Behind China's 'One Belt, One Road' Initiative and Establishment of the Asian Infrastructure Investment Bank. *Journal of Contemporary China* 26 (105): 353–368.

Yu, Hong. 2022. Is the Belt and Road Initiative 2.0 in the Making? The Case of Central Asia. Journal of Contemporary Asia. Online first. Available at https://www.tandfonline.com/doi/abs/. https://doi.org/10.1080/00472336.2022.2122858. Accessed 29 Oct 2022.

Yu, Hong. 2023. Establishment of the Asian Infrastructure Investment Bank: Is China Taking a Leadership Role in Regionalism in Asia? In *Chinese Regionalism in Asia: Beyond the Belt and Road Initiative*, eds. Tiang Boon Hoo, and Jared Morgan Mckinney, 73–90. Routledge: London and New York.

Zhou, Wenlong. 2018. Pan Yuen, Director of the Investment Operations Bureau: The Goal of the AIIB is to Promote Regional Economic Development. *Lianhe Zaobao*. Available at https://www.zaobao.com.sg/zfinance/news/story20180219-836164.

Chapter 10
Belt and Road Initiative 2.0 in the Making: How Far Can It Go?

The shifting global geopolitical environment amidst the power rivalry between the United States and China and the once-in-century global COVID-19 pandemic have pushed China to rely more on the domestic market, demands and resources for generating economic growth at home. The Chinese central government has for the past few years proposed and implemented a new development paradigm of "dual-circulation" (domestic and international) strategy, which emphasises the domestic market and demands as the primary force to drive development.

Meanwhile, the other side of China's circulation strategy is to open up its domestic economy to the world and to gain wider international market access for the Chinese firms. The Belt and Road Initiative is at the heart of international circulation under this strategy. The international market is crucial to hundreds of export-oriented manufacturing industries located in the Chinese coastal provinces, where millions of Chinese workers working in these industries rely on foreign markets and imports of intermediate goods and materials from abroad.

The completion and subsequent operation of the China-Laos Railway, the Phonon Penh-Sihanoukville Expressway and many other BRI infrastructure projects demonstrate that the BRI remains on track. According to China's Ministry of Commerce (2021), compared to the corresponding figures in 2018 and 2019, Chinese direct investment to the BRI countries recorded modest increases to US$18.1 billion in 2020 and US$20.3 billion in 2021. It indicates that China is still pumping money into the BRI-related projects abroad despite the changing global geostrategic environment and the global COVID-19 pandemic. Nevertheless, compared to when the initiative was initially launched in 2013, many new and complex challenges are facing implementation of the BRI.

Despite China's claims that the BRI is an economic cooperation initiative that will foster economic growth and industrial development for the participating countries, to create trade and investment opportunities and promote stability and peace in the world, the perception of China in general and the BRI in particular throughout the world is becoming increasingly negative. For example, according to a survey report

H. Yu, *Understanding China's Belt and Road Initiative*, Asia in Transition 26,
https://doi.org/10.1007/978-981-99-9633-9_10

by the ISEAS-Yusof Ishak Institute (2020), among member states of the ASEAN attitudes towards China have become increasingly complex and cautious. Most of the Southeast Asian elites surveyed believe that "China is a revisionist power and intends to turn Southeast Asia into its sphere of influence", with 63.6% of the respondents having little or no confidence in China's BRI. Moreover, the Pew Research Centre's Global Attitude Survey on China (2020) shows that the developed Western nations are also adopting increasingly negative attitudes towards China.

Meanwhile, mixed reactions and suspicion regarding the BRI from the participating countries are a product of a lack of trust in China and the motivations behind its push for the initiative. Many BRI countries are unclear as to whether or not the initiative will truly bring a win–win outcome with equal benefits and prosperity for all parties. China therefore needs to take practical steps to adjust its approach to promoting the initiative in response to the new regional and global new geopolitical environment. In the post-COVID-19 era, the international community needs to rebuild to create an open world economy and resilient regional and global industrial chains. And China's participation will be very important.

To achieve sustainability of the BRI, China needs to improve openness and transparency in its overseas infrastructure projects, pay more attention to the sustainability of borrowing in developing countries along the route and consider the long-term fiscal impact of borrowing for infrastructure projects on relevant countries (Yu 2022a). Excessive borrowing could pose a threat to financial sustainability for the borrowing countries. According to Horn et al. study (2019), low-income countries that have encountered huge debt burdens associated with China's BRI investment include Laos, Pakistan, Mongolia, Kyrgyzstan and Djibouti.

10.1 Readjustment of BRI Implementation[1]

China needs to calmly assess the progress made over the past decade since the implementation of the BRI and face up to the challenges. Against the backdrop of mounting pressure and serious challenges faced by BRI implementation, this initiative has reached a crossroads' moment requiring recalibration and readjustment. Given the diversity of BRI countries and their individual domestic conditions, China acknowledges that it is difficult for them to replicate China's own development model centred on domestic infrastructure development.

The construction and operation of BRI projects should fully take into account the feelings of local residents and communities and benefit the people and local communities of countries along the route, so that the BRI projects can truly integrate into those countries. For Chinese enterprises to successfully "go global", they need to accept and adapt to global standards and prevailing international rules, establish sustainable development principles and play the role of responsible investors. They

[1] An initial version of this chapter was first published as an academic article at (Yu 2023).

need to pay equal attention to the economic benefits of their overseas investment projects, the voice of the local community and sustainability of the environment.

In response to the international scepticism and criticisms of BRI implementation, during the second BRI summit in 2019, Xi pledged to deliver a multilateral BRI that would generate benefits for all participating countries. China has made adjustments to its BRI strategy through diversification and expansion of industrial sectors and cooperation areas under the BRI framework. BRI implementation was initially centred on infrastructure financing and construction, but its scope has now been expanded to include areas such as green and digital economy and health care.

10.1.1 Renewable Energy Sector

In order to deliver on its promise of a high-quality BRI, China is planning to build a green Silk Road, pay attention to the ecological protection and natural environment sustainability of countries along the route and minimise the potential environmental impact of investment projects on the BRI countries. In June 2021, China and 28 countries, including Singapore, Thailand and Kazakhstan, jointly launched the BRI Green Development Partnership Agreement, pledging to support the green and low-carbon development of the BRI countries, increase financing for low-carbon and environmentally friendly projects and promote the use and development of renewable energy.[2]

In September 2021, the Chinese authorities pledged not to approve any new overseas coal power generation projects and to vigorously support BRI countries in developing green and low-carbon energy. Chinese enterprises have strong manufacturing capacity and rich experience in the renewable energy sector. China is the world's largest producer of renewable energy equipment (e.g. wind and solar), accounting for 36% and 39% of the world's total solar photovoltaic capacity and total wind power installed capacity, respectively. China will be able to provide renewable energy equipment and transfer relevant technologies to countries along the Belt and Road routes, which will help them in their energy transition.

In addition, the Chinese authorities and Chinese firms have started to incorporate environmentally sustainable objectives into their BRI implementation plans and Chinese firms have started to assess the environmental impact of projects in countries along the BRI route, focus more on financing the construction of low-carbon clean energy projects and promote low-carbon development in BRI countries. China is seeking to place equal emphasis on the economic and environmental sustainability of BRI projects. In September 2021, the Nanoujiang Cascade Hydropower

[2] These countries include Afghanistan, Bangladesh, Brunei, Cambodia, Chile, Colombia, Fiji, Indonesia, Kazakhstan, Kyrgyzstan, Laos, Malaysia, Maldives, Mongolia, Myanmar, Nepal, Pakistan, the Philippines, Saudi Arabia, Singapore, Solomon Islands, Sri Lanka, Tajikistan, Thailand, Turkmenistan, United Arab Emirates, Uzbekistan and Vietnam.

Station in Laos, which was invested and constructed by the China Power Construction Group Co., Ltd., came into full operation. This hydropower station can supply 127.2 million kilowatts of stable and reliable clean energy, which is sufficient to meet more than 12% of Laos' electricity needs. In the process of project construction and operation, Chinese enterprises trained local Laotian technical talents in water resources' utilisation and management, to assist in the transformation of local energy use and promote sustainable development.

Prior to 2019, China's investment in overseas energy projects had been strongly tied up with carbon-intensive fossil fuels such as coal. Coal power generation is the world's single biggest cause of carbon emissions. However, in line with China's plan to cut domestic coal production and the overcapacity of coal-related equipment manufacturing at home, Chinese firms and banks have been willing to finance and build coal-fired power plants abroad. According to the findings of a World Resource Institute report published in 2018, from 2014 to 2017, 95% of overseas energy investments by Chinese state-owned enterprises were in fossil fuels, and 61% of energy-sector loans funded by the China Development Bank and Export–Import Bank of China were also channelled into fossil fuels (Zhou et al. 2018).

According to data from the Council on Foreign Relations (2021), 40% of BRI lending for the energy sector in Pakistan went to coal-fired power plants in 2018, which have had a major effect of increasing local carbon emissions. Many of the BRI energy and transport projects were built without conducting proper environmental impact assessment studies (Yu 2022b), which could generate long-lasting negative environmental consequences for the recipient countries. In response to climate change, Bangladesh, Egypt and some other developing countries have updated their energy development plans to promote energy diversification strategy and restrict new coal-fired power plants.

Meanwhile, leveraging on its strength as the global renewable energy superpower, China is promoting the green BRI by gradually shifting the focus of its overseas energy investments to more renewable power projects. The share of renewables had risen to 57% (or US$11 billion) of China's total energy investment in 2020, compared to the 2019 figures (Nedopil 2021). For example, China sent an official letter to Bangladesh in February 2021 announcing that the Chinese side intends to phase out coal project investment in Bangladesh, including the proposed US$433 million Gazaria 350-megawatt coal-fired thermal power plant (Green Belt and Road Initiative Center April 2021). Given that Bangladesh is one of the world's biggest recipients of coal financing, along with Indonesia, Vietnam, South Africa and Pakistan, and 70% of all coal-fired power plants built in the world today are funded by China, China's announcement to phase out coal investment in Bangladesh is both symbolic and significant. China could be expected to make similar announcements in other BRI countries too.

However, China's endeavour for a clean and green BRI has limitations. Some data convey a contradictory message from the Chinese side regarding BRI-affiliated investments on the energy sector. Although China's investment in renewables has increased, the share of carbon-intensive coal investment in its total energy-sector investment went up to 27% in 2020 from 15% in 2018 (Nedopil 2021). This signals that China has yet to make a decisive move towards investing primarily in environmentally friendly BRI projects. Chinese firms and banks so far have not stopped financing or building carbon-intensive coal-fired energy projects in the BRI countries, despite international calls to stop funding coal-fired power plants. For example, China's State Development Bank has recently financed a coal-fired power plant in Pakistan and the Export–Import Bank of China has funded a new coal investment project in Serbia (Ma et al. 2021).

While China is moving towards developing a green Silk Road and Chinese firms have taken steps towards mediating environmental impact of the BRI projects, conducting due environmental and social impact assessment and mediation is both costly and time-consuming. The extent to which the Chinese side and the participating countries will in the future pursue a sustainable path for BRI implementation by ramping up environmental safeguards remains to be seen.

10.1.2 Health Care

The "Health Silk Road" (or HSR) has become an important part of China's promotion of the BRI since the outbreak of the COVID-19 pandemic. Chinese President Xi Jinping repeatedly said that any vaccine developed and put into use by China would be used for the global public good in the fight against the pandemic. Vaccines, as the ultimate weapon to end the pandemic, had become one of the most sought-after strategic commodities in the world during the pandemic.

China's rapid development of several effective COVID-19 vaccines, mainly comprising Sinovac and Sinopharm vaccines, has become the starting point for China's foreign promotion of the HSR. In 2021, Sinopharm and Sinovac vaccines were successively approved by the World Health Organisation (WHO) as new COVID-19 vaccines for emergency use, and they were also the first two vaccines developed by non-Western countries and to have their safety and efficacy recognised by the WHO.

China has become the world's largest exporter of coronavirus vaccines. Based on the Chinese-made vaccines, China has been actively promoting the Health Silk Road regionwide and worldwide since late 2020. By January 2022, China had exported more than 2 billion doses of COVID-19 vaccines to more than 120 countries (Bridge Consulting, 2022). Chinese vaccine manufacturers are also working with overseas partners to set up overseas filling and production facilities for Chinese vaccines in Indonesia, the United Arab Emirates, Egypt, Malaysia and Brazil. This provides an opportunity to deepen cooperation between China and the BRI countries in the areas of public health and capacity manufacturing.

Expanding its export of coronavirus vaccines will also help China to enhance its soft power and global influence. Furthermore, according to the Lowy Institute's vaccine donation data (2021), China is the second-largest COVID-19 vaccine donor after the United States. The United States had so far donated 91.9 million doses of vaccines abroad, while China had donated 38.9 million doses by 2021.

Other BRI adjustment measures adopted by the Chinese authorities and Chinese companies in the past several years include project refinancing and debt deferment and shifting the focus of third-party market cooperation on energy investment to more environmentally friendly projects such as wind and solar power. Moreover, due to pressure from foreign governments and the local community in the past few years, Chinese firms' business operations and practices in the host countries have become more localised.

Chinese companies' "localisation" strategy in relation to BRI projects covers employee recruitment, raw materials and equipment procurement and revenue contribution. In addition, Chinese enterprises investing and building Belt and Road projects overseas have started to pay more attention to the traditional customs, cultural diversity and differences of countries along the route. Chinese enterprises are taking the initiative to go into the community, fulfil their social responsibilities, engage in dialogue with local people and communities and become integrated into local society as long-term investors and responsible stakeholders.

Another major readjustment to BRI implementation is that China has shown its willingness to take refinance projects in the low-income developing countries. Malaysia's East Coast Rail Link (ECRL) project is such a case in point. The ECRL is a flagship project between China and Malaysia under the BRI, and it is also the largest Chinese investment to Malaysia. China and Malaysia signed the ECRL construction agreement in 2016, and the project was officially launched in 2017 during the then Malaysia's Prime Minister Najib's era.

Faced by heavy criticism and pressure from the then Prime Minister Mahathir's administration regarding lack of openness and transparency of the project design and financing, and the expensive construction cost, China agreed to debt refinancing and project redesign measures for the ECRL project, and financing restructuring arrangements were concluded in 2019. According to this supplementary bilateral agreement, China offered the concession to Malaysia of lowering the construction cost of the ECRL project to RM44 billion, which was roughly 35% of the originally agreed cost. Meanwhile, the total cost of the ECRL project was reduced by roughly 25% after the contract renegotiation, to RM66.02 billion from the original cost of RM85.97 billion (see Table 10.1).

Table 10.1 Cost comparison of the ECRL project

Cost breakdown	Original cost (RM billion)	Amended cost (RM billion)
Construction cost	66.78	44.00
Land cost	7.55	8.92
Project cancellation/suspension cost	N.A	1.00
Interest during construction	11.09	11.70
Operating expenditure	0.55	0.40
Total	85.97	66.02

Source Ministry of Transport, Malaysia

The construction of the ECRL project has been resumed since this financial restructuring. The ECRL case reflects China's flexibility on BRI implementation, in response to doubts over debt sustainability and requests from the low-income recipient countries to lessen their debt burdens (Yu 2019). A lesson that China has learnt from the ECRL project is that changing political sentiments towards the Chinese investments among governments in the BRI countries could pose serious operational challenges and risks to the completion of the infrastructure projects.

In addition, in June 2020, China acted on the G20 initiative to suspend debt repayment "for the poorest countries" by announcing its consent to a temporary suspension of debt repayment (due by the end of 2020) for 77 developing countries and territories. China further supported the extension of the G20's Debt Service Suspension Initiative (DSSI) for the eligible countries to December 2021 (Ministry of Foreign Affairs of China 2021a).

Based on the World Bank/International Monetary Fund's Debt Sustainability Framework for Low-Income Countries, China's Ministry of Finance issued the "Debt Sustainability Framework for Participating Countries of the Belt and Road Initiative" in April 2019. This introduced a form of debt sustainability analysis for the BRI countries, while the Debt Sustainability Framework is non-mandatory.

Chinese authorities, such as the Ministry of Foreign Affairs and Ministry of Finance, claim that China has already offered debt relief in the form of emergency loans and extended loan maturities to the poorest countries affected by the COVID-19 pandemic and domestic economic crises. China also claims that it was the biggest contributor to a programme to temporarily suspend interest payments by borrower countries during the global pandemic.

The need to safeguard domestic financing stability does, however, restrict China's flexibility in refinancing and debt reduction for BRI infrastructure projects. The renegotiation of contracts for BRI projects could have impact in terms of domestic economic slowdown and capital flight that might threaten China's domestic financial stability. The Chinese banking institutions have no intention of writing off debt for the BRI countries, but delaying debt repayment and debt restructuring are open for negotiation. During the annual meeting of the Boao Forum for Asia in April 2021, Hu Xiaolian, then Head of the Export–Import Bank of China, who is one of the largest Chinese creditors for foreign lending, said that China would consider delaying debt repayments for borrower countries which are struggling to repay their debt due to domestic economic crises deriving from the severe impacts of the COVID-19 pandemic. However, China would not offer debt reduction or debt relief for these countries, because it would harm Chinese commercial interests and safety of the Chinese lenders' loans.

Moreover, China is seeking to cooperate with the participating countries and the established multilateral financial institutions to jointly enhance debt management capacity of the borrowing BRI countries, through adopting a flexible approach of "third-party market cooperation" under the BRI umbrella (Ministry of Foreign Affairs of China 2021b). China's MOF has already signed MOUs with various multilateral development banks in order to forge partnerships that will advance progression of the BRI., China's central ministries have also signed such agreements with 14 countries, such as France, Italy, Japan, Switzerland and Singapore, to enhance third-party market cooperation on infrastructure financing and construction in both BRI and non-BRI countries. For example, among these countries, France and Japan have not signed up for the BRI.

Cases of third-party market cooperation between Chinese firms and foreign companies include the following: the State Grid of China and Singapore Power collaborated to co-invest in an energy network project in Australia involving the gas transmission line from Northern Territory to eastern Australia; China Communications Construction Group collaborated with a German firm to build the Maputo-Katembe Bridge and Linkroads Project in Mozambique and China Railway Group cooperated with an Italian firm working on a water supply project in Beirut, Lebanon.

These readjustments to BRI implementation demonstrate that, despite certain limits and restrictions, China can apply adaptability and flexibility. The implementation of the initiative has been evolving over time, and in the future a more open China will play a pivotal role in the world economy. Through the BRI, China and the participating countries will improve interregional connectivity, expand bilateral trade and two-way investment and drive the Chinese economy to become deeply integrated in the global economic system. Expansion of the BRI's circle of friendly countries can create a positive environment for China's international development and help China respond strategically to the changing global geopolitical situation.

Central Asian countries have both geographical proximity and close economic ties with China. Those Central Asian states of smaller size and with limited capabilities have asymmetrical relations with China, their giant neighbour. Proposals for China's contemporary continent-based Silk Road initiatives were first put forward in Central Asia. The Silk Road Economic Belt, which forms the continental component of the Belt and Road Initiative, was launched by President Xi Jinping during a speech at Nazarbayev University in the Kazakh capital in September 2013. Literally, the seeds of the Belt and Road Initiative were sown in Kazakhstan.

Alongside the ASEAN countries, Central Asia is one of the core regions in China's push for the BRI implementation. It is therefore worthwhile examining how the readjustment of BRI implementation is playing out in the Central Asian countries.

10.2 BRI Implementation in Central Asia

Central Asia (see Map 10.1 for the geographical location of Central Asian countries) is recognised as a geographical region that comprises five countries: Kazakhstan, Uzbekistan, Tajikistan, Kyrgyzstan and Turkmenistan. These countries declared independence from the Soviet Union in December 1991. Although they have abundant energy and other mineral resources, Central Asian countries are characterised as having weak economies and underdeveloped industries. Moreover, in many Central Asian countries, political and social instability have been fuelled by rampant corruption and cronyism.

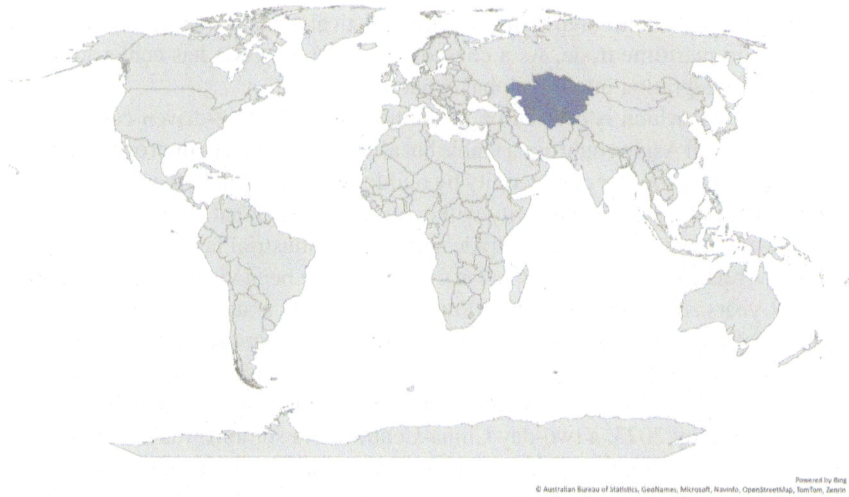

Map 10.1 Location of Central Asian Countries

The unprecedented turmoil in Kazakhstan in the beginning of 2022, sparked by petrol price increases, was a vivid example of the vulnerable and volatile political and social situation in Central Asia. In Almaty, the epicentre of Kazakhstan's unrest, gunfire echoed through the government buildings and streets. Kazakh President Kassym-Jomart Tokayev called the unrest a "Coup attempt". In response to an urgent appeal by President Tokayev, the Russia-led Collective Security Treaty Organisation (CSTO), for the first time since its inception, sent massive numbers of troops to Kazakhstan to help to restore local public order and safeguard critical infrastructure facilities such as airports. The unrest in Kazakhstan was due to more than the petrol price hike, as it can also be attributed to accumulation of political, social and economic problems which have been left unresolved by the government.

Central Asia is one of the key regions for China's neighbourhood diplomacy in general and its push for the BRI in particular. Geographically, Central Asia plays an indispensable role in connecting China with the vast Eurasian continent. Central Asian countries are situated in prime locations in relation to overland trade routes linking East Asia with Europe. China sees the region as a crucial overland passage alternative for the maritime trade to Europe. Access to Central Asia is thus vital in guaranteeing open passage for the Silk Road trade routes. Historically, Central Asia was a key participant in the ancient Silk Road trade until its decline by the mid-fifteenth century. Uzbekistan's Samarkand is an ancient Silk Road city; hence, many Central Asians are familiar with the Silk Road concept and tend to be more amenable to the concept of the BRI.

The geographical isolation imposed by their unique landlocked status has motivated the Central Asian states to welcome and participate in the BRI. A lack of both intra-regional and cross-border connectivities (e.g. insufficient road, rail and air networks) has long constricted the economic development of the Central Asian countries, largely due to high transport and logistical costs for accessing the sea to participate in maritime trade. As a consequence, Central Asia has achieved only a low level of integration into the global economy.

China's BRI, which is centred on promoting infrastructure-driven connectivity, offers the Central Asian countries a viable but affordable option to improve their intra-regional and cross-border connectivity by building transport and other infrastructure projects. The enhanced connectivity will empower the regional countries to unleash their growth potential, to promote trade and pursue industrial take-off.

China's relations with Central Asian countries have been visibly picking up pace in recent years. In September 2022, President Xi made a state visit to the Central Asian countries of Kazakhstan and Uzbekistan. As Xi's first foreign visit since the outbreak of the COVID-19 pandemic in 2020, this trip signals the significance of Central Asia in China's foreign policy and its global diplomatic outreach.

On 18–19 May 2023, a two-day China-Central Asia summit was held in the city of Xi'an, the ancient capital of China and the Eastern starting point of the ancient Silk Road. It was symbolic as the first in-person gathering of such kind since diplomatic relations were established between China and the five Central Asian nations in 1992. It was attended by China's President Xi Jinping and the presidents from all five Central Asian countries.

The China-Central Asia summit was replete with symbols of the ancient Silk Road. The venue chosen for the summit was Tang Paradise, a large theme park with buildings and gardens incorporating elements of the Tang Dynasty (618–907 BC), during which period the ancient Silk Road arguably reached its zenith. This clearly signalled China's President Xi Jinping desire to convey to the Central Asian leaders that the historical bond between China and Central Asia under the ancient Silk Road should not only be cherished but revived under the BRI.

During the summit, Xi Jinping pledged to offer RMB26 billion (about US$38 billion) in a package comprising both financing support and grants in order to promote bilateral cooperation between China and the Central Asian countries under the BRI umbrella and support those nations' domestic development (Ministry of Foreign Affairs of the People's Republic of China 2023a). As stated in the China-Central Asia Summit Xi'an Declaration, the Central Asian leaders endorsed China's greater engagement with the region under BRI implementation (Ministry of Foreign Affairs of the People's Republic of China 2023b). This summit is perceived as a diplomatic victory for China and a major achievement for its outreach endeavour under the BRI. The Chinese and Central Asian leaders agreed to institutionalise their summits and hold meetings every two years, hosted alternately by the six countries. The second summit will be held in Kazakhstan in 2025. Beijing is expected to gain much from its deepened relations with the Central Asian nations, while both Moscow and Washington struggle to match Beijing's investment commitment to the region.

As reflected in the summit's joint declaration, the bilateral cooperation between China and Central Asia is multidimensional, focusing mainly on connectivity, trade and economic aspects, but also covering cultural and people-to-people exchange, agricultural development, national capacity building, security and the high-tech sector. Nevertheless, while the joint declaration was heavy on pledges and rhetoric, it was short on concrete projects and action roadmaps. The leaders agreed to speed up work on the planned construction of China-Kyrgyzstan-Uzbekistan (CKU) railway, which could become a flagship project in Central Asia under the BRI. The geological survey for this railway construction plan was completed in October 2022. On the one hand, the construction of the CKU railway will facilitate the exports of Chinese-made products to the markets of the Middle East, Iran, Turkey, the Caucasus and Europe by shortening transport distance and reducing logistics cost. On the other, the railway will help to transform the landlocked region of Central Asia into a transcontinental transport hub connecting East Asia, South Asia, the Middle East and Europe.

New geopolitical realities in Central Asia are unfolding, whereby Chinese influence is rapidly growing in the region via the BRI implementation. Beijing's pursuit of close partnerships with Central Asia forms part of China's broader plan to deepen political, economic and security relations with the BRI countries within a new multipolar world order that could counter the United States-led global order. Due to the growth of China's global influence, Kazakhstan, Uzbekistan, Tajikistan, Kyrgyzstan and Turkmenistan all anticipate reaping economic benefits from spillover to the region of China's rapid development dividend. The Central Asian countries also view the BRI as offering an alternative to the conventional Russian domination of the region's political, economic and strategic spheres.

The BRI could be instrumental in facilitating cross-border trade and investment across the Belt and Road countries through its focus on infrastructure connectivity improvement. Baniya et al. (2019) showed that the BRI-linked transportation projects, through improvement of economic corridors, could increase the total amount of exports among the participating countries by 4.6% and by 7.2% when border delay issues are reduced.

BRI implementation in Central Asia has also increased China's access to resources that it needs to power economic growth at home, since the Central Asian countries have abundant reserves of oil, gas, gold, coal and other mineral resources. For example, 21% of China's imports of zinc and lead come from the Central Asia region (Umarov 2020).

Central Asia is situated in the key node for the China–Europe Railway Express, which is a flagship project for overland connectivity under the BRI. All routes of the China–Europe Railway Express service will have to pass through Kazakhstan before heading towards other Eurasian countries as well as Europe. According to a Ministry of Commerce of China source (2022), the number of trains increased from 80 in 2013 to 12,406 in 2021, with the numbers of outbound and return trips becoming more balanced (Fig. 10.1). By 2021, the capacity of train cargo shipments had risen to 1.46 million TEUs. The Railway Express is thus emerging as a viable transportation means for trade on the Eurasian continent.

Despite the Central Asian nations having abundant agricultural, energy and other mineral resources, realisation of their development potential has been hampered by the low level of intra-country and intercountry infrastructure connectivity. All Central Asian states are landlocked and geographically isolated with the outside world. From the Central Asian perspective, their geographical isolation attributed by their landlocked condition drives the Central Asian countries to embrace the BRI,

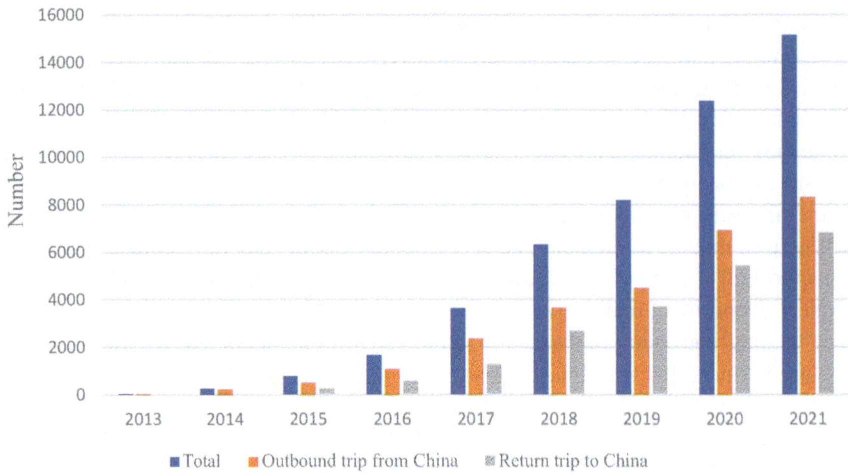

Fig. 10.1 Operation of the China–Europe Railway Express. *Sources* Office for the CCP Central Leading Group for BRI and State Railway Corporation of China (2021)

which promises for better connectivity, trade opportunities and access to the huge Chinese market. Enhanced connectivity will be crucial to unleash economic growth potential of landlocked Central Asian countries. A lack of connectivity, including infrastructure underdevelopment and the relatively high transport and logistics costs, constraints the economic development of the regional countries in Central Asia.

The BRI-affiliated infrastructure projects will help the Central Asian countries to develop new trading routes (via Afghanistan, Pakistan and China) and thus to diversify their trade. Central Asian countries are keen to circumvent Russian hegemony by reducing the trade and economic dependence on Russia since their independence.

Enhanced intra-regional connectivity through the development of roads, railways, civil aviation and telecommunication facilities under the BRI cooperation framework will also help to boost regional economic integration among the Central Asian countries.

Pursuit of enhanced connectivity and developing new trade routes have dominated the geopolitical and geoeconomic calculations of the Central Asian countries to embrace the BRI for the past decade. The rail and road network, civil aviation and telecommunication facilities are all badly needed to upgrade and improve. According to the World Economic Forum (2019), Central Asian countries (e.g. Tajikistan and Kyrgyzstan) lag behind many other countries in global rankings on infrastructure readiness. Improvement of transportation and other infrastructure in the Central Asian countries is essential in order to overcome their landlocked geographical disadvantage, boost local economic growth and increase their participation in regional as well as global trade networks.

In addition, Central Asian nations aspire to increasing their manufacturing capacity in such as the textile and garments, food processing and transport equipment industries, but they need investment, technology and management skills and expertise in order to make meaningful inroads. Based on China's strength in the infrastructure construction sector, Central Asia views China as a much-needed source of foreign investment for improving the region's infrastructure connectivity. Numerous China-funded large-scale transport and other infrastructure projects have either been completed or are under construction in the region, including highways, bridges, power plants, tunnels and airport upgrading.

Meanwhile, from a security perspective, China views Central Asia as crucial to safeguarding national security in its Western Region in general and Xinjiang in particular. Kazakhstan, Tajikistan and Kyrgyzstan share a 3300-km border with Xinjiang, which is arguably the region of China most beset by domestic security and stability problems.

Xinjiang is a highly sensitive issue in China's relations with the Central Asian states. There are roughly 1.5 million ethnic Kazakhs, 180,000 ethnic Kyrgyz, 50,000 ethnic Tajiks and 10,000 ethnic Uzbeks living in Xinjiang (Umarov 2020). Understandably, Central Asians feel a strong ethnic and religious kinship with the Uyghurs. The China image and its reputation in Central Asia have been somehow damaged since the early 2010s following the tightening up security measures and policies against the ethnic minorities in Xinjiang, including Uyghurs, Kazakhs, Kyrgyz and Tajiks. Although the respective governments in the Central Asian states insist that the Xinjiang issue is an internal matter for China, many in Central Asia have criticised Beijing's heavy-handed ethnic policies in Xinjiang and its harsh and discriminative treatment of the Uyghur minority, with some going further by waging protests.

Almaty is the largest and the most populous city in Kazakhstan and Centra Asia as a whole. It is also merely 350 km away from Xinjiang. China has watched the developments in Kazakhstan closely, since maintaining stability in Kazakhstan is vital for access to the Silk Road routes, and the safety of the China-funded projects and Chinese personnel in Kazakhstan. On 7 January 2022, President Xi sent a verbal message to Kazakh President Tokayev, demonstrating solidarity with the Kazakh regime, in which he stated, "China firmly opposes any deliberate attempt by external forces to provoke unrest and instigate 'colour revolutions' in Kazakhstan, as well as any attempt to harm the China-Kazakhstan friendship and disrupt the cooperation between the two countries" (Ministry of Foreign Affairs of China January 2022).

China, Kazakhstan, Tajikistan, Uzbekistan and Kyrgyzstan, together with Russia, are the founding members of the Shanghai Cooperation Organisation (SCO), which is a Eurasian political, economic and security alliance founded in June 2001. For the past 20 years, China has conducted joint military exercises and military training with armies from Russia and the Central Asian countries under the provisions of the SCO framework. China has also supplied security equipment to Central Asian countries such as Tajikistan.

Although China has become the largest trading partner as well as an important source of foreign investment for the Central Asian countries, gradually displacing Russia's economic dominance in the region, it is not currently able to challenge Russia's military and security clout in Central Asia. China is merely able to react to events taking place there, as reflected from the case of turmoil in Kazakhstan. The five Central Asian countries still have strong historical connections to Moscow, and Russia will continue to be their dominant military partner and security guarantor for the foreseeable future.

10.3 China's Economic Ties with Central Asia: Development and Issues

Discrepancy between China and the Central Asian countries' data on customs figures, mainly due to official corruption and the existence of a sizeable shadow economy, makes it difficult to estimate the actual bilateral trade volume. Nevertheless, without doubt, China's trade ties with Central Asian countries have been strengthening over the past decade and the BRI trade routes are playing an important role in boosting bilateral merchandise trade between China and Central Asia.

In 2022, according to data published by the Ministry of Commerce of China (2021), China's total trade volume with the five Central Asian countries amounted to US$70.2 billion, with China enjoying a trade surplus. China has become the largest trading partner for Uzbekistan, Kyrgyzstan and Tajikistan and the second-largest trading partner for Kazakhstan. Except for Turkmenistan (which exports large volumes of natural gas to China under the bilateral energy agreement), in 2019, the Central Asian countries all had trade deficits with China, though the situation varies from country to country.

China's trade with Central Asia accounts for a small fraction of the former's total foreign trade. While China's trade dependence on Central Asia is extremely low (Central Asia accounted for merely 1% of China's total volume of trade in goods in 2019), China is among the Central Asian region's most important trading partners. In 2019, 22% of the Central Asian countries' exports went to China, while 37% of their imports came from China. China enjoys a huge trade surplus with the countries in Central Asia, but the latter's trade deficit has increased over the years. Energy and mineral resources and agricultural raw materials still dominate the Central Asian countries' exports to China, while their imports from China mainly include China-made household appliances, machinery, electronics and telecommunication equipment (see Table 10.2). This asymmetrical trade relationship is detrimental to Central Asia's pursuit of industrialisation, and it is not sustainable.

Central Asia's economies are highly dependent on the energy and mineral extraction sectors. They need to diversify in order to accelerate economic growth. The economic diversification strategy long pursued by the respective governments in Central Asian countries has so far achieved little progress. The five Central Asian states all still have large agricultural sectors and weak manufacturing industries, in addition to outdated infrastructure facilities and limited exposure to global value chains.

According to the "Chinese Global Investment Tracker" data, from 2013 to 2022, the value of the accumulated volume of Chinese investments and China-funded

Table 10.2 Decoding the trade commodity structure between Central Asia and China

Country	Chinese exports	Chinese imports
Uzbekistan	Electronics; household appliances; plastic products	Gas; natural uranium; cotton
Turkmenistan	Electronics; textiles and apparel products; chemical products	Gas; minerals; cotton; woollen products
Tajikistan	Textiles; household appliances; electronics	Minerals; gold; aluminium; cotton; leather
Kyrgyzstan	Textile; household appliances; electronics; leather	Copper; leather; mineral
Kazakhstan	Household appliances; textile and apparel products; electronics	Oil; natural gas; mineral

Source Compiled by the author

projects in Central Asia was US$12.4 billion. Kazakhstan is the top destination for Chinese outbound investments to Central Asia under the BRI. The volume of Chinese investments and China-funded projects in Kazakhstan was worth US$9.19 billion between 2013 and 2022, accounting for 74.1% of China's total investment in Central Asia. The volume of Chinese investments and contracts in Uzbekistan amounted to US$1.27 billion during the same period, accounting for 10.2% of China's total investment in Central Asia. In contrast, the other three Central Asian states combined accounted for only 15.7% of Chinese outbound investment to the region during the same period (Fig. 10.2).

Thus, most of these Chinese investments in Central Asia were directed into joint ventures in the industrial sectors of oil, natural gas, mining and infrastructure construction. For example, the China National Petroleum Corporation (CNPC)

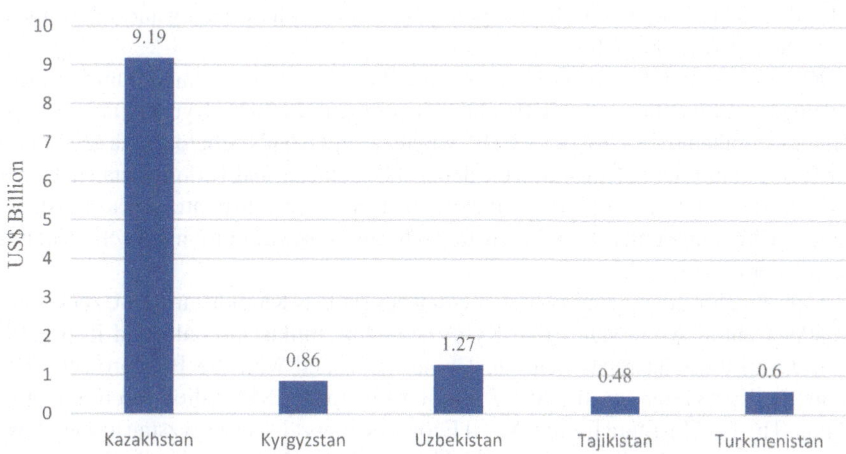

Fig. 10.2 China's investments and contracts in Central Asian Countries between 2013 and 2022. *Source* American Enterprise Institute (2023), "China Global Investment Tracker"

is one of the largest foreign investors in Kazakhstan. It has engaged in the acquisition, exploration and production of oil and gas, as well as in the sale of oil and refined products. Meanwhile, another Chinese mining firm, Zijin Mining, holds a 75% share in Zarafshon Joint Venture, which operates in Tajikistan's Penjikent Region and mines nearly 70% of the volume of gold produced in the country annually (Asia-Plus 2020).

While Chinese investment in Central Asia has been shoring up local manufacturing, its impact in terms of developing the local workforce via skills training has been limited. The fact that Chinese firms have brought in many Chinese workers with them indicates a need to create more jobs for the locals. Indeed, the rapid influx of Chinese workers to Central Asia as a result of Chinese investment has generated negative perceptions and anti-Chinese resentment in the local society. The locals' concern about the disproportionate use of immigrant Chinese employees in the China-funded projects and Chinese companies provoked anti-China protests of various scales in Kazakhstan and Kyrgyzstan in 2018 and 2019, respectively (see Gerber and He 2022).

The Chinese investment that flowed into the Chinese firms was also used to purchase Chinese-made equipment and intermediary goods, as well as to hire Chinese workers to carry out project construction and business operations in Central Asia. During a meeting with the senior management team of the CNPC in November 2019, Kazakhstan's President Tokayev expressed rare concern over the low wages of Kazakhstani workers employed by CNPC. In addition, he asked for the share of Kazakhstani content in the CNPC's procurement of goods and services to be increased (Office of the Prime Minister of the Republic of Kazakhstan 2019).

Publicly available information on Chinese investments to the Central Asian countries is limited. There is a lack of transparency on the specific details of projects, for example, project financing and loan repayment structure, project operation and management. The Export–Import Bank of China and State Development Bank are the two major Chinese financial institutions for providing loans in Central Asia for BRI-related projects. These two Chinese policy banks are both owned by and subordinate to the State Council of China.

Kyrgyzstan and Tajikistan have become the two Central Asian countries most indebted to China due to the BRI-related investment. In 2021, Kyrgyzstan's debt to China accounted for 30.5% of its GDP, whereas Tajikistan's debt to China accounted for 16.1% of its GDP. Meanwhile, the debts of Uzbekistan and Turkmenistan to China accounted for 16.0% and 13.1% of their GDP, respectively. In contrast, Kazakhstan's debt to China amounted to 6.5% of its GDP, the lowest figure among the Central Asian nations (Fig. 10.3).

Consequently, compared to bigger countries such as Kazakhstan and Uzbekistan, smaller Central Asian states like Kyrgyzstan and Tajikistan could find it difficult to keep up the loan repayments to China associated with the BRI projects. For example, Kyrgyzstan owed US$1.7 billion of its total US$4 billion foreign debt to China. The Kiel Institute for the World Economy report lists Kyrgyzstan among low-income countries that have encountered huge debt burdens associated with China's BRI investment. In addition, Tajikistan's debt owed to China was US$1.38 billion, accounting for almost 50% of Tajikistan's total external debt (See Horn et al. 2019).

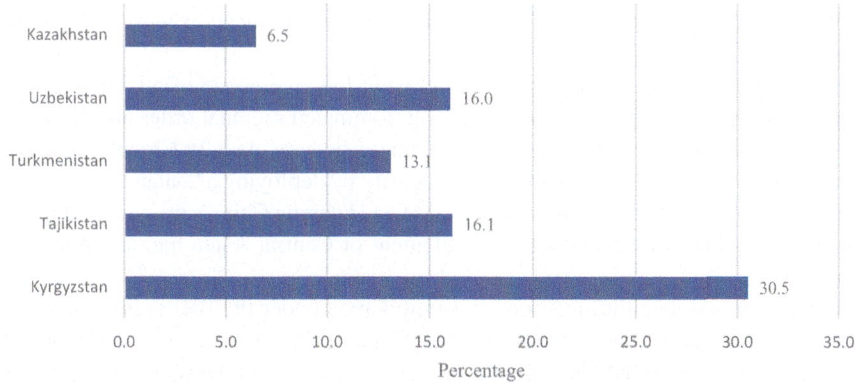

Fig. 10.3 Ratio of Central Asian countries' accumulated debt to China to their GDP in 2021. *Source* Author's own compilation and calculation based on the individual country information available

The BRI-linked projects in Central Asia are still lacking in transparency. Key financial details of many BRI-linked infrastructure projects have been kept from public oversight, including the terms of their loan structure and the length of the lease. Furthermore, the Central Asian countries are vulnerable to debt distress related to the BRI projects. As the case of Central Asia demonstrates, the smaller the country and the closer it is to China geographically, the more it will be indebted to China.

Given China's aim to enhance its international image through its push for BRI implementation in the region and beyond, it has no desire to deliberately drive the recipient countries into a debt trap or force them to borrow from China. However, if these issues are left unaddressed, they could make difficult for China to win the hearts and minds of locals and deter the Central Asian countries from cooperating fully with China's BRI in the future. They could also potentially jeopardise the BRI by fostering strong opposition to the China-funded projects under its umbrella.

The anti-China protests sparked in several Central Asian countries reflect both scepticism and a lack of trust among the local community in the region over China's push for the BRI. China has to do more in order to convince the Central Asian countries that implementation of BRI is a win–win situation for both parties.

China looms large in the region through the BRI platform, which is shoring up China's political and economic influence. China is becoming the most influential external power in Central Asia, although Russia still maintains strong political, cultural and defence ties in the region as a legacy of the Russia-led Soviet Union. Although China and Russia are competing for influence in the region, it is in both countries' interests to maintain stability in Central Asia.

There is concern among the Central Asian countries that they could become too economically dependent on China through BRI implementation and eventually lose autonomy over their foreign policy by being forced to adopt pro-China diplomacy. The Central Asian countries do not want to be drawn into China's orbit of development; neither do they want to be seen as passive recipients of China's BRI implementation, due to lack of consultation and communication with the Central Asia side.

The Central Asian countries wish to prevent the emergence of a China-centric regional order that might replace the Russia-dominated regional order and are keen to avoid tilting too far towards any of the major powers, namely China, Russia or the United States. Safeguarding national security by deploying a "balance of power" strategy of putting their national interests first and keeping China's growing influence in check has become an indispensable element of Central Asian nations' relations with China.

Therefore, while building strong ties with China under the BRI is important for the Central Asian nations in order to attract Chinese investment and technology and gain better access to the Chinese market, building on relations with other powers including Russia, the United States, European Union, Japan, India and South Korea is equally crucial. Hedging their bets by diversifying their foreign relations is the best option for the Central Asian countries in responding to the intensifying rivalry between the major powers and mounting pressure to choose sides.

10.4 Readjustment of BRI Implementation in Central Asia

Pressure from overseas authorities and citizens, including in the Central Asian countries, to increase provision for local manufacturing industries, local jobs and tax revenue has led China to make several major readjustments to the BRI and the related project implementation in Central Asia since 2019. A Joint Communique of the Leaders' Roundtable of the Belt and Road Forum (BRF) was released immediately after the second BRF. The Joint Communique emphasised the need for high quality of infrastructure projects, debt sustainability, project transparency and environmental sustainability and respect for internationally accepted practices, norms and standards (The Second Belt and Road Forum for International Cooperation 2019).

First, there has been a gradual shift of Chinese investment in the region, from the energy and mining sectors to agriculture and industries. China has started to do more to help Kazakhstan, Kyrgyzstan, Tajikistan and Uzbekistan to industrialise by setting up manufacturing and developing processing plants for raw materials. In addition, Chinese firms are helping to modernise textiles, cement, steel and glass factories in Tajikistan, Kyrgyzstan and Uzbekistan.

As well as building local industrial capacity and localising the workforce, Chinese firms are helping to upgrade local workers' skills through training. In Tajikistan, some Chinese companies have steadily increased their local hires and skills' training for local workers both onsite and in China. For example, 97% of CNPC's workforce and 80% of Huawei operations workforce are locals (Klev and Yau 2021). In May 2021, during a meeting with the foreign ministers of the five Central Asian countries in China's Xi'an city, China's State Councillor and Foreign Minister announced that China would further support upskilling of the local workforce by setting up a vocational training centre called the "Luban Workshop" (named after a legendary

Chinese craftsman) in each of the five Central Asian countries over the next three years (Ministry of Foreign Affairs of China May 2021c). In November 2022, Tajikistan Luban Workshop, the first Luban Workshop established in Central Asia, was put into operation (Luban Workshop 2022). It focuses on skills training in the renewable energy and civil engineering sectors for local Tajikistan students through targeted training courses designed by China and taught by the Chinese teachers using Chinese teaching equipment.

To enhance the "localisation" of the BRI projects, China has already opened 11 Luban workshops in Thailand, Pakistan, Kenya and a few other countries since 2016. A report issued by the Lowy Institute in May 2021 states that since 2019, the Chinese-aided and Chinese-built overseas projects have become more localised in terms of local job creation, and local tax revenue contribution, citing country cases including Tajikistan.

Second, while the BRI was centred on large-scale infrastructure financing and construction in the earlier phrase, its scope has now been expanded to include domains such as digitalisation and health. By leveraging on its advanced digital technology and its leading tech firms, China intends to use the Digital Silk Road (DSR) to cement its position as a leading international technological power through increasing digital access among the urban and rural populations of developing countries via the BRI platform.

Digital network infrastructure plays a pivotal role in the development of modern industries and economies, and safeguarding national economic and defence security. There are only a handful of firms in the world capable of providing 5G network infrastructure, China's Huawei being one of them. A substantial amount of the telecommunication network hardware in the BRI countries, such as data processing equipment, has been provided by Huawei, ZTE and other Chinese tech firms due to their products being competitive in terms of both cost and quality.

Although the Chinese government has not clarified in detail the structure and role of the DSR, Chinese tech firms such as Huawei and ZTE are already investing in digital infrastructure and related industries across the globe, including 5G cellular networks, fibre-optic cables, big data, cloud computing, artificial intelligence and satellite navigation systems (its own Beidou system). China is engaged in digital infrastructure projects in 80 countries, with the value of the projects amounting to US$79 billion (Cheney 2019).

In 2019, Uzbekistan signed a cooperation agreement with Huawei, China's leading tech company, to launch development of digital infrastructure facilities and surveillance capability for government agencies, including law enforcement bodies. In addition, in 2019, Uzbekistan used loans from China to purchase Huawei technology with a value of US$150 million to upgrade its cellular networks (ITUC 2021).

A third area in which China is actively promoting the HSR is through what is commonly known as its Vaccine Diplomacy. Central Asia's already difficult economic situation was worsened by the COVID-19 pandemic. In response, China has already delivered over 37 million doses of Chinese-made vaccines to the Central Asian countries, the majority of which were delivered under sales agreements with the respective countries. Uzbekistan is the largest recipient country of Chinese vaccines

Table 10.3 China's COVID-19 vaccine delivery to Central Asian countries (in million doses)

Country	Total delivered	Purchased	Donated
Uzbekistan	26.99	26.99	0
Kazakhstan	4.50	4.50	0
Kyrgyzstan	4.15	2.35	1.80
Tajikistan	2.30	2.0	0.30
Turkmenistan	0	0	0
Total	37.94	35.84	2.10

Source Bridge Consulting (2022)

in Central Asia, whereas Turkmenistan has so far not ordered any vaccine from China. In terms of vaccine donation, only 2.1 million doses of Chinese-made COVID-19 vaccine have been donated to Central Asia, of which Kyrgyzstan received 1.8 million doses and Tajikistan 0.3 million doses (Table 10.3).

Given China's growing clout in Central Asia, it is hard to imagine the countries in the region achieving future development without cooperation with China. China claims that the goal of the BRI is to pursue high-standard, transparent, shared, green and sustainable development in partnership with the recipient countries. While China has made some major readjustments to BRI implementation in Central Asia since 2019 in response to local demands and criticism regarding its outreach approach and business practices, the BRI in Central Asia has not yet become the global initiative based on high standards of transparency, environmental and financial sustainability and shared development that was promised by China.

10.5 Conclusion

The Central Asian nations are situated in prime locations along overland trade routes linking East Asia with Europe and China with the vast Eurasian continent. Through opening up the vital Silk Road trade routes, BRI implementation has helped to expand China's economic interests and influence in Central Asia.

In the light of China's asymmetrical economic relations with the various Central Asian countries, these countries will need to walk a tightrope of maximising the economic and infrastructure development benefits of the BRI while minimising the threats to national sovereignty and risk of social backlash. Central Asia's strategic location at the crossroads between Europe and Asia means that the Central Asian states are having to find a balance in the face of competition for regional influence among the world's great powers.

China's push for the BRI in Central Asia has met with both challenges and resistance. Many BRI projects lack transparency as well as proper consultation and support from the local community. Moreover, the existing high debt stress in several regional countries, attributed to the financing for the BRI-related projects, could potentially jeopardise future cooperation by the Central Asian countries with the BRI.

BRI implementation is based on a China-centric approach, rather than being a credible multilateral endeavour, as claimed by the Chinese government. As shown in the case of Central Asia, the BRI is built on bilateral deals, with no multilateral involvement in overseeing the BRI or making investment decisions. The anti-China protests in several Central Asian countries in 2018 and 2019 reflect both strong suspicion and resentment among the local community in the region over China's push for the BRI.

Despite its attempts to localise BRI implementation in the face of local pressure, China has yet to convince the Central Asian countries that the BRI is a win–win situation for both parties. There is currently a lack of any vigorous internal review or public debate on BRI implementation within the Chinese society or among public intellectuals and business elites. It therefore remains to be seen how far China is willing to go with this readjustment process in the long run.

China should work together with the Central Asian countries to build a high-quality Belt and Road Initiative, based on mutual openness and cooperation. Multilateralism is the only effective way to boost the transparency and credentials of the BRI and achieve equal benefits for all parties.

Moreover, the Chinese companies should shift their focus from building large-scale infrastructure projects in Central Asian countries towards working with local partners on "small but beautiful" projects. These projects, including such as rural roads, bus stations, electricity transmission plants, water wells and rural telecommunications networks, should be primarily aimed at improving the people's living standards and helping the local community to share in the benefits of economic development. These smaller projects are more visible to the local community and could help to enhance local people's sense of gain under the BRI cooperation framework.

Although BRI implementation in Central Asia will be affected by the Chinese economic slowdown and the shifting global geostrategic environment, China is likely to persist in its determination to push for the BRI. This ambitious initiative is important for the Chinese economy at home and gaining global market access for the Chinese firms and Chinese-made goods and is even more significant for China's pursuit of its geopolitical and geoeconomic ambitions.

References

American Enterprise Institute, 2023. *Chinese Global Investment Tracker*. https://www.aei.org/china-global-investment-tracker/. Accessed 15 May 2023.

Asia-Plus. 2020. Resources and Facilities: How Much has China Gone into Tajikistan? https://asiaplustj.info/ru/news/tajikistan/politics/20200111/resursi-i-obekti-naskolko-kitai-uglubilsya-v-tadzhikistan. Accessed 16 Jan 2022.

Baniya, Suprabha, Nadia Rocha, and Michele Ruta. 2019. *Trade Effects of the New Silk Road: A Gravity Analysis*. World Bank. http://documents.worldbank.org/curated/en/623141547127268639/pdf/WPS8694.pdf. Accessed 29 Apr 2019.

Batsaikhan, Uuriintuya, and Marek Dabrowski. 2017. Central Asia—Twenty-Five Years After the Breakup of the USSR. *Russian Journal of Economics* 3 (3): 296–320.

Bridge Consulting. 2022. *China Covid-19 Vaccine Tracker*. https://bridgebeijing.com/our-publications/our-publications-1/china-covid-19-vaccines-tracker/. Accessed 7 Feb 2022.

Burna-Asefi, Sophia Nina. 2022. Uzbekistan Looks South foe New Trade Routes. *The Diplomat*. Available at https://thediplomat.com/2022/04/uzbekistan-looks-south-for-new-trade-routes/. Accessed 15 July 2023.

Cheney, Clayton. 2019. China's Digital Silk Road: Strategic Technological Competition and Exporting Political Illiberalism. *Pacific Forum Working Paper* 8 (19): 1–23.

Council on Foreign Relations. 2021. *China's Belt and Road: Implications for the United States*. Independent Task Force Report No. 79. https://www.cfr.org/report/chinas-belt-and-road-implications-for-the-united-states/. Accessed 20 Jan 2022.

Gerber, Theodore P., and Qian He. 2022. Sino-Phobia in Russia and Kyrgyzstan. *Journal of Contemporary China* 31 (133): 38–56.

Green Belt and Road Initiative Center. April 2021. *China's Coal Investments Phase-Out in BRI Countries—Bangladesh Case*. https://green-bri.org/chinas-coal-investments-phase-out-in-bri-countries-bangladesh-case/. Accessed 5 Feb 2022.

Horn, Sebastian, Carmen Reinhart, and Christoph Trebesch. 2019. China's Overseas Lending. KIEL Working Paper No. 2132, Kiel Institute for the World Economy. https://www.ifw-kiel.de/fileadmin/Dateiverwaltung/IfW-Publications/Christoph_Trebesch/KWP_2132.pdf. Accessed 15 Jan 2022.

ISEAS-Yusof Ishak Institute. 2020. *The State of Southeast Asia: 2020 Survey Report*. https://www.iseas.edu.sg/wp-content/uploads/pdfs/TheStateofSEASurveyReport_2020.pdf. Accessed 5 Feb 2022.

ITUC, Belgium and the Friedrich-Ebert-Stiftung. 2021. *Belt and Road Initiative in Central Asia: Desk Study*.

Lemahieu, Hervé, and Leng Alyssa. 2021. *Asia Power Index Key Findings 2021*. Lowy Institute. https://power.lowyinstitute.org/downloads/lowy-institute-2021-asia-power-index-key-findings-report.pdf. Accessed 17 Jan 2022.

Luban Workshop. 2022. The Launch Ceremony of the First Luban Workshop in Central Asia. http://www.lubanworkshop.cn/html/2022/jsjc-lb_1201/461.html.

Ma, Xinyue, Gallagher Kevin, and Chen Siqi. 2021. *China's Global Energy Finance in the Era of COVID-19*. GCI Policy Brief 006, Global Development Policy Center at the Boston University. https://www.bu.edu/gdp/files/2021/02/GCI_CGEF_PB_FIN.pdf. Accessed 20 Jan 2022.

Ministry of Commerce of China. 2021. China's Trade and Investment Cooperation under the Belt and Road Initiative 2021.

Ministry of Foreign Affairs of China, 2021a. *On April 2, 2021, Foreign Ministry Spokesperson Hua Chunying hosted a regular press conference*, 2 April 2021. Available at http://sg.chinaembassy.gov.cn/fyrth/202104/t20210402_8918118.htm. Accessed 1 September 2023.

Ministry of Foreign Affairs of China. 2021b. *High-Quality Belt and Road Cooperation: Partnership on Connectivity*. Report on the Findings and Recommendations from the Meetings of the Advisory Council of the Belt and Road Forum for International Cooperation in 2019 and 2020.

Ministry of Foreign Affairs of China. May 2021c. *Wang Yi Talks About the Eight-Point Consensus and Ten Outcomes of the 'China + Five Central Asian Countries' Foreign Ministers' Meeting.* https://www.fmprc.gov.cn/web/wjbzhd/202105/t20210512_9137291.shtml. Accessed 16 Jan 2022.

Ministry of Foreign Affairs of China. January 2022. *Xi Jinping Sends a Verbal Message to Kazakh President Kassym-Jomart Tokayev.* https://www.mfa.gov.cn/mfa_eng/zxxx_662805/202201/t20220108_10480233.html. Accessed 18 Feb 2022.

Ministry of Foreign Affairs of the People's Republic of China. 2023a. Keynote Speech by Xi Jinping at the China-Central Asia Summit. https://www.fmprc.gov.cn/zyxw/202305/t20230519_11079936.shtml.

Ministry of Foreign Affairs of the People's Republic of China. 2023b. China-Central Asia Summit Xi'an Declaration (Full Text). (中国 – 中亚峰会西安宣言). https://www.fmprc.gov.cn/zyxw/202305/t20230519_11080194.shtml.

Nedopil, Christoph. 2021. China's Investments in the Belt and Road Initiative (BRI) in 2020. International Institute of Green Finance at the Central University of Finance and Economics.

Office for CCP Central Leading Group for BRI & State Railway Corporation of China. 2021. *Report of the China-Europe Railway Express Development.* https://www.ndrc.gov.cn/fzggw/jgsj/kfs/sjdt/202208/P020220818311703111697.pdf.

Office of the Prime Minister of the Republic of Kazakhstan. 2019. *The Head of State Received Wang Yilin, Chairman of the Board of Directors of CNPC Corporation.* https://primeminister.kz/ru/news/glava-gosudarstva-prinyal-predsedatelya-soveta-direktorov-korporacii-cnpc-van-ilinya. Accessed 15 Jan 2022.

Pew Research Center. 2020. *Unfavorable Views of China Reach Historic Highs in Many Countries.* https://www.pewresearch.org/global/2020/10/06/unfavorable-views-of-china-reach-historic-highs-in-many-countries/. Accessed 16 Jan 2022.

Stronski, Paul and Nicole Ng. 2018. *Cooperation and Competition: Russia and China in Central Asia, the Russian Far East, and the Arctic.* Washington D.C: Carnegie Endowment for International Peace.

The Second Belt and Road Forum for International Cooperation. April 2019. *Joint Communique of the Leaders' Roundtable of the Second Belt and Road Forum for International Cooperation.* http://www.beltandroadforum.org/english/n100/2019/0427/c36-1311.html. Accessed 29 Apr 2019.

Umarov, Temur. 2020. *China Looms Large in Central Asia.* Carnegie Moscow Center.

Van der Klev, Dirk, and Niva Yau. October 2021. *How Central Asians pushed Chinese Firms to Localize*, 1–49. Carnegie Endowment for International Peace.

Van Noort, C., and T. Colley. 2021. How Do Strategic Narratives Shape Policy Adoption? Responses to China's Belt and Road Initiative. *Review of International Studies* 47 (1): 39–63.

World Economic Forum. 2019. *The Global Competitiveness Report 2019.* https://www3.weforum.org/docs/WEF_TheGlobalCompetitivenessReport2019.pdf. Accessed 30 Apr 2022.

Yu, Hong. 2019. Reflections on the Belt and Road Initiative. *China: An International Journal* 17 (4): 8–23.

Yu, Hong. 2022a. China's Ten-Year-Old BRI Needs a Revamp. *ThinkChina.* Available at https://www.thinkchina.sg/future-china-chinas-ten-year-old-bri-needs-revamp. Accessed 23 Nov 2022.

Yu, Hong. 2022b. China Wants to Win the World over with the BRI, but Something's Amiss. *ThinkChina.* https://www.thinkchina.sg/china-wants-win-world-over-bri-somethings-amiss. Accessed 30 Apr 2022.

Yu, Hong. 2023. Is the Belt and Road Initiative 2.0 in the Making? The case of Central Asia. *Journal of Contemporary Asia* 53 (3): 535–547.

Zhou, Lihuan, et al. 2018. Moving the Green Belt and Road Initiative: From Words to Actions. Working Paper, World Resource Institute. https://files.wri.org/d8/s3fs-public/moving-green-belt-and-road-initiative-from-words-to-actions.pdf. Accessed 14 Jan 2022.

Chapter 11
Reflections on the Belt and Road Initiative at Its 10th Anniversary

The Belt and Road Initiative (BRI) reaches the 10th anniversary of implementation in 2023. In 2013, Xi Jinping, China's President, announced the land-based "Silk Road Economic Belt" and the sea-based "Maritime Silk Road of the 21st Century" during his state visits to Kazakhstan and Indonesia, respectively. The land-based and sea-based initiatives were subsequently combined to form the Belt and Road Initiative, or BRI in short.

The BRI, which comprises various routes by land and by sea, is China's global outreach strategy for connecting China with the world (Yu 2019). A total of 150 countries (38 from Asia, 27 from Europe, 52 from Africa, 11 from Oceania and 22 from the Americas) and 32 international organisations had already signed up for China's BRI by December 2022. Although this documentation is not legally binding, such a positive global response lends credibility to the BRI. The BRI countries combinedly account for about 60% of global population and 40% of global GDP.

The world has seen the unfolding of a successive wave of competing regional and global initiatives, all of which aim to accelerate interregional connectivity through infrastructure investment and development. Examples include the Russia-led Eurasian Economic Union (EAEU), ASEAN-Korea Infrastructure Fund, Japan's Partnership for Quality Infrastructure, the European Union's Global Gateway plan and the G7 Partnership for Global Infrastructure and Investment (PGII). However, many of these competing connectivity initiatives are still at the vision stage, without concrete achievements. None of these initiatives so far have been able to compete with China's BRI from the perspective of the sheer scale, geographical coverage and geoeconomic influence (Yu 2022a).

China's BRI is perhaps one of the most prominent and ambitious infrastructure development initiatives in the history of the world (if not the most prominent). According to the "China Global Investment Tracker" statistics, worldwide Chinese investments and contracts under the BRI framework amounted to US$369.12 billion

H. Yu, *Understanding China's Belt and Road Initiative*, Asia in Transition 26,
https://doi.org/10.1007/978-981-99-9633-9_11

between 2013 and 2022 (American Enterprise Institute 2023). To promote the initiative to the world, the Chinese authorities have proactively mobilised various political, economic and diplomatic resources over the past decade. Other countries cannot match the huge infrastructure promises of China's aspirational BRI or the relentless pursuit of its execution.

The BRI is China's ambitious outreach to the world, which aims to forge better interregional connectivity through developing infrastructure projects and redefine China's relations with the BRI countries (Ebel 2023). The China-Laos Railway and the Mombasa-Nairobi Railway in Kenya, upgradation of Piraeus Port in Greece and the Lahore Rail Transit Line in Pakistan represent just a few among the hundreds of infrastructure projects completed and now operational under the BRI framework, which gives a glimpse of the initiative's current impact across the world in geopolitical and geoeconomic terms.

There are five components to the BRI, namely policy coordination, connectivity, trade, financial integration and people-to-people exchanges. The BRI is centred on physical infrastructure connectivity. The aim is to forge an extensive regional network of infrastructure, ranging from roads, railroads, airports, seaports to energy plants and digital communication facilities. Given the scope and scale of the Chinese-funded infrastructure projects along the Silk Road countries, BRI implementation is transforming the geoeconomic landscape in Asia and beyond.

China is a global champion for infrastructure financing and construction through leveraging its highly competitive manufacturing and construction industries. For example, in the field of technological capacity and infrastructure construction, fourteen Chinese construction firms are listed among the top 20 largest infrastructure contractors in the world. Chinese firms are not merely the leading players; in fact, China structurally dominates the global infrastructure construction industry.

BRI implementation so far has been executed mainly through the Chinese state-owned enterprises and banks. China's push for the BRI is driven by both domestic economic and global geostrategic factors. From the domestic perspective, the initiative is important for stimulating Chinese industrial and economic growth at home, to secure market access for the Chinese firms in the BRI countries. From the global geostrategic perspective, to accompany its economic rise, China is keen to play a key role in reshaping the international system and rules in China's favour. The BRI serves as an important platform for China to push for its ambitious agenda on regional and global governance reforms.

Against the backdrop of the changing global geostrategic landscape, centred on the strategic competition between the United States (US) and China, and the rippling effects of the global COVID-19 pandemic, China's aim is to use the BRI to mitigate the external shock and uncertainty by promoting close regional trade and economic integration via improving interregional connectivity.

The BRI is a modern version of the century-old Silk Road linking the vast Eurasian continent to East Asia. The BRI's historical association with the Silk Road would increase the appeal of participation among regional countries and beyond, encouraging China to utilise the BRI brand to boost its soft power abroad.

Table 11.1 Estimated infrastructure needs by region, 2016–2030 (US$ billion in 2015 prices)

Region	Projected annual GDP growth	2030 UN population projection (US billion)	2030 projected GDP per capita (2015 US$)	Climate-adjusted estimates		
				Investment needs	Annual average	Investment needs as % of GDP
Central Asia	3.1	0.096	6202	565	38	7.8
East Asia	5.1	1.503	18,602	16,062	1071	5.2
South Asia	6.5	2.059	3446	6347	423	8.8
Southeast Asia	5.1	0.723	7040	3147	210	5.7
The Pacific	3.1	0.014	2889	46	3.1	9.1
Asia and the Pacific	5.3	4.396	9277	26,166	1744	5.9

Source Asian Development Bank (2017)

The initiative is President Xi Jinping's signature project, and it is directly associated with his legacy. The Belt and Road concept fits well into Xi's world view of "building a global community for a shared future". To borrow from Xi's own words: "China is willing to work with all sides to build a community with a shared future for mankind through the high-quality development of the Belt and Road cooperation". Followed the 20th National Congress of the CCP which was held in mid-October 2022, Xi's leadership and grip on the Party State have been further cemented by his gaining an unprecedented third term as the CCP general secretary.

Connectivity based on infrastructure development is the central pillar to China's BRI. It is the key selling point in encouraging the regional countries' participation. Many of the developing countries lack both technological know-how and the capacity to raise the significant amounts of capital to fund the required infrastructure projects. The developing nations desperately need foreign investments, production capacity and technological know-how in these industries as they hasten the pace of industrialisation and infrastructure upgrading.

As estimated by the Asian Development Bank, Asia and the Pacific countries will require over US$26.1 trillion for climate-adjusted infrastructure development up to 2030 (Table 11.1). No plan proposed by a single country or grouping could come close to filling the developing nations' infrastructure investment gap. Vast capital is required for infrastructure upgrading in developing nations, and the risks are high.

China had previously undergone spectacular economic growth since the reform and opening up policy in the early 1980s. Nevertheless, the Chinese economy has been continuing to slow down substantially since 2010. At home, the weakening of economic comparative advantages such as supplies of cheap skilled labour and land costs, population ageing and regional development disparity means that

China's economy is now facing significant headwinds from these challenging and long-standing structural issues.

Although the Chinese economy showed promising growth recovery in early 2022, with year-on-year quarterly growth of 4.8%, the local outbreaks of COVID-19 variants in several cities (e.g. Shanghai and Chengdu) still had an economic toll in that year and contributed further to curbing industrial output and domestic demand, putting severe downward pressure on economic growth. In July 2022, the World Bank downgraded its assessment of China's real economic growth rate to merely 3 per cent for 2022, primarily due to the pandemic outbreak and its Zero-COVID-19 policy. This is the lowest growth rate in over 40 years, excluding the growth rate of 2.2% recorded in 2020 during the initial pandemic outbreak in Wuhan.

China's economic slowdown has adversely affected the BRI, putting further strains on the initiative and forcing the Chinese authorities to recalibrate the scope and form of its implementation (Yu 2022b). The economic slowdown at home could make it hard for China to sustain its once rapid growth of lending associated with the BRI projects into the future. Although the grants and loans provided by the Chinese banks are essential in financing BRI-related infrastructure projects abroad, the need to prioritise domestic economic stability will force Chinese banking institutions to lend more domestically, rather than spending billions of dollars overseas as before. Furthermore, China's economic slowdown could generate negative spillovers for many countries' exports to China due to weakening domestic industrial production and decreasing consumption demands in China.

Meanwhile, many BRI countries have suffered as a result of the challenging global geostrategic environment and the domestic economic crises in the wake of the global coronavirus pandemic. Slowdown in BRI implementation is likely as some infrastructure projects currently under construction or at the planning stage may have to be scaled back or suspended indefinitely. These countries encounter difficulty in debt repayment for the Chinese-funded BRI infrastructure projects, which undermines their ability to host further BRI projects or even to contemplate massive capital expenditure on infrastructure construction.

For example, Sir Lanka, an important BRI country in South Asia, is facing its worst economic, political and social crisis in decades. It is struggling with repaying external loans and the interest associated with borrowing for infrastructure construction, partially deriving from BRI projects financed by Chinese firms and banks. In 2017, after failing to pay back its debt to China, Sri Lanka had no choice but relinquish control over its Hambantota Port to the Chinese firms and agreed to cede a fairly large chunk of nearly coastal land (approximately 15,000 acres) to the Chinese on a 99-year lease. The case of Hambantota Port has been widely reported by the international media and serves as a real-life lesson for other BRI countries seeking to avoid any similar situation when encountering domestic economic crises.

China is a major creditor of many BRI countries, such as Sir Lanka, Pakistan, Laos, Zambia, Angola, Kenya, Ethiopia and Myanmar. These countries' economies have been hit hard by the COVID-19 pandemic, which have further escalated their domestic economic and fiscal crises. According to the recent debt sustainability analysis by both the World Bank and International Monetary Fund, one-third of low-income developing countries participating in the initiative face a high risk of debt distress. Nearly two-thirds of emerging market economies that have embraced the initiative face rising debt vulnerabilities, which calls for critical scrutiny of countries whose debt exceeds the indicative threshold of 50% of GDP or whose total financing needs exceed 15% of GDP.

If more foreign governments follow the examples of Zambia and Sri Lanka and demand debt restructuring or ask for debt forgiveness, this could present a dilemma for China on making concessions to keep BRI projects alive or accept their termination in the recipient countries struggling with debt repayment.

BRI projects can significantly improve connectivity, boost trade, investment, economic growth and improve the living conditions of the recipient countries on a sustainable basis, but only if China is willing to collaborate with the BRI countries by allowing the participating economies to fully account for the potential costs of debt-financed infrastructure.

Reliable information on the financing terms and conditions for BRI infrastructure projects is currently scarce. In order to effectively address the issue of debt sustainability in relation to BRI infrastructure projects, China should address the issues of transparency and lending management. The lack of transparency surrounding the terms and scale of financing for the BRI poses serious risks to borrowing and creditor countries, and to the eventual success of the Initiative. Debt transparency is essential for borrowers and creditors to make informed decisions, ensure the efficient use of available financing and safeguard debt sustainability, as well as citizens' ability to hold governments accountable.

To promote sustainable BRI development, China should adhere to the guidance of the Belt and Road Debt Sustainability Analysis Framework (hereinafter referred to as the Analytical Framework) on overseas lending. The debt situation in borrowing countries and their prospects of repaying the debt incurred through BRI projects should be examined in detail, and transparency and debt sustainability analysis should be applied in relation to the BRI debt. The Analytical Framework, which was adopted after the second BRI summit in 2019, is based on the Debt Sustainability Framework (DSF) of the International Monetary Fund and the World Bank, taking into account the national conditions and development practices of the BRI countries.

China and 26 other countries have also jointly formulated the Guiding Principles for Financing the Belt and Road Projects, which clearly define the need to build a transparent, friendly, non-discriminatory and predictable financing environment, emphasise sustainable economic and social development and take into account debt sustainability when mobilising funds. In addition, private sector participation in the BRI financing through public–private partnerships can promote high-quality infrastructure development and enhance project financing transparency.

BRI implementation is likely to face more headwinds and challenges in the post-pandemic era, in view of the unfavourable global geostrategic environment and the Chinese economic slowdown. As the BRI approaches its 10th anniversary, it is at a crossroads.

Internally, China's self-imposed Zero-COVID-19 strategy (or the Dynamic Clearing policy) was another major challenge impeding Beijing's push for BRI implementation worldwide. In the face of surging COVID-19 cases and highly infectious virus variants, the Chinese central and local authorities had imposed draconian Zero-COVID policies to curb the virus's spread, including frequent city-lockdowns and sealing off the country physically from the world for almost three years. These strict lockdown and control measures had made it extremely difficult for Chinese officials, business executives and engineers to travel abroad to conduct in-person promotion and management of BRI projects, as well as causing disruption in supplies of critical raw materials and equipment for infrastructure construction projects.

The pandemic has also pushed up construction and labour costs of BRI infrastructure projects due to supply chain disruption, soaring energy prices and manpower shortages. For example, a budget overrun of the Chinese-funded Jakarta-Bandung high-speed rail project has been reported. The estimated construction cost for the 142-km-long high-speed railway has increased by 20% to US$7.9 billion.

From the external perspective, first, several countries in the region and beyond are pushing back against this initiative on the grounds that the BRI-affiliated infrastructure projects, funded by investments from China, are costly and impractical, with issues of corruption in internal transactions. In the perception of these recipient countries, the terms of their infrastructure deals favour China, leaving these countries to bear the financial burdens and risks.

BRI implementation also has been weak in terms of compliance with internationally recognised standards on such as transparency and open bidding, and social, labour and environmental protection. In addition, some BRI infrastructure projects have been scaled back or suspended amidst concerns over rising debts.

Second, excessive borrowing could pose a threat to financial sustainability and lead to a dependency trap. According to a paper published by the National Bureau of Economic Research, low-income countries that have encountered huge debt burdens associated with China's BRI investment include Laos, Pakistan, Mongolia, Kyrgyzstan and Djibouti (Horn et al. 2019).

Having said that, it is important to bear in mind that it is not a sin for developing countries to engage in growth-oriented infrastructure borrowing. A distinction must be made between use of debt as investment to remove growth bottlenecks or to support spending and consumption. Many low-income developing countries lack infrastructure development funds and can only borrow externally.

Since the BRI investments focus on infrastructure construction, the increase in debt of borrowing countries in the short and medium terms is conducive to their sustainable development in the long run through boosting trade and economic growth. After the infrastructure is built, the economy will develop faster, creating jobs, raising income levels and earning foreign exchange through exports. A virtuous circle could be embedded (Yu 2023).

Looking back on the Chinese development experience over the past four decades, the biggest bottleneck China has faced in its development which is infrastructure underdevelopment. Without infrastructure, there is no way to promote trade or develop an agricultural, manufacturing or service economy. From China's own experience, in order to develop, countries must first overcome infrastructure bottlenecks, which a Chinese saying encapsulates as "to get rich, build roads first".

As a World Bank report (2019) shows, the BRI transport corridor will help in two important ways: shortening transport times and increasing trade and investment. It is estimated that travel times could be reduced by up to 12% in countries along the transport corridor routes and by an average of 3% in the rest of the world, indicating that non-BRI countries and regions will also benefit.

External development financing is required for cash-strapped countries with underdeveloped infrastructure. It is perfectly normal for developing countries to seek to accelerate infrastructure construction using financing tools, given their huge investment needs and domestic financial restraints. The salient question is how to balance infrastructure development needs and domestic financial sustainability.

Third, Russia's war in Ukraine could also potentially cause collateral damage to the BRI, as China's land-based connectivity with the European Union via the China–Europe express may be jeopardised. The China–Europe Express is crucial for overland-based connectivity between China, Eurasian countries and the European Union. China has tried hard to support, promote and make it profitable since 2016. The value of goods transported by the freight trains was US$74.9 billion in 2021, with two-way trips reaching 14,000. Almost half of the routes and lines (78 lines reaching 180 cities in 23 European countries by 2021) pass through Russia. Due to the massive sanctions imposed on Russia, European firms may choose not to ship goods via Russia in the future. It is difficult for the freight rail service to operate along the Eurasian continent when there is a major war going on in Europe.

The strategic competition between China and the United States has prompted China to view Russia as one of its indispensable allies; preserving this strategic partnership has thus become crucial. From the long-term perspective, China's alignment with Russia through its refusal to condemn Russia's aggression in the Ukraine war has deepened the strategic distrust between China and Europe, making Beijing's BRI push in the European countries more challenging.

Nevertheless, neither the shift of the global geostrategic environment nor domestic economic slowdown will stop Beijing's will to push for BRI implementation. First, the developing BRI countries known as the Global South, from Asia to Africa, from the Pacific Islands to Latin America, are still facing bottlenecks for boosting trade within or across their borders due to chronic infrastructure shortage and underdeveloped interregional connectivity. Thus, the economic growth potential of the developing countries remains largely untapped, since infrastructure readiness lays the foundation for industrial take-off and economic prosperity. These countries are welcoming foreign investment, including the Chinese investment, in their infrastructure construction sector. The majority of the countries in the Global South have participated in the BRI and aligned with China's development agenda.

Despite the impact of the COVID-19 pandemic and the challenging global geostrategic environment, China's investment in the BRI countries has remained robust, and Chinese firms are still pumping money into the infrastructure projects abroad. According to official data from the Ministry of Commerce of China, Chinese direct investment to the BRI countries had increased from US$12.6 billion in 2013 to US$20.9 billion in 2022, accounting for 17.9% of China's total outbound direct investment.

Chinese construction companies have built new roads, rail lines, airports, seaports, power plants and 5G telecommunication facilities across the BRI countries since 2013. The annual growth of the contract values of new construction projects undertaken in the BRI countries was 10.2% between 2013 and 2020 (Ministry of Commerce of the People's Republic of China 2022). A case in point is the Port of Piraeus in Greece. Since a Chinese firm took over the operation and management of the port's terminals in 2016, this firm has invested in upgrading the port and related facilities. The port of Piraeus has now been transformed into one of the busiest commercial ports in the Mediterranean Sea and has become a poster child for the BRI.

Second, in response to the criticisms from the BRI countries and the shortcomings exposed by infrastructure project financing and construction, the Chinese authorities have adopted readjustment measures for its implementation over the past few years. For example, in response to pressure from the governments and local communities in the BRI countries, the Chinese firms have been more willing to employ local workers and provided skills training by setting up in various countries Luban Workshops, the Chinese version of vocational training colleges, named after a legendary Chinese craftsman.

China has been making efforts to modify the original initiative in the form of the BRI 2.0. The BRI 2.0 is intended to expand the Belt and Road cooperation to new areas such as the digital and health fronts in the BRI countries in the post-COVID-19 era, departing from the initial infrastructure-centred outreach approach. The BRI 2.0 also seeks to make Chinese-funded projects more commercially viable and financially sustainable for the recipient countries, as well as to promote greening and localisation of BRI projects. Moreover, China is encouraging the BRI countries to align their own development strategies with the initiative.

To reduce the domestic financial burden, China is shifting from a bilateral approach to a more multilateral approach to project financing through collaborating with multilateral development banks and private investors. To achieve sustainability of the BRI as a whole, China must focus more on sustainability of financing for developing nations along the BRI routes and lower the long-term financial impacts of loans for infrastructure projects. China is seeking to cooperate with participating countries and multilateral financial institutions to jointly enhance debt management capacity of the borrowing countries. It is therefore adopting "third-party market cooperation" as a flexible approach in its pursuit of cooperation with other countries under the BRI umbrella. However, making a break from the past unilateralism of the BRI is easier said than done.

Third, China has also made efforts to gradually institutionalise the initiative over the past several years. The Green Investment Principles (GIPs) for the Belt and Road, which were co-initiated between China and the United Kingdom, are a case in point. The GIP is a set of principles for promoting green investment in the BRI countries, and it includes seven principles at three levels, namely strategy, operations and innovation. The GIP has expanded its membership to 40 global institutions (including the big four state-owned commercial banks and two state policy banks in China) and 11 supporters from 15 countries[1] (although a few countries so far have not signed up for the BRI).

BRI projects are vulnerable to both geopolitical and geoeconomic risks, due to their lengthy gestation periods and high costs. BRI project implementation is affected by developments in bilateral relations, domestic situations in the host countries and external shocks such as the pandemic and the Ukraine war. It would be desirable for China and the BRI countries to jointly institutionalise the BRI-related collaboration mechanisms and framework in order to uphold policy continuity.

Fourth, the determination of the Chinese leadership and government to push for the BRI remains constant as the initiative enters its second decade of implementation. This determination appears primarily through its push for closer cooperation with the BRI countries and with the countries of Global South more generally. Xi Jinping calls for expansion of China's circle of friends, with the BRI central to this mission.

As the U.S.-China rivalry intensifies and China's relations with several traditional major trading partners, such as Japan and Canada, turn sour, the Belt and Road Initiative has apparently become even more important for China. China's trade, investment and economic ties with the BRI countries are the foundations of its global outreach.

Following the almost three-year-long imposition of the Zero-COVID-19 policy, in late 2022, the Chinese authorities suddenly shifted to a "live with COVID-19" strategy by lifting all restrictions and started to reopen the domestic economy and China's borders with the outside world. This policy shift will facilitate China's push for the BRI abroad and the Chinese companies' engagement in business overseas.

While the BRI has been a centrepiece of China's foreign policy initiative since 2013, it is not China's only outreach strategy. To advance its national economic interests and its geostrategic ambition, China has also become a key player in many regional cooperation institutions, such as BRICS, SCO and RCEP. China's endeavour to play a more influential role in both regional and global affairs is multipronged and extends beyond the BRI.

China will need to modify its model of BRI implementation in response to both internal and external challenges. China's engagement with opposition political parties, civil society, non-governmental organisations, media and business leaders of the BRI countries, which are beyond the orbit of government and ruling parties' control, has been limited. To succeed, it would do well to focus more on the economic benefits of overseas investment projects, the voices of the local communities and environmental sustainability. A balance will be required to secure win–win situations.

BRI infrastructure projects are built to benefit the interests of the many rather than the elite few. Therefore, thorough feasibility study of the BRI projects is needed, including the economic viability of the projects, their environmental and social impacts, as well as the debt sustainability of the recipient countries. BRI project design, planning and construction should integrate consultation with relevant local

[1] These fifteen countries include China, United Arab Emirates, Kazakhstan, Thailand, Morocco, France, Germany, Singapore, Pakistan, the United States, Mongolia, Japan, Luxembourg, the United Kingdom and Switzerland.

stakeholders and closer observation of BRI project implementation from the perspectives of the BRI countries should be encouraged. BRI countries have a vital role to play in shaping successful outcomes of BRI cooperation and implementation.

The BRI is an evolving strategy, and it has demonstrated to be incredibly adaptable and flexible in practice. To reassure the BRI countries of an equal partnership under the BRI framework and to promote the BRI's image of collective ownership of the international community, China is making efforts to erase the China-centric image associated with the initiative.

11.1 BRI Remains Central to China's Foreign Policy Agenda

The third Belt and Road Forum for International Cooperation (or the BRF in short) convened in Beijing from 17 to 18 October. This event was China's biggest diplomatic charm offensive in 2023. The message that Beijing wanted to send to the world is clear: don't bet on the BRI fading away. This initiative will continue to move forward as planned. On the part of the BRI countries attending the BRF event, it enables them to get a sense of how Beijing will promote the BRI and its provision of funding for the prioritised sectors when the BRI enters the second decade.

The BRI has been transformed from a regional infrastructure plan, designed to connect China with the Eurasian countries, to a global initiative aiming to support infrastructure project financing and construction in almost every corner of the world, and underdeveloped and developing countries in particular. The BRI has already in many ways reshaped the regional landscape of infrastructure financing and development for many BRI countries. China has used its rich capital reserves and infrastructure development expertise to tie together the BRI countries across the regions.

To that end, the BRI has been a success. In total, 152 countries had already signed up to the initiative by June 2023, the majority being Global South countries.[2] China regards the collective Global South countries which are crucial for its economic and diplomatic agenda. The improved infrastructure connectivity, ranging from railways, seaports, highways, airports to power plants, has thus helped to facilitate the bilateral trade between China and the BRI countries. China's influence in the region and the world has rapidly increased to accompany its push for BRI implementation.

International reactions to the BRI have been largely divided along geopolitical lines between the West and the Global South countries. Although many in the West criticise the initiative's shortcomings and suspect Beijing's geopolitical motivation behind its implementation, the Global South countries in general overwhelmingly support China's BRI and praise its achievements in improving infrastructure connectivity in the developing countries.

[2] The term Global South countries broadly refer to developing and underdeveloped countries in Asia, the Pacific, Africa and Latin America.

Many have raised questions about the initiative's long-term sustainability amid the economic slowdown in China, the growing scepticism towards China's geopolitical ambitions, as well as the possible impact of the fast-changing global geopolitical environment. Nevertheless, the BRI remains central to China's foreign policy and its global outreach. It is the Chinese leader's belief that the BRI will not only bring benefits to the world but also to China's own development. President Xi explained this as follows: "as the saying goes, the one who gives roses to others will have the fragrance lingering on their hands", during his keynote speech to the 3rd BRF.

During the 3rd BRI, President Xi unveiled an eight-point action plan for the BRI implementation in the next decade, which covers the following major areas: first, China has committed to providing another RMB780 billion (or roughly US$107 billion) to fund the BRI for the next five years, including RMB700 billion financing windows from both the Export–Import Bank of China and the State Development Bank, which are two Chinese policy banks, and injecting RMB80 billion-yuan capital into the Silk Road Fund, which is a state-owned investment vehicle. All three are major Chinese financial institutions engaged in financing BRI-affiliated infrastructure projects.

Compared to the previous announcement made by President Xi during the first BRF in 2017, there is to be no scaling back of Beijing's ambitions for financing infrastructure projects for the developing countries under the BRI umbrella despite concerns over China's domestic economic slowdown and its various daunting external and internal challenges. It is unlikely that the West in general and the United States in particular can even attempt to match the size of Chinese investment to the developing countries under the BRI. Nevertheless, as many low-income and developing BRI countries are facing serious domestic economic and fiscal crises after the global COVID-19 pandemic, they now have much less capacity to host new BRI projects or take on additional Chinese lending affiliated with the BRI projects.

Second, China will be emphasising the construction of so-called "small but beautiful" projects in the developing countries as the BRI enters the second decade, in contrast to its focus on building mega infrastructure projects in the first decade. The "small but beautiful" projects, which are more financially and environmentally sustainable, will be able to bring more direct benefits to the locals in the recipient countries, in the forms of raising their income and improving their livelihood and local environment. To China, financing "small but beautiful" projects is a high-yield, low-investment and less risky option.

It signals that China might shift away from funding big-ticket infrastructure projects. The Chinese financial institutions have already learned the hard lesson that infrastructure financing and development in the developing countries are indeed difficult and risky. China's banks will in the future be more selective regarding their funding of infrastructure projects overseas. The new BRI-affiliated projects are expected to be more targeted, smaller in scale, cost-effective and lower risk. It is expected that China will focus on quality rather than quantity of BRI projects in its decisions on outbound investment and lending.

The BRI in the second ten years may focus on promoting standard-setting and strengthening skill training for the locals. It will prioritise funding for green and digital infrastructure projects by advocating for the green and Digital Silk Road.

Third, China will promote green development under the BRI framework. Leveraged on its strengths as the world's largest manufacturer for renewable energy equipment, such as solar panels and wind turbines, and its strong production capacity, China anticipates further promoting green infrastructure projects in order to facilitate exports of Chinese-made renewable energy products to the BRI countries. China has already recently announced removal of all restrictions in the manufacturing sector for foreign investment access.

Fourth, China will advance the DSR and promote the digital economy among the BRI countries. Chinese companies such as Huawei (the world's leading 5G telecommunication equipment manufacturer), Alibaba (the leading firm in e-commerce), ByteDance (the owner of social media TikTok) and Tensent (the maker of WeChat) are strongly competitive in digital industries such as 5G communications, e-commerce, big data and quantum computing. These Chinese high-tech firms need to unlock foreign market access to keep their revenue flowing and further enhance their international competitiveness. Beijing intends to use the DSR to cement its position as a leading international technology power through increasing digital access among the urban and rural population of developing countries (Sim 2023).

Many BRI countries are increasingly seeing the value that digital industries could bring to their economic and industrial growth. For example, in Southeast Asia, the leaders of both Malaysia and Indonesia have already said that their countries would like to work with China to expand cooperation in the digital economy. With the state's push for the DSR, Chinese firms are likely to receive more preferential state policy support and favourable lending from the Chinese state-owned banks in their bid to expand their business operations overseas.

The Chinese authorities have expressed their confidence to compete with the West-backed infrastructure development plans for the developing countries, in the fight for influence over the Global South. During the BRI press conference (Ministry of Foreign Affairs of China October 2023c), in response to a question from a Chinese journalist, Wang Yi remarked:

> We may as well compete internationally who can build more roads, railways and bridges for developing countries, and who can build more schools, hospitals and gymnasiums for the people in low-income countries. We are confident.

China will closely tie in its own development and expansion of its trade and investment with the Global South countries. The BRI in its second decade could be more consequential for the BRI countries and the world. On 18 October 2023, China's Ministry of Foreign Affairs concurrently published a list of 89 various multilateral cooperation documents and another list of 369 practical cooperation deliverables after the conclusion of the BRF event (Ministry of Foreign Affairs of China 2023a, b). Nevertheless, few of these documents or deliverables contain concrete, practical and substantial proposals.

Xi Jinping and other Chinese leaders view the Initiative as a valuable tool for projecting Chinese power and influence abroad amidst the intensifying power competition between China and the United States. With the advancement of the BRI, China's leader envisions promoting an alternative world order in China's favour to replace the rule-based liberal global order championed by the United States. As Xi (2023) clearly stated in his speech:

> The BRI promotes connectivity, mutual benefit, common development, cooperation and win-win outcomes. Ideological confrontation, geopolitical rivalry and bloc politics are not a choice for us. What we stand against are unilateral sanctions, economic coercion and decoupling and supply chain disruption.

Against the backdrop of the China-U.S. power rivalry and the deteriorating relations between China and the Western countries, to sustain Chinese economic growth and to ensure its economic security, Beijing is attempting to pursue a diversification strategy that will secure access to the BRI countries' markets for Chinese-made goods and Chinese capital while gradually reducing its dependence on the traditional markets in the West. For the Global South countries, China's offer of infrastructure financing and development is apparently more attractive than anything the United States and other Western countries can currently offer.

Although it will take a long time for the BRI countries to fully replace the markets in the Western countries, China's overall trade volume with the BRI countries has already substantially increased over the past decade. In 2013, China's exports and imports to the BRI countries amounted to US$569.19 billion and US$471.36 billion, respectively. By 2020, China's exports and imports to the BRI countries had risen to a record high of US$783.86 billion and US$569.91 billion, respectively. According to the data released by China's Ministry of Commerce (2021), in 2021, the BRI countries combinedly accounted for nearly 30% of China's total foreign trade.

The BRI is an evolving and adaptive concept and policy. The initiative will, in the second decade, not look the same as in its first decade. China's aim is for the BRI to be as flexible and inclusive as possible in order to meet the needs of participating countries in different regions. In the face of an evolving and adaptive BRI, the West will have to think hard on how to compete with China's BRI, economically as well as geopolitically, rather than just opposing it and hoping that it will diminish over time.

References

American Enterprise Institute. 2023. The China Global Investment Tracker. Updated on 16 May 2023. https://www.aei.org/china-global-investment-tracker/.

Asian Development Bank. 2017. *Meeting Asia's Infrastructure Needs*. https://www.adb.org/sites/default/files/publication/227496/special-report-infrastructure.pdf. Accessed 5 May 2023.

Ebel, Pippa. 2023. *China's Belt and Road Initiative: Ten Years On*. Council on Geostrategy, Explainer No. GPE16.

Horn, Sebastian, Carmen M. Reinhart, and Christoph Trebesch. 2019. *China's Overseas Lending.* Working Paper 26050, National Bureau of Economic Research. Available at https://www.nber.org/system/files/working_papers/w26050/revisions/w26050.rev0.pdf. Accessed 22 June 2022.
Ministry of Commerce of the People's Republic of China, 2021. *China's Belt and Road Trade and Investment Development Report 2021.*
Ministry of Commerce of the People's Republic of China. 2022. *2021 Statistical Bulletin of China's Outward Foreign Direct Investment.* China Commerce and Trade Press.
Ministry of Foreign Affairs of China. 2023a. List of Multilateral Cooperation Outcome Documents of the Third Belt and Road Forum for International Cooperation. Available at https://www.mfa.gov.cn/zyxw/202310/t20231018_11163409.shtml. Accessed 21 Oct 2023.
Ministry of Foreign Affairs of China. 2023b. List of Practical Cooperation Deliverables of the Third Belt and Road Forum for International Cooperation. Available at https://www.fmprc.gov.cn/eng/zxxx_662805/202310/t20231020_11164541.html. Accessed 22 Oct 2023.
Ministry of Foreign Affairs of China. 2023c. Remarks by H.E. Wang Yi at the Press Conference of the Third Belt and Road Forum for International Cooperation. Available at https://www.fmprc.gov.cn/eng/zxxx_662805/202310/t20231020_11164742.html. Accessed 22 Oct 2023.
Sim, Dewey. 2023. Belt and Road Scheme Earns a Hi-Tech Revamp. *South China Morning Post.*
World Bank. 2019. https://www.worldbank.org/en/country/china/overview#:~:text=Following%20China's%20swift%20reopening%20after,in%20demand%2C%20particularly%20for%20services. Updated on 20 Apr 2023.
Xi, Jinping. 2023. Building an Open, Inclusive and Interconnected World for Common Development. Keynote Speech at the opening ceremony of the Third Belt and Road Forum for International Cooperation. Available at https://www.fmprc.gov.cn/eng/zxxx_662805/202310/t20231018_11162854.html. Accessed 21 Oct 2023.
Yu, Hong 2019. *Reflections on the Belt and Road Initiative.* China: An International Journal, 17(4), November 2019, pp. 8–23.
Yu, Hong. 2022a. China's Ten-yYar-Old BRI Needs a Revamp. *ThinkChina.* https://www.thinkchina.sg/future-china-chinas-ten-year-old-bri-needs-revamp.
Yu, Hong. 2022b. China's Slowing Economy will not Deter BRI Outreach. *ThinkChina.* https://www.thinkchina.sg/chinas-slowing-economy-will-not-deter-bri-outreach.
Yu, Hong. 2023. Why China's BRI is not a Debt Trap? *ThinkChina.* Available at https://www.thinkchina.sg/why-chinas-bri-not-debt-trap.

Index

H. Yu, *Understanding China's Belt and Road Initiative*, Asia in Transition 26,
https://doi.org/10.1007/978-981-99-9633-9

The manufacturer's authorised representative in the EU is Springer Nature Customer Service Centre GmbH, Europaplatz 3, 69115 Heidelberg, Germany. If you have any concerns regarding our products, please contact ProductSafety@springernature.com

Printed and bound by CPI Group (UK) Ltd, Croydon, CR0 4YY

30/09/2026

02225318-0005